Sal Carson

The Life of a Big Band Leader

A pictorial history by
Jim Goggin

Over 760 Illustrations

Order this book online at www.trafford.com
or email orders@trafford.com

Most Trafford titles are also available at major online book retailers.

Note for Librarians: A cataloguing record for this book is available from Library
and Archives Canada at www.collectionscanada.ca/amicus/index-e.html

Printed in Victoria, BC, Canada.

ISBN: 978-1-4269-1411-9 (Soft)

*We at Trafford believe that it is the responsibility of us all, as both individuals
and corporations, to make choices that are environmentally and socially sound.
You, in turn, are supporting this responsible conduct each time you purchase a
Trafford book, or make use of our publishing services. To find out how you are
helping, please visit www.trafford.com/responsiblepublishing.html*

*Our mission is to efficiently provide the world's finest, most comprehensive
book publishing service, enabling every author to experience success.
To find out how to publish your book, your way, and have it available
worldwide, visit us online at www.trafford.com*

Trafford rev. 9/4/2009

Trafford PUBLISHING® www.trafford.com

North America & international
toll-free: 1 888 232 4444 (USA & Canada)
phone: 250 383 6864 ♦ fax: 812 355 4082 ♦ email: info@trafford.com

This book is dedicated to the memory of

Sal Carson

An unforgettable person

Forward

Every effort has been made to locate copyright material that appears in this book as required under copyright law. For some materials the publisher is unable to locate the copyright owner. In such cases copyright holders are invited to contact the publisher who will be pleased to make the necessary arrangements at the first opportunity.

Also what I have done is record events that were reported to me and I assume the events to be true.

Because of my close relationship with the musicians that I write about they have sent me photos and clippings over the years. Of course the gifts were welcomed, but quite often they did not include the name of the photographer, the newspaper, or the important where or when. I have done my best to include this data, but working with a copy of a copy does not make it a simple problem. In this book most of the photos were in the Sal Carson collection where he had the same problem I had in correctly identifying the photographs and clippings. We did our best and any omissions were not intended.

Jim Goggin

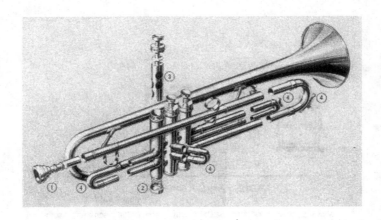

Introduction

Sal Carson lead his first orchestra when he was a teenager attending Claremont Junior High School. By the time he was in the ninth grade his band was playing proms throughout the Bay Area.

Some of his favorite big bands that he listened to were: Count Basie (his favorite), Jimmy and Tommy Dorsey, Benny Goodman, Harry James and Jimmy Lunceford.

It is enjoyable to read about Sal's personal experience with Harry James and Tommy Dorsey as well as backing stars such as Vic Damone, Duke Ellington, Bob Hope, Frankie Laine, Helen O'Connell and Andy Russell plus many more.

There's even a story about a flying saucer and an unforgettable ride on a B-17 when Sal was in the World War II Air Force.

As a result of being the leader of the 40 piece San Francisco 49ers Band, Sal became known as the "San Francisco's Music Man". After reading about his accomplishments you will probably agree that the title was justified.

For me, Sal Carson ranks right up there with the finest men I have ever known. How lucky I am.

SAN FRANCISCO'S MUSIC MAN

SAL CARSON
ORCHESTRA
INTERSTATE 80 ROCK SWING BAND
DIXIELAND BAND & COMBO'S
FORMER S.F. 49ER BAND

127 HARDIE DRIVE • MORAGA, CA 94556
TEL/FAX: (925) 254-1881
www.jazznow.com/SalCarson/SalCarson.html   e-mail: SalCarson@yahoo.com

Chapter 1
1920-1939

On November 1, 1920 (Or was it November 2) Salvatore Carcione was born in San Francisco much to the delight of Guiseppe and Silvia Carcione.

The birth certificate is somewhat confusing. Angelina Cesana, the attending midwife, certified she was present at the birth of the child on November 2, 1920, but the date of her signature was 7/11/20. Angelina used the European way of dating by indicating the day ahead of the month. She probably signed the certificate later.

After Sal, the Carcione's had three daughters, Sylvia, Valeria and Gloria. Guiseppe was born in Italy and came to the USA around 1900 when he was only four or five years old. He became a barber and located on the fifth floor of the Bank of America Headquarters building. The bank's founder, A.P. Giannini, was one of his customers which included the Bechtel family. Appointments were needed to get a haircut which was unusual in those days. As successful as he was as a barber he had a night job.

"He had a beautiful tenor voice and sang at a series of concerts plus being with the San Francisco Opera Company. He took private lessons and practiced religiously".

Sal went to many operas with his mother and his father would often take him to rehearsals. He remembers being introduced to Mr. Merola who was the director of the opera company. "I was very impressed with the rehearsals of the orchestra, singers and seeing my Dad on stage".

The former Silvia Roventini was a stay at home housewife who not only was pretty, but could play the piano well. She purchased a banjo from a door to door salesman when Sal was about eight years old. He took lessons and became a member of the Eddie Peabody Club. Peabody was a popular banjo player and often on a nation-wide radio station.

Just for the record, Peabody was born February 19, 1902 in Reading, MA and died November 7, 1970 in Covington, KY.

The banjo lessons really got Sal interested in music so he started his first band when he was in the eight grade at Claremont Junior High School. By the time he was in the ninth grade his seven or eight piece band was playing proms in Oakland schools.

He practiced his banjo, but he also enjoyed sports, especially baseball which was a good thing as you will discover later on in this book.

When he was about fifteen years old his Dad took him to the Golden Gate Theater where Horace Heidt's Orchestra was playing. Heidt was a well-known band leader and quite popular. Later on in life he had his own television show.

"I will never forget the trumpet player coming up to the microphone and playing a beautiful solo 'The Rose in Her Hair'. A pretty solo. I was impressed and from that day on I wanted a trumpet so my dad bought me one".

He took lessons from Leo De Mers, "a wonderful trumpet player" and Sal's interest in music took a big leap even though his Dad told him "Get into singing".

What bands influenced him? Count Basie was his favorite. Other bands he listened to were Jimmy and Tommy Dorsey, Benny Goodman, Harry James (the first record he purchased was by the James band) and Jimmy Lunceford. "There were also a number of very good society type bands such as Dick Jurgens, Freddy Martin, Russ Morgan and Alvino Rey. All were in the Bay Area so there was considerable competition".

The orchestras he admired encouraged him to enlarge his own band to about 16-17 pieces and to become a commercial band. He required all his band members to be good readers and looked for musicians that could double on more than one instrument. They rehearsed at least once a week and started to "making some good money for those days". Remember that during the depression $150.00 a month was considered good, that is if you could find a job. In 1935 the estimated unemployed was 20.1%.

When Sal got a band going at University High School they were doing quite well and he had a "really good vocalist whose name was Sue Miller. She was with the band for about three years. Sue was a stunning, beautiful girl". One day a fellow came up to the bandstand and told Sal, "I am going to marry that girl". He did and they still are.

At first they played the high school prom circuit in Oakland and San Francisco then moved up to the University of California dances, fraternities, sororities, clubs, etc. which makes one wonder if Sal received help in changing from a small band to a standard size swing band. For that matter where did they get arrangements? They, at first, used stock arrangements which does not suggest a special "signature" to their approach to music, but it is a logical start.

Well, who helped them? Maurice Anger an already established Bay Area band leader would come to their rehearsals and tried to help them plus bringing some arrangements. Anger was a good arranger and pianist. Sal always considered the help he got from Maurice Anger to be unforgettable.

By the time Sal was about twenty years old, had left high school in his senior year to be a full-time musician. Many students found it necessary to drop out of school during the depression, besides his band was doing very well.

His parents could not have been pleased about his decision to leave school, but understood his passion for music. Sal spent many night hours at the famous Sweet's Ballroom in Oakland listening to the touring big bands such as Les Brown, Les Hite, Jimmy Lunceford and others. It was more than just listening, he "went to school".

When Gene Krupa's hot band was at Sweet's, Sal entire band was there including Dick Lotter, a superb trumpet player who was in Sal's band. Later on Lotter, who was from Alameda, became a member of Krupa's band. He also was with Russ Bennett's band.

They also listened to Gary Nottingham who was Sweet's house band. Sal played at Sweets for two weeks in 1946 when Nottingham took a break.

He remembers the headliner was Stan Kenton who "came out with that new style. He had five trumpets. I admired Kenton".

I asked if some of Kenton's music was in the form of a concert rather than dancing. "Yes, I would say so. The way his arrangements were. Musicians especially appreciated what he did".

When he was nineteen he sold corsages at the University of California stadium before football games.

He also sold Christmas wreaths. He had a day job during the week at San Francisco Insurance Company's Fire Adjustment Section. During lunch Sal could be found in the company's basement practicing his trumpet for his night job.

Sal Carson knew what he wanted to be and with practice, determination and hard work he followed the path he selected so let's join him on his trip.

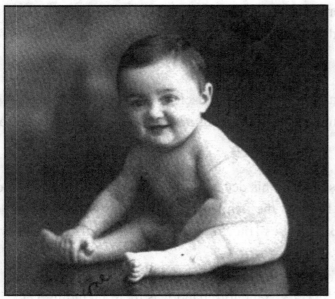

Ss. Peter & Paul's Church

Salesiana of St. John Bosco
655 Filbert Street, San Francisco, California

Certificate of Baptism

✳ This is to Certify ✳

That *Salvatore Giuseppe Carcione*

Child of *Giuseppe Carcione*

and *Sylvia Roventini*

born in *San Francisco, Calif.*

on the *1st* day of *November* 1920

✳ Was Baptized ✳

on the *2nd* day of *January* 1921

According to the Rite of the Roman Catholic Church

by the Rev. *Thomas J. Deehan*

the Sponsors being *Annuto Sudici*

and *Rose Roventini* as appears

from the Baptismal Register of this Church.

Dated *January 30, 1986*

Rev. Armand Oliveri Pastor.

A happy Salvatore when he was about eight months old.
(right) Certificate of Baptism indicates he was born November 1.
(Below) Birth certificate.   Sal was told he was born November 1, not 2.

1 PLACE OF BIRTH. Dist. No. **3801**	STATE OF CALIFORNIA		
(To be inserted by Registrar) CITY AND COUNTY OF SAN FRANCISCO	DEPARTMENT OF PUBLIC HEALTH VITAL STATISTICS STANDARD CERTIFICATE OF BIRTH	Local Registered No. **7960**	

No. **1864 Green** St.;

2 FULL NAME OF CHILD **Salvatore Carcione**

PERSONAL AND STATISTICAL PARTICULARS

3 SEX OF CHILD **Male**	4. Twin, Triplet, or Other	5 Number in Order of Birth (To be answered only in event of plural births)	6 DATE OF BIRTH **November 2, 1920** (Month) (Day) (Year)
FATHER		**MOTHER**	
7 FULL NAME **Guiseppe Carcione**		13 FULL MAIDEN NAME **Silvia Roventini**	
8 RESIDENCE **1864 Green St.** City State		14 RESIDENCE **1864 Green St.** City State	
9 COLOR OR RACE **White**	10 AGE AT LAST BIRTHDAY **25** (Years)	15 COLOR OR RACE **White**	16 AGE AT LAST BIRTHDAY **19** (Years)
11 BIRTHPLACE **Italy** (State or country)		17 BIRTHPLACE **California** (State or country)	
12 OCCUPATION (a) Trade, profession or particular kind of work **Barber** (b) General nature of industry, business, or establishment in which employed (or employer)		18 OCCUPATION (a) Trade, profession or particular kind of work **Housewife** (b) General nature of industry, business, or establishment in which employed (or employer)	
18 (a) Was a prophylactic for Ophthalmia Neonatorum used? **Yes** If so, what? **Nitrate of silver**		19 Number of children born to this mother, including present birth **1** 20 Number of children of this mother now living **1**	

21 CERTIFICATE OF ATTENDING PHYSICIAN OR MIDWIFE*

I hereby certify that I attended the birth of this child, who was **alive** at 6 A.M. on the date above stated.
(Born alive or stillborn)

(Signature) **Angelina Cesana**

Dated **7/11/19 20**
(Physician, midwife, father, etc.)

Address **839 Union St.**

22 Filed **Nov. 9, 1920** **William C. Hassler**
Registrar or Deputy

Silvia Carcione.   Sal's mother when she was
about 21.

Guiseppe Carcione.   September 20, 1919.

**SAN FRANCISCO
O P E R A
C O M P A N Y**

SEASON 1926

EXPOSITION AUDITORIUM
September 21st to October 6th

GAETANO MEROLA, General Director

EDW. F. MOFFATT, Business Manager
HOWARD G. HANVEY, Director of Publicity
GIOVANNI GRANDI, Technical and Scenic Director
Casts, Dates and Repertoire Subject to Change

**Tuesday Evening, September 21st
at 8:15 o'clock sharp**

San Francisco Opera Company playbill for 1926.

1948 photo of Sal's mother.

Sal when he was a Boy Scout with a Scout counselor.

(Left) Another playbill.

Sal's band, 1935

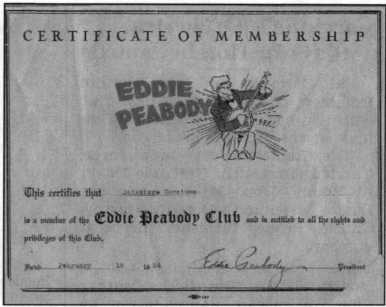

Eddie Peabody Club certificate.   February 19, 1934

(Left) Publicity photo of Eddie Peabody.   He was a Commander during World War II for all U.S. Navy bands.

Jack Joyce, 1935

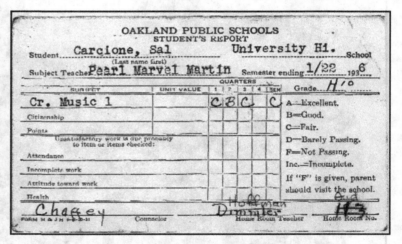

A "C" in music?   My guess is Ms. Martin had a tin ear.

(Right)
Rhythm Ramblers card.

Carcione's Orchestra Plays in Hotel Alameda

Sal Carcione and his Rhythm Ramblers of the U. C. Study Club will now be heard on Friday evenings at the Hotel Alameda.

The Ramblers are Jack Joyce, Garried Grossmith, Gertrude Davis, Al Young, Don Geyer, Jim Kaar, Dave Jesser, and Bob McCarthy. Charles Presley furnishes the vocal numbers.

The orchestra also plays once a month at the Twentieth Century Club for private dances given by the ?'s? Club.

Ramblers clipping, ca. 1937.

Romaine Photo, 1936 0r 1937.   (l to r)   Sal, Jimmy Kaar, Bob Davidson and Mr. Unknown.

Vol. 4 No. 1.   July, 1937

JULY - INVITATIONAL TWO BALL MIXED FOURSOME

GOLF - P. M.   - - -   DINNER & DANCING in the EVENING

SUNDAY - JULY 25th 1937

*****

Vacation time....Recreation time...for all Members who are in town that week
end this will be the MAIN EVENT of the Summer Season. Sal Carcione and his
Rhythm Ramblers who made such a hit at our May Dinner Dance will again furnish
us with syncopation that makes an enjoyable party.

Invite your friends for both GOLF and DINNER. Golf Entry Fee - 50¢ each player
and Dinner and Dancing - $1.25 per plate. Many are planing small parties for
this one...please phone your reservations; so that proper table arrangements
can be made.

*****

LADIES INVITATIONAL DAY - FRIDAY - JULY 30th

Starting time reservations open on Friday, July 23rd....sign up with John Carse
for golf. LADIES: - This is the perfect day to invite guests to the Club for
luncheon and bridge. Your reservations phoned to the Club Office will be
appreciated.

*****

SUMMER ACTIVITIES BRIEFLY SUMMED UP: Men's Summer Eclectic - dates & details
to be announced soon..........Nat'l Amateur Sectional Qualifying - at Olympic
Club at Lakeside.........8 Sequoyahans to take test.....Northern California
Open at Pebble Beach, Sat. July 31st - Walter Wauhab and Fred Schultz to carry
Sequoyah bid for honors........Clubhouse porch furniture sparkles with new
colors........Brings great joy nd pride.....Window trim also gets fresh coat
of paint to bring new color and vigor to Clubhouse outlook..........New
No. 10 and No. 14 greens permanently open for play..........Golf course in
fine playing condition.........BIG WEEK OF GOLF - California State Championship
at Del Monte and Pebble Beach..August 15 to 20th........SEPTEMBER FIRST........
EVERYBODY COMES BACK TO SEQUOYAH FOR REAL CLUB ENJOYMENT!

******

Sequoyah Country Club News. July 1937.

Sal's card and his business manager.   Wow, things were picking up.

Who's Who Dinner To Be Held In Cafeteria On Wednesday Evening

Studnt Body Officers, Class, and Club Presidents, Editors of U-N-I, and Social Affairs Committee Members Are Invited To Attend and Discuss Problems

Student body officers, class and club presidents, Daily U-N-I editors, honor students, committee chairmeen and members of the Social Affairs Committee will again meet at the semi-annual Who's Who dinner, Wednesday, to discuss school problems. It will be held between 6 and 9 p. m. in the cafeteria, and will include dancing to the music of Sal Carcione's orchestra.

Barbara Cochrane is in charge of th event with the following committee: Ruth Dodds, Chairman of decorations; Nancy Smith, chair-place cards; Sue Marx, chairman of publicity; Roberta Whaley, chairman of invitations; Jean Schmidt, chairman of the seating chart; Marian Badger, entertainment chairman; Frances Wilzinski, reception committee chairman; Mary Locke, in charge of menu; Marian Hills in charge of table cloths; Madeleine Minturn, ticket chairman; Phyllis Foulkess, Who's Who book, and Tom Taveretti and Hal Sams, clean-up chairmen.

Who's Who Dinner, ca late 1937.

1938 photo at Sal's home. (l to r) Back row: Les Hawk, Al Willis. Front row: Hal? Jack Bingham, Sal, Jack Joyce, Jim Swift, Ralph Willits.

Holy Names Girls Plan Dance

Girls of Holy Names Central High School will hold an informal dance Friday night at the Lake Merritt Hotel.

Agnes Vinson, student body president, heads an arrangements committee for the annual affair.

Sal Carson's orchestra will furnish the music.

Patrons and patronesses will include Mr. and Mrs. B. J. Fanning, Mr. and Mrs. A. F. Balwick, Mrs. E. H. Vinson, Mr. and Mrs. B. W. Bates, Mr. and Mrs. H. C. Andrews and Mr. and Mrs. G. V. Strabler.

Three clippings, ca late 1930's.

Baseball – Track dinner, ca late 1930's.

Dream Comes True For Sal Carson

Tuesday will be something more to Sal Carson and his popular orchestra than Armistice Day; it will be his bow to many of his old-time friends and associates at Claremont Junior High and University High Schools, where he first began to dream of having an orchestra of his own.

That dream has come true. The Carson Orchestra and its popular leader are regular featues at some of the leding hotels on both sides of the bay. Tuesday evening they are to play at the Armistice Day dance at Sweets Ballroom . . . the first opportunity many of his friends have had to dance to his music since the old school days. Since then Sal has changed his family name of Carcione to Carson, by which he and his group of talented musicians are universally known. But the family home is still at 370 Sixty-third Street and Sal is the same as in the old days, though his name has been changed and he has "arrived" musically speaking, in the entertainment world.

De Molays Plan Dance Tonight

Under the chairmanship of Chester Nelson, the second annual "Starlite Serenade" dance of the Oakland Chapter, Order of De Molay, will be held at the Oakland Club this evening.

Music for the affair will be furnished by Sal Carcione and his 10-piece orchestra with Miss Alice La Vonne as soloist. A star theme will be carried out with novelty

LOIS VAUGHN

musical arrangements and decorations.

Hostess for the evening will be Miss Lois Vaughn with the following members serving on the committes: Al Rossi, Harvey Lo Sassi, Ed Collier, Werner Johnson, Alvin Pressler and Harvey Croswhite. Guest of honor will be Master Councilor William Howard.

Carcione's Orchestra To Provide Music At Baseball-Track Dinner

Singing At The Table Between Courses Will Be Featured; At Least An Hour of Dancing And A Variety of Games To Be Provided After Dinner

Dance music for the baseball-track dinner, to be held on Wednesday, June 8, from 6 to 9 p. m. in the cafeteria, will be provided by Sal Carcione and his nine piece orchestra. The general theme for the dinner will be sports, in honor of the players on the baseball and track teams and their coaches.

Singing at the table between courses will be a featured attraction at the dinner. At least an hour of dancing will follow dinner, and a large variety of games will be available.

Tickets for this affair are on sale now in the front hall for 35 cents. The amount of tickets, however, will be limited to 55 because a total of 89 invitations have been sent out to coaches and their wives and to members of the faculty as well.

Committee chairmen in charge are Juin Palmgren, place cards; Tris Coffin, clean-up; Pat Hardy, seating chart; Cay Wilding, publicity; Cay Wilkie, reception; Ruth Dodds, invitations; Jane Ginn, tickets; Evelyn Stuart, entertainment; Caddie Dodge, menu; Bobbe Reed, serving; and Dolores Duckworth, decorations. General chairman of the affair is Margie Meads, commissioner of social affairs.

Club Plans 'Nautical' Dance

More than 150 of society's younger sets will attend the "nautical" dance tonight which members of the Aeolian Yacht club, juniors, are giving at the club.

Everybody's going in seafaring clothes, and there will be a prize for the most appropriately dressed couple. Music is to be furnished by Sal Carcione's orchestra. The "Big Apple" is to be among features.

There's to be a mile of dinner parties preceding the dance. Howard and Jack Frey who, with Paul Gutleben, William Simon and Harry Millar, head the committee of arrangements, are giving a large cocktail party at their home.

Another Carcione gigs.

Dinner Dance Band Chosen

Preparations Being Made For Holy Names Affair

Following the formal acceptance of the invitation extended by the Associated Students of Saint Mary's to Holy Names College, Oakland, to attend a supper dance on the campus April 5, preparations for the function are advancing rapidly. Robert Johnson, chairman of the dance disclosed.

After a series of auditions of popular orchestras, Sal Carcione and his sensational nine piece orchestra has been chosen to supply the music for the affair. Maestro Carcione is widely acclaimed throughout the Bay area for his talented musical and vocal renditions.

The supper dance will be held in the Saint Mary's refectory from 7:30 to 11:30 p.m. on April 5. Charlotte Campi, representative from Holy Names, is making preparations for the attendance of 75 girls.

Gigs, gigs, and gigs.

Could the Masked Troubadors be Sal's band?

Italian Federation Plans Dance Here

A dance will be held tonight at Ligure hall, Forty-eighth street and Shattuck avenue, under auspices of the Italian Catholic Federation girls' drill team No. 40. Sal Carcione and orchestra will furnish the music. Elda Croce is in charge.

Rally Dance In Gym Today

First Boys' League Dance Of Term Will Be Held After School In Gym

The Masked Troubadors, A Mystery Orchestra, Will Furnish The Music For The Event; First String Football Players Will Be Guests of Honor, a Special Feature

Today the first Boys' League dance of the semester, a Spade Day Dance in accordance with the Tech-Uni football game tomorrow, will be held after school in the combined gyms.

Twenty-two of the first string football players will be guests of honor at the dance. The entire line-up for tomorrow's game is expected to attend as an added feature. A group of the stars who appeared in the recent Follies will form a major part of the floor program.

Mystery Orchestra To Play

The masked Troubadors, a mystery orchestra, will furnish the music for the dance. The orchestra, which charges $18 for an hour and a half of playing, will be unmasked towards the end of the dance.

Tickets are still selling at the price of 10 cents and may be purchased at the bank, from Boys' League salesman, or at the gym door just before the dance.

Term's Only Rally Dance

"This is the only rally dance to be held this term and is hoped that the student body will back it 100 per cent" stated Marshall Hunt, Boys' League president.

An attempt is being made to establish the Spade Day Dance as a tradition in the school and reactions from this the first dance will help to determine whether this plan can be carried out.

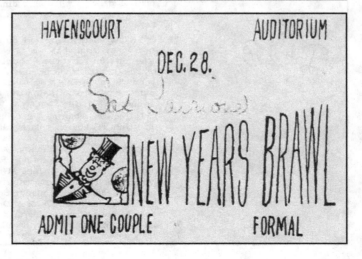

HAVENSCOURT   AUDITORIUM
DEC. 28.
Sal Carcione
NEW YEARS BRAWL
ADMIT ONE COUPLE   FORMAL

Sal Carcione's orchestra to play at Dads' Club dances Friday nights

Jazz time, ragtime, swing—that's what Sal Carcione and his orchestra play at the Friday night dances.

Attendance which was small during vacation increased greatly with the opening of school, and with each appearance the orchestra has gained in popularity.

Last year with the proceeds from the dances the Dad's Club bought purple caps and belts for the band and an excellent microphone. This year with similar cooperation the dad are planning to get colorful capes for the band and new instruments.

Mr. H. P. Simpson, president of the Dads' Club and chairman of the dances, announced that plans are well on the way for a mammoth free dance to be held in the near future.

Attractions include the nine-piece orchestra, blonde Sue Miller, vocalist, and the giving of door prizes.

Loudspeaker system will be used for football games this year, according to Mr. R. J. Simpson, president

Loudspeaker will also be used at the noon dances this term. Mr. Simpson says that it costs only two cents an hour to run the speaker.

Guiseppe Carcione's barber shop in the Bank of America Building, San Francisco

Musician Is Interviewed By Inquisitive Daily U-N-I Reporter

By Jim Dugan

Inspired by his love of music, in 1935 Sal Carcione started an orchestra of four, himself and three others. They were all students of Claremont Junior High School which he attended at the time. The orchestra was composed of a trombone, piano, clarinet, and a banjo. With much success at Claremont, Sal's band played at noon dances and later at other schools. While at Uni his orchestra increased to nine members.

Then playing at the Cal campus, Sal reduced the band to eight men, later having a regular nine piece orchestra. Sal is in great hopes of playing at the big hotels soon. He has just finished two appointments at special fraternities at Cal.

Sal intends to enter the orchestra in the musicians union. He had changed his plans because of the Follies that occurred last Friday.

Spade Day Dance Is To Be Established As New School Tradition

Marshall Hunt States Dance Is Big Success; Wide Acclaim Shown By Student Body

Due to the wide acclaim shown by the student body for the Boys' League dance last Thursday, the spade day dance is to be established as a tradition of the school.

Dance Successful

Marshall Hunt stated that the dance was a success both financially and in the showing of school spirit. He added that there is a need for a dance to be held before a great game like the Tech-Uni clashes because of the spirit created by such an affair. He also stated that this tradition would set a definite time for Boys' League to hold their dances.

Over two hundred tickets were sold for the dance which featured Sal Carcioni and his band. Marshall stated that he wished to thank Sal on behalf of the Boys' League for the fine music furnished by his new and improved orchestra at the dance.

Review of Follies Says Annual Fete Was Big Success

By Dorothy Anderson

With the swing music of Sal Carcione's orchestra, the curtain rose upon the twenty-third follies in the history of the school, and if this writer does say so it went over with a bang.

Featured among the outstanding acts, the "Noble Lord" by Percivale Wilde caused the most comment among the First Nighters. It really had "it". The play put on show the comical talent of Dustin Lake and Elsie Wiley.

Elsie was a title hunter and Dusty was a title holder. When the curtain opened we heard a screech of a maiden in distress and unconsciously (as always) Dusty came on the stage and immediately went to her rescue. He saw through her little plot and led her on up an exciting climax.

Another act that had an interesting theme was "Hill Billy Interlude" with a cast of two, Lois Bugbee and Mary Fulmer with Pat Chapin at the piano. It was an illustration of he popular and current song, "The Martins and the Coys."

A positively beautiful and interesting interpretation was a Javanese dance. It was given by Carmencita Harland, and she had on a white satin gown and a silver head dress. While she danced a blue silver light was played on her.

I believe that the audience did not fully appreciate the talent and beauty expressed in this dance, as they were restless and made quite a bit of noise.

French Bolero by Barbara Lee Thomas and Darrel Argubright was a second Rogers and Astaire act. That is all that can be said for it.

The cream of the school dancers was a "Little Bit of Harlem" tap danced by Theodore Nix. Bob Hill, the master of ceremonies, was good and he added a bit of color to the Follies, but he really should have had a larger part.

Sal Carcione Furnishes The Music For Whoosies Dance

Scrapbook Signed By All Who's Who Members Present At The Dinner Last Evening; Big Current Problems Discussed

.. By Jeanne Taylor

Approximately 200 recognized leaders of the student government met together at the traditional Whos Who Dinner to dine and discuss problems. They did well as far as the dinner was concerned but the discussion failed to get a foothold.

Said one diner to his dinner mate, "If you enter the discussion I'll break your neck," the idea behind this being that Sal Carcione's orchestra was waiting to play in the next room and the students were anxious to dance.

After dinner Barbara Cochrane, Commissioner of Social Affairs turned the meeting over to Harvey Short, Student Body President who conducted the discussion. The only problems discussed was the policy of rewarding students who serve the school. Most of whoosies agreed that on a whole students are not very willing to work would be detrimental to the school spirit Another point brought up was that the finished work should be enough reward to the students, that and service.

Harvey Short expressed hope that most of the student body will feel that they should be willing to do things for their school and not expect specific awards but be proud to be helping their student government.

More clippings.

Alumni To Dance At Woodrow Gym Today

Fall Colors Thanksgiving Motif Planned for Decorations

Fall colors and a Thanksgiving motif will be carried out at the Woodrow Wilson Alumni Dance today, from 3:30 to 5 o'clock in the combined gyms at Woodrow.

All former Wilson graduates are invited to go and renew old friendships. The admission is ten cents and the proceeds will be used to pay for the expenses. Posters are being circulated in the various high schools announcing the affair.

As each person enters the gyms he will write his name on a piece of paper and put it in a box. A door prize, probably a box of candy, will be given to the person whose name is drawn.

Homemade candy will be sold at the dance by the H9 girls. The profits will be used to purchase picture cuts for the school paper. Patricia Beldin, vice-president of the Woodrow student body, has secured Sal Carcione's orchestra.

Horace Heidt was born May 21, 1901 in Alameda, CA.   Died December 1, 1986 in Sherman Oaks, CA

William "Count" Basie, Sal's favorite band, was born August 21, 1904 in Red Bank NJ.   Died April 26, 1984 in Hollywood, CA

Les Brown.   Born March 14, 1912, Reinerton, PA.   Died January 4, 2001 in Los Angeles, CA

Benny Goodman.   Born May 30, 1909, Chicago, IL. Died June 13, 1986 New York City, NY.

Jimmy Dorsey.   Born February 29, 1904, Shenandoah, PA.   Died June 12, 1957, New York City, NY.

Tommy Dorsey.   Born November 19, 1905, Shenandoah, PA.   Died November 26, 1956, Greenwich, CT.

Harry James.   Born March 15, 1916, Albany, GA.   Died July 5, 1983 Las Vegas NV.

McFadden's Ballroom News. June 14, 1934

Jimmy Lunceford. Born June 6, 1902, Fulton, MS. Died July 12, 1947 Seaside, OR.

Les Hite Again

Les Hite and his great band will be here again on Friday evening, June 22nd. This band now on tour, has made a big hit every performance and on each occasion has been prevailed upon for a return engagement. At the present rate he could stay in Northern California for months but a movie contract will soon take him to Hollywood. Mae Diggs, his Vocalist, is without question the most clever and versatile singer and dancer that has ever appeared in this area. She has everything.

Les Hite. Born February 13, 1903, Du Quoin, IL. Died February 6, 1962, Santa Monica, CA

Freddy Martin. Born December 9, 1906, Cleveland, OH. Died September 30, 1983, Newport Beach, CA. (Some have his date of death as October 1, 1983)

Gary Nottingham. Born September 2, 1901 in Wisconsin. Died January 12, 1962, Oakland, CA. Photo courtesy of the San Francisco Public Library

Gary Nottingham (middle), Mr. Unknown (left) and Matt Saxton, ca 1940's. Photo Courtesy of Jack and Bette Tulley. Jack, a trumpet player, worked at Sweet's and had a long stay with the US Army Band in Washington, D.C.

Publicity photo of Gary Nottingham and four gals in the 1940's. Courtesy of the San Francisco Public Library.

Sweet's down the block from 14th and Franklin Sts., Oakland.   March 1958.

Russ Bennett and Gary Nottingham.   Two band leaders.   Photo courtesy of Jack and Bette Tulley.   Photo ca 1940's.

Dick Jurgens.   Born January 8, 1910, Sacramento, CA., where he died October 5, 1995

Gene Krupa was born January 15, 1909 in Chicago.   He died October 16, 1973 in Yonkers, NY.   His recordings with Anita O'Day and Roy Eldridge were terrific.

At the Masonic Hall, Oakland, ca 1939. (l to r)   Bill Grant, Sal, Les Hawk, Jim Kaar, Lauren Kell, Grover Daniels, Mr. Unknown, Art Oppedal and Ms. Unknown.

Alvino Rey, another local band leader, was born July 1, 1911, Oakland, Ca.   He died February 24, 2004 in Draper, VT.

Something Sentimental

By

Frank Ryerson, Irving Taylor and Vaughn Monroe

Vaughn Monroe.   Born October 7, 1911, Akron OH. Died May 21, 1973, Stuart, FL.

Sweet's Ballroom, Oakland, CA., ca 1940's

Chapter 2
1940's

The 1940's started with optimism for our country and Sal. Employment was going up, the big band business was at a peak besides that President Franklin Delano Roosevelt told the country, "Your boys are not going to be sent into any foreign wars".

Sal and some band members took the very new bridge that went from Oakland to San Francisco and provided a turn-off to the World's Fair in the man-made Treasure Island.

While it was true some were concerned about a wild leader in Germany, but all of that seemed a long way off.

It is my understanding the World's Fair was not making as much money as was hoped for, but guys like "Count" Basie and Benny Goodman drew immense crowds which made a considerable improvement in the Fair's financial difficulties..

Bill Grant, the pianist for Sal, was extremely talented and played in a style employed by "Fats" Waller. Grant and Sal enjoyed going to Treasure Island to catch the music.

The rest of the year consisted of a series of gigs, rehearsals and looking for more gigs.

In April or May 1941 Sal drove up to Lake County and stopped off at various resorts in an effort to book his band for the coming summer. One of the resorts was Hoberg's, but they already had a band for the summer. OK, that one didn't work out for that year, but George Hoberg and Sal seemed to "hit it off:" well. So I have devoted a chapter to Hoberg's. Sal made one more stop, around 7:00pm, at Forest Lake Resort where he met Vince Emerson, the owner, who reminded Sal of Dwight Eisenhower, who later became our president and was as "nice as could be". They had a lengthy and cordial conversation which ended with Sal's band being hired for the Memorial weekend. It was a two-three days gig and Sal considered it to be his first real big gig. He changed his name to Sal Carson, not legally, but shorter.

His eight piece band had good musicians and well rehearsed. The band was a hit resulting in a packed house every night. Emerson hired them for the summer of 1942, six nights a week. Once again they were a good draw. Everyone was happy.

Another special memory of that gig was in June 1942 when he met Kathleen Glenn who later changed her last name, but more about that in the next chapter.

Another highlight was the band recorded (78's) for the first time and the records sold rather well. "Honey Dear" with vocal by Sal did well and was an often requested tune. The arranger was Dave Zuntqua who also played tennis. Because they packed the house so often George Hoberg came down to hear the band which led to a special relationship.

After Labor Day, 1942 the band was at the Trianon Ballroom in Sacramento, but other things came into play. December 7, 1941 the Japanese Air force bombed Pearl Harbor in Hawaii and Sal's men started to be drafted. So, Sal turned over what was left of his band to Danny Boyle after Sal enlisted in the Air Force. It was "I might as well" decision because the draft was taking away band members and those not drafted were subject to be picked up by big name touring bands. "We got hit by Dick Jurgens, Jimmy Dorsey and others". His military career is the subject of Chapter 3.

Sal was discharged from the Air Force in 1945. So back again to Forest Lake Resort in June, 1946. The owner, Vince Emerson, had passed away leaving his son, Don in charge, but he was not yet twenty-one years old. George Hoberg was a good friend of the family so he helped oversee the resort until Don became twenty-one and he was very successful after that.

In 1946 Sal's band was at Sweet's Ballroom in Oakland to fill in for the vacationing Gary Nottingham the long-time house band leader at Sweet's.

The Black and White Ball in 1946 had a billing at the Fairmont of Ernie Heckscher, Ray Hackett and Sal's band. All three were at the Gold Room. Hackett and Heckscher were well-known society bands in San Francisco. This was a case when one band completed their set another replaced them.

Lu Watters with Turk Murphy had the 6:00am slot in the Fairmont's Rose Room. 6:00am? That's about the time Watters' band would go to bed.

I asked Sal what he thought about The Yerba Buena Jazz Band. "It was a very good band. I really appreciated that type of music and enjoyed playing it, but there just wasn't enough money in it. They play it for the love of that music. If I could have made more money playing Dixieland I would have, because I enjoyed it and I have a feel for that music".

"Harry James, Benny Goodman, The Dorseys, Glenn Miller were making the bucks. Not as much, but up there were Dick Jurgens and Freddy Martin".

At that time Sal was with Music Corporation of America (MCA) and they had good bookings. "They booked us into the Hotel Utah for one month and we had a wonderful band".

Here's what Sal said about MCA: "I was not in society, really. We competed with the other bands around, but MCA did not believe we could get $5,000 a week such as Heckscher. They put us in the $1,500 a week group. I became disgusted with MCA and later on I left them".

In the 40's Sal, Kathleen and Ardiene DeCamp were driving in Sal's new car at night on the way to a gig at the Hotel Utah. Ardiene, by the way, was Sal's first vocalist at Hoberg's and was well received by the audience.

"While driving about 65-75 miles per hour in the desert part of Utah we were surprised by something flying above us keeping up with our speed for about an hour. It was late at night and I was tired from driving so while curious as to what it was I just kept driving and forgot about the incident.

"Some ten years later I ran into Ardiene and she said to me, 'Remember the time in Utah when we saw a flying saucer flying over us?' It hit me. I never really saw a flying saucer, but I knew something went over us. Later on there were numerous reports of saucers and maybe it was one".

For two winters in the 40's Sal worked at the Ahwahnee in Yosemite with a nine piece band from 9:00 to 11:00pm. He considered the Ahwahnee to be a class place and the band was treated "very nicely". His vocalist was Sharon Carnes. Sal played trumpet fanfares for the special dinners, Thanksgiving, Christmas, New Years Eve. He also soloed at Camp Curry in the evening for the Fire Falls. The tune was "Indian Love Call". It was really a fun gig for him and his band members.

What follows is an excerpt of one of the interviews I had with Sal:

Sal: I had a very funny experience one night. I was not staying at the Ahwahnee so after the job I was walking out of the entrance to go to my cabin. There were a lot of spotlights out there. I could see a bear here and there.

Jim: (Laughs)

Sal: At least three or five.

Jim: That would get your attention.

Sal: It certainly did. I had several drinks that night. I really did and I was walking out and the bears got bigger and bigger.

Jim: (Laughs)

Sal: To this day it seems to me there must have been ten bears out there. I was almost "goo-goo". I did not feel comfortable as I never saw bears before and maybe they were hungry. I don't know. Besides that I remember the Ahwahnee as a good engagement. Remember Bill Hammett? He was a young protégé, superb trombone player who was with us. Later he was the band leader at the Hyatt Regency for tea dances. After Del Courtney. Eventually he joined the Teddy Wilson Band.

Sal in the 40's

A trio at the Treasure Island, 1940. (l to r) Sal, Harry Larkin (fan of the band) and Bill Grant who played piano patterned after "Fats" Waller.

Treasure Island post cards and matches.

OCTOBER 15, 1940

PREPARE FOR ANNUAL FOLLIES

Principals in the annual University High School dramatics club show to be presented Friday night are shown above. They are "Dectective" Stanley Blum arresting Robin Adair Clark on a "tip" from Peggy Jacobs.—Tribune photo.

University High Drama Club To Give Annual Follies Friday

The University High School Dramatic Club will present its annual follies Friday night in the school auditorium, according to Mrs. Marguerite Squire, dramatics instructor.

The presentation will be staged with a "Grand Hotel" theme. It will feature a skit concerning the love affairs of Robin Adair Clark, who becomes embroiled in the affairs of an international spy ring.

Music for the show will be played by Sal Carcione and his orchestra. Carcione, a University High graduate, has played for several previous follies.

Other principal roles in the skit will be played by Peggy Jacobs, Archer Howard, Dorothy Shertzer, Stanley Blum, Vernon Jesperson and Edward Wheeler.

During the program vocal solos will be sung by: Kenneth Alexander, Carol Dutter, Jerrie Madsen, Henry O'Connell, Miss Shertzer, Robert Turpin and Elmerlee Williams.

Instrumental numbers will include a brass quartet formed by Gene Boaz, Robert Evans, Olin Scholm and Lloyd Glick. Jean Lutey, drums, and John Raposelli, accordion, will play a novelty duet, while Louise Borland and Beverley Hocking will play a piano duet.

Peggy Horn is student chairman in charge of the follies. Faculty advisers include: Miss Caryl Cuddeback, dancing; Mrs. Pearl Martin, music, and Miss Squire, dramatics.

University High School Follies, October 15, 1940

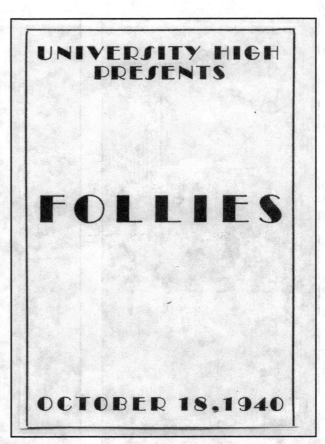

UNIVERSITY HIGH PRESENTS

FOLLIES

OCTOBER 18, 1940

Follies Program cover, October 18, 1940

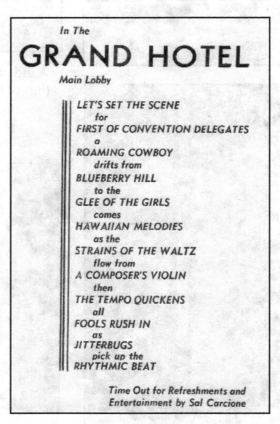

In The

GRAND HOTEL

Main Lobby

LET'S SET THE SCENE
for
FIRST OF CONVENTION DELEGATES
a
ROAMING COWBOY
drifts from
BLUEBERRY HILL
to the
GLEE OF THE GIRLS
comes
HAWAIIAN MELODIES
as the
STRAINS OF THE WALTZ
flow from
A COMPOSER'S VIOLIN
then
THE TEMPO QUICKENS
all
FOOLS RUSH IN
as
JITTERBUGS
pick up the
RHYTHMIC BEAT

Time Out for Refreshments and Entertainment by Sal Carcione

Inside portion of program

Special Events

Three More Days Until The Follies; Friday, October 18

Only three more days! Not until Christmas but until the Follies. For Friday, October 18, at 8 o'clock the curtain will go up, on this term's Follies.

The script, written by Peggy Horn and her script committee, will have the theme of "Grand Hotel," which was chosen in a contest held by the Special Events committee. The contest was a tie for Lorraine Lewis, a H12, and Martha Shaw a L12, both suggesting the theme of a "Hotel lobby."

The Follies will also include specialty numbers which are singing, music, and plenty of jokes.

For several years candy has been sold at the Follies. It will be sold again this term by members of the Special Events committee and others. As a special attraction this year, one out of every fifty bags of candy will have a slip of paper in it.

The owner of the lucky bag will be given another one free. Don't worry if your allowance is a little short this week, for the candy will only be 5 cents a bag.

Harold Oxsen, who made such a big hit at last year's operetta, will sing "Grand Hotel" during intermission.

Sal Carcione and his orchestra will also play. Sal is a graduate of Uni, and while he was still attending Uni he organized his band of students from here and other high schools. He has played for us several times at dances and at the Follies.

Follies clipping, October 18, 1940

Forest Lake Resort flyer, 1941

Sal and Kathleen, Forest Lake, 1942

1941, now called Sal Carson's Band at Forest Lake Resort
(l to r) Sal, Grover Daniels Hal Pugh, Al Caprio, Fred Ditto, Dick Kouch, Les Hawk, Mel Mederias

Vince Emerson, August 1941

Vince Emerson, Ca 1940's.

Four sides, 78's

The Sacramento Tower Bridge
opened in December 1935.
Sal's last gig before going into the
Air Force (1942) was in Sacramento
at the Trianon Ballroom.

CA 1939 photo of the Fox Senator Theater, 910 K Street, Sacramento. The Trianon Ballroom was on the second floor. There was a bowling alley with just a few lanes in the basement of the building.

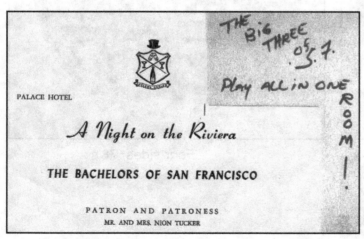

PALACE HOTEL

A Night on the Riviera

THE BACHELORS OF SAN FRANCISCO

PATRON AND PATRONESS
MR. AND MRS. NION TUCKER

THE BIG THREE OF S.F.
PLAY ALL IN ONE ROOM!

St. Patrick's Day Dance, March 17, 1946

Black and White Ball, A Night on the Riviera, 1946

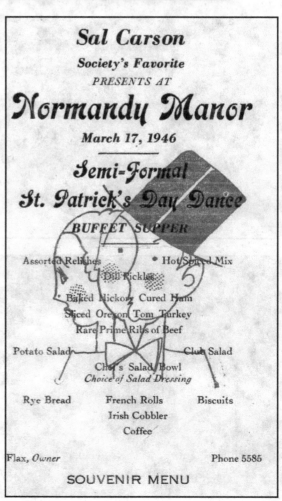

Sal Carson
Society's Favorite
PRESENTS AT

Normandy Manor

March 17, 1946

Semi-Formal
St. Patrick's Day Dance

BUFFET SUPPER

Assorted Relishes • Hot Spiced Mix
Dill Pickles
• Baked Hickory Cured Ham
Sliced Oregon Tom Turkey
Rare Prime Ribs of Beef
Potato Salad Club Salad
Chef's Salad Bowl
Choice of Salad Dressing
Rye Bread French Rolls Biscuits
Irish Cobbler
Coffee

Flax, *Owner* Phone 5585

SOUVENIR MENU

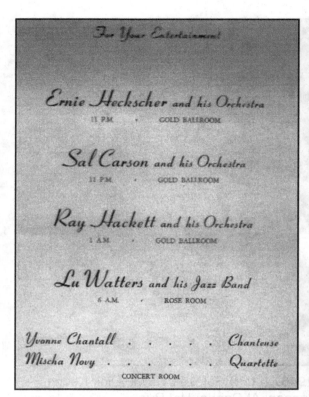

For Your Entertainment

Ernie Heckscher and his Orchestra
11 P.M. • GOLD BALLROOM

Sal Carson and his Orchestra
11 P.M. • GOLD BALLROOM

Ray Hackett and his Orchestra
1 A.M. • GOLD BALLROOM

Lu Watters and his Jazz Band
6 A.M. • ROSE ROOM

Yvonne Chantall . . . . . Chanteuse
Mischa Novy . . . . . . Quartette
CONCERT ROOM

Black and White Ball program at the
Fairmont Hotel.

Fairmont Hotel post card.

Ernest Massey "Ernie" Heckscher. Very popular
orchestra. He was born July 19, 1916 in England.
Died January 16, 1996, Rancho Mirage, CA

Lu Watters played at 6:00am in the Rose
Room. Lu was born December 19, 1911
in Santa Cruz, CA. He died November 5,
1989 in Santa Rosa, CA

Stan Kenton.
Born
December
15, 1911,
Wichita, KS.
Died, August
25, 1979
Los Angeles,
CA

The Sal Carson Orchestra at Sweet's Ballroom in 1946. (l to r) Sal, Les Hawk, Dick Kouch, Mel Mederias, Grover Daniels, Bob Hanson, Al Caprio, Hal Pugh

At Sweet's in 1946. (l to r) Les Hawk, Dick Kouch (possibly), Hal Pugh and Sal.

Barn Dance, 1946

Holiday Greeting, 1948 from Yosemite

Yosemite match cover
and post cards, 1948

More Yosemite post cards.

The Ahwahnee Hotel, coaster and match cover.

Sharon Carnes worked with Sal's band in Yosemite

Holmes Band Walk Out in Frisco Culinary Strike

by DIXON GAYER

San Francisco—Hotel Mark Hopkins presented the first musical liability to Local No. 6 late last month when the Culinary Workers' Union threw a picket fence around that spot where Herbie Holmes' young band was playing. Herbie and the band were among the first to walk out, much to the delight of the several hundred pickets who surrounded the swank Nob Hill hostelry. So far the Mark is the only hotel to be hit by the line but the union is threatening other name hotels for near-future closings. Such closings would put Paul Whiteman and Freddy Martin orks on the local 6 board bill. Holmes' band was doing a fine job for an unknown in this city of names.

Woody Herman took in the third highest gate ever recorded at Sweet's ballroom in Oakland recently. Never let it be said that he let the crowd down, either. Kicks were numerous, solid and varied. Erskine Hawkins followed with a less successful night both musically and financially.

Sal Carson's local crew hit town last month after a terrific ten week jump at Hoberg's resort in Lake County. The Hoberg spot went union for the first time this summer and following the Carson bash promises to continue in those footsteps. Sal's three tenor band is soft like fuzz on peaches yet kicks are there.

Maurice Anger, non-union headache for local 6 and who intimates that he will go union if the army goes 'way from his baton and piano, is at present holding a terrific session with local draft doctors and appears to be winning out. Maurice, who probably plays the most solid piano in the area, says, "If I get out of this mess I can thank God that a musician's life is an unhealthy one." However, local fingers will still be crossed for a few days until Maurice knows definitely.

U. of C. Gets Krupa

University of California Dormitory Association is clapping hands over the purchase of Gene Krupa, band and company for their Men's Gym fracas. Southern California MCA booked the deal. Local Cabbages, Kings and Things campus agency OK'd the deal and checked the contract and swore because they couldn't get a percentage. It is rumored, however, that they may glean an MCA campus representation for future deals.

Don Kaye, whose band sells at Berkeley's Claremont hotel sans effort and sans reproach, and Bob LeMarr, drummer in the aggregation, are out airplane shopping. Both boys fly about a bit, having private licenses, and have decided to sink that old hourly rental into buying a plane of their own. If the plane stays up as terrifically as the band has, both Don and Bob will live to have long grey beards getting tangled in their airplane prop, baton and drumsticks.

Dixon Gayer column (Downbeat?) 1948 or 1949

One might surmise I made this up.

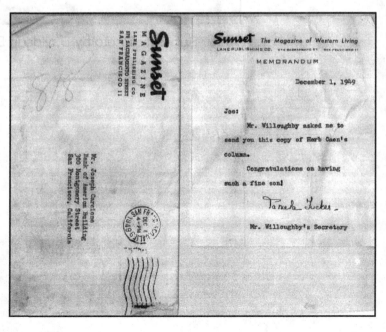

Letter to
Joseph Carcione,
December 1949

Sgt. Sal. Photo by Davidson Bros. ca 1943

Chapter 3
The Air Force Gig

Sal made his decision to join the Air Force and wasted no time by going to a recruiting office located in Sacramento since his last gig was in that city. It turned out the officer knew Sal from San Francisco. "I thought this is great and believed he would assign me to a military band in San Francisco".

Right? Wrong. He was sent to Camp Kearns near the City of Taylorsville, Utah. And it was in the winter.

The Air Force wanted an isolated place to build a training base that would be safe from any attacks by the Japanese yet be on the main rail route to the Pacific Coast.

The War Department purchased 5,000 acres of land. Camp Kearns in 1942 where living conditions were described as horrible. Camp Kearns was closed in 1946 and some of the first residential homes in what is now called Kearns were built from materials left over from the base buildings.

If you are trying to find Kearns, Utah on a map it is located West of Taylorsville near West Jordon and North of Provo. To say the winters in Kearns were cold is a gross understatement. So the band rehearsed in the barracks every day. "Had a party every night to 10:00pm. I did play reveille and taps every day".

On November 25, 1942 Sal was sent to the 56th Army Air Force Band at Sergeant Bluff, Iowa near Sioux City. "The band was an eight piece one, but I built it up to about 14-15 pieces and eventually I had two groups. One a dance band and the second was a typical marching band".

They rehearsed every day in the morning and again in the afternoon. He had his library shipped to him, organized band stands and obtained more arrangements from Maurice Anger. The government sent some scores including material used by Count Basie and Harry James. In addition, Sal did some arranging.

Later on his well-rehearsed band had a thirty minute radio spot on CBS which went out to the entire Middle West. Their programs were put on transcriptions for listening in other locations.

Sal was called upon to play taps which required flying to various camps. Can you believe that?

After he had the band "working together" he would play for the enlisted men one night, the NCO Club another night and the Officer's Club still another night.

They also played at some nearby towns for occasions such as a Red Cross Drive, USO affairs, theaters, etc.

Some private events supplemented their nightly income by $5.00 each per gig.

Sal said about a fourth of the band members became professional musicians. Two came to mind: Bill Barnhoff went to Lawrence Welk who would only hire very good musicians.. Another musician was Ralph Markovich who he ran into one time in Reno. He was backing "Fat's" Domino at the Harrah's Club.

Another very good alto player was Sam Shrieber who became the leader of the Washington Redskins Football Team Band. "One time we were told to have the band at the airport to greet General Arnold coming in from Washington, D.C. A big general. The plane was late and it was cold. I mean real cold. Below zero".

Jim: Tough on the chops in that kind of weather.

Sal: I remember one of the trumpet players had a problem because it was so cold. The general arrived and as I recall he was 45-60 minutes late. The general gets off the plane and it was pouring down rain. The general balled the hell out of the guy for having us stand there all that time.

Jim: Good for him.

Sal: And he had it coming.

Jim: He was trying to impress General Arnold.

Sal: Takes care of the men. I remember that day as he was something. He released us for the rest of the day. General Arnold was a top level guy.

By 1943 Kathleen Glenn became Sal's wife and they were able to find housing off base. Their daughters Kathy and Jo Anne were born in Sioux City. His housing was convenient so he would leave every morning about 8:00am and return at 5:00pm.

Of course he continued playing with his band about six nights a week, loving what he did.

Sal really enjoyed telling me about Colonel William Calhoun who was in charge of the base even though he was only about twenty-four years old. "A very likeable guy and handsome".

But let Sal tell you:

Sal: Calhoun ran flights over Berlin and came back to head up the base. We became very close friends. He had a little Ford convertible and I had a twelve cylinder Lincoln convertible with red leather. An incredible car. I would be driving down in Sioux City and he pointed a finger at me. Just like a kid.

Jim: He obviously liked you.

Sal: We were really good friends. He was a nice guy. One morning he called and said, "Sergeant Carcione, this is Colonel Calhoun. See if you can get permission to fly to New York with me". I told him I would see if I could (laughs) so I called Warrant Officer Ledbetter who was in charge of the military band. He was not too popular, by the way. He could hardly say no.

Jim: (Laughs) That's right.

Sal: I drove to the base and there was a B-17 which was my first time in one. There was Colonel Calhoun and another pilot and me. Just the three of us and we went to New York.He talked to me all the way about music and he said, "look out the window to the right".We were approaching the Statue of Liberty. I will never forget that. Went right by the Statue of Liberty, "zoom!" I will never forget the sight. So we looked around New York.

Stayed at a very nice hotel. He stayed at another hotel because he was the Commanding Officer. He picked us up that evening and we went on the town for three nights. I had never been in such big night clubs and, for that matter, had never been in New York City before.

So he flew me there and I was on my own at times. So just walked and wandered around.I walked into this one restaurant bar and Tommy Dorsey happened to be playing there later that night. I went to Dempsey's and I remember going into I think, it was the El Nido, a night club, The Waldorf, and anyway I had a good time in New York.

Jim: Did you meet Tommy Dorsey at that time?

Sal: No, I didn't meet him at all. I didn't hear the band. I just walked into the club, in and out. Grabbed one of his tent cards. I wandered around New York. Interesting how much traffic even then.

So anyway it was very nice he invited me. I was quite flattered. On the way back from New York to Sioux City Base, I was in the nose pit.

Jim: With the machine gun. (laughs)

Sal: Boy, what a thrill when we landed. So that was a big experience, flying in a B-17.

Yes, a big experience. Sal will never forget nor will he forget the birth of their second child Jo Anne on September 3, 1945.

He received an Honorable Discharge on November 21, 1945.

Post card – Downtown
Provo, Wasatch Mountains

On the air, CBS, WNAX ca
1940's that's Bill Barnhoff to
Sal's left.

Band photo. Bill Barnhoff standing   ca 1940's

A happy drummer. ca 1940's

Sal on WNAX,   ca 1940's.

No, it's this key. Pete Prestigiacomo on the right.

4 band members. ca 1940's

Sal and three band members. Ca 1940's. On the far right is Pete Prestigiacomo.

Clippings.
ca 1940's

Vocalist Dorothy Fields (l to r) in front: Pete Prestigiacomo, Lou Machek, Jack Fulton (blocked just a portion of his sax). In back: Charlie Fulmer, Frederick Lyman and far right is Sal.

The Band's New Vocalist

DOROTHY FIELDS, whose singing is lovely too, is another reason for the popularity of Sal Carson's all-soldier dance band. Accompanying Mrs. Fields' chorus on "Sentimental Journey" are (left to right, front row) Cpl. Pete Prestigiacomo, Sq. D; S/Sgt. Lou Machek, Sq. M; Sgt. Jack Fulton, Sq. A, on saxes, and, (left to right, back row) Sgts. Charlie Fulmer and Frederick Lyman, Sq. A, on guitar and bass, respectively. Other members of the band not shown in this picture are S/Sgt. Buss Crookshank, Sq. D, drums; Cpl. Mel Routman, Sq. D, trumpet, and PFC Jack Buckley, 17th wing, piano. Sal Carson is fronting the band with his trumpet. Other members of the organization are S/Sgt. Frank Grover, sax, Cpl. Pete Bonham, piano and Sgt. Joe Sakakian, Sq. D, drums.

Clipping of Dorothy Fields with Sal's band. ca 1940's

St. Patrick Festivities at U. S. O. Bring, Entertain Center's Largest Assembly

More Than 1,200 Uncle Sam's Nephews and Nieces Attend

It took 1,232 soldiers, sailors, and marines to do it but they did and the Nebraska street U. S. O. now has a new record for Sunday attendance and also proudly acclaims one of the most successful programs ever to be presented to the swarms of Uncle Sam's nephews and nieces who attended the St. Patrick's frolic Sunday night.

While playing hosts to hungry G. I.'s, members of the Sioux City Teachers' association served more than 300 persons at a buffet supper which featured the day's entertainment and floor show. Miss Nora Lemcke was social chairman and Miss Eliene James was program chairman.

Staff Sergeant Bob Hunan served as master-of-ceremonies for the show which included musical selections by Peggy Joyce Britton accompanied by Joyce Tronsareau and a pantomine and dance by Vernon Cowgie. Members of the U. S. O. hostess corps and women escorts for the service men were participants in a contest for the best and most original St. Patrick's necktie for their partners. The contest was won by Mrs. Frank Flannery.

Marriage Tonight

Judges were Technical Sergeant Varge Daniel and his fiancee, Miss Evelyn Collum, both of Cisco, Tex. Young Daniel, a veteran of two years service in the south Pacific and Miss Collum will be married tonight at the home of Rev. T. G. Lilley, pastor of the First Presbyterian church. Following the ceremony, the couple will be given a reception at the U. S. O. center in true military style.

The center was in a setting of green decorations for the dance through the courtesy of Central high school students. Sergeant Sal Carson's orchestra played for dancing. Miss Betty Barney was vocalist.

At the Sergeant Bluff, U. S. O. center Sunday night, officials distributed the first 300 copies of the center's new song book, "Songs Service Men Sing, which was compiled by Mrs. D. D. Dewey, program chairman, and Miss Fay Walker. Many copies will be sent to men overseas who have requested the book, Mrs. Dewey said, and the local demand, too, has been large.

Supper and Music

A buffet supper served by the Rose Croix chapter, Order of Eastern Star, highlighted the evening's entertainment, which was followed by a musical program by pupils of the Edna McLaughlin studio. Dancing concluded the day.

Members of the Riverside Methodist church will sponsor the treats tonight and an air base orchestra will play for dancing, the chairman stated. Wednesday night will be bridge night, and hosts will be Mayflower Congregational church members.

In the afternoon a group of air base soldiers will try their hand at the culinary arts with a spaghetti feed. All the cooking will be strictly G. I. style done by the boys themselves.

Clippings. ca 1940's

USO Formal Dance Tonite

Don't forget that big annual USO Formal Fall Dance, tonight is the night. This big event will be held at the Skylon Ballroom starting at 8:30. Music will be furnished by the Air Base Band under the able direction of Sgt. Sal Carson.

The Military Misses will be the host for the evening. All the Base military personnel are cordially invited to attend this big night of dancing with beautiful gals.

ODDS and ENDS. Pvt. Alexander S. Bovee, who authors "General Supply News" columns, is from San Francisco, where he was a purchasing agent for a machine tool company. He's now a QM clerk and married. . . . Genial . . . easy-going Cpl. Stephen L. Bailey (Atlanta, Ga.) says he stood guard once after reaching this base over a year ago and was then placed in the same or similar work in post-EM days. His wife is employed by the Singer Sewing Machine company at Atlanta . . . From the "Navigator" we learn that Cpl. Don Schuerholz who has been keeping track of his losses in a family gin-rummy tournament, now owes some $20,000 to his wife. That should give her the household dictatorship. . . . PFC Sid Peller, a pre-Med student at NYC before entering, plays chess in his spare time when he can find an opponent . . . A band conducted by Sgt. Sal Carson was one of two selected on a competitive basis from San Francisco to appear on "Fitch Bandwagon" radio program. Sal organized his first band, a unit of kids, when he was in the ninth grade . . . Lt. Robert A. Warner, an assistant provost marshal, is from Darien, Conn. He served with the state police . . . PFC Gene Romel Signor, Los Angeles clerk in combat S-2, who helps keep the maps in the war room up-to-the-minute, worked in the engineering dept. of the Hughes Aircraft plant. He was also assistant editor of their employee paper, "Hughes News" . . . After the final performance of "Sound Off II" Sgt. Harry Steinburg asked Sgt. Carol Miller if he wouldn't take some long underwear (GI) back to the base for him. Sgt. Miller says he doesn't mind doing these favors, but he does wish Sgt. Steinburg would drop around to Unit F and pick up the underwear . . . Humorous moment: Violent explosion of flash bulb and a shower of glass particles when S/Sgt. Dallas McKee is snapping a photo of round table discussion at first orientation session.

IMPROVISING: The Tuesday nite dances, which brings to the base all those lovely Military Misses certainly fulfills a GI's dreams. Judging from the increasing crowds each week, GIs know it . . . about time that someone gave credit to the two solid dance orchestras we have on the base. The boys are playing on "their own time" and enjoy doing it. Two distinctive styles are heard—"The Tenor Band," under the direction of Sgt. Sal Carson, plays soft and sweet with a light and pleasant "lift"; while "The Bombardiers," under the baton of Pvt. Sam Schriber, swings out with the jam and jive. They're doing a grand job and more of us should remember to tell them so . . . Among the many newcomers to the band is M/Sgt. Emerson Hill who has taken over the duties of first sergeant and assistant director of the Military Band. Sgt. Hill has left an enviable record behind him as director of the Salt Lake band and what is our fortunate gain is their terrific loss.

Clippings. ca 1940's

find an opponent . . . A band conducted by Sgt. Sal Carson was one of two selected on a competitive basis from San Francisco to appear on "Fitch Bandwagon" radio program. Sal organized his first band, a unit of kids, when he was in the ninth grade . . . Lt. Robert A. Warner, an assistant provost marshal, is from Darien, Conn. He served with the state police . . . PFC Gene Romel Signor, Los Angeles clerk in combat S-2, who helps keep the maps in the war room up-to-the-minute, worked in the engineering dept. of the Hughes Aircraft plant. He was also assistant editor of their employee paper, "Hughes News" . . . After the final performance of "Sound Off II" Sgt. Harry Steinburg asked Sgt. Carol Miller if he wouldn't take some long underwear (GI) back to the base for him. Sgt. Miller says he doesn't mind doing these favors, but he does wish Sgt. Steinburg would drop around to Unit F and pick up the underwear . . . Humorous moment: Violent explosion of flash bulb and a shower of glass particles when S/Sgt. Dallas McKee is snapping a photo of round table discussion at first orientation session.

Princess theater ad. ca 1940's

Iowa Lakes post card.

Soldiers Enjoy Gala Fourth at Sergeant's Bluff

The Sergeant Bluffs USO and Monahan Post Legionaires were hosts to the Air Base soldiers in a gala Fourth of July celebration. A chicken dinner, outdoor concert and dancing in the club made the historic date one to remember.

An excellent chicken dinner began the events of the evening. A feature of the dinner being the service by the members of Monahan Legion Post, Sioux City. They dished it out on the line and took on kitchen duty for the occasion. And what's more, they seemed to enjoy doing KP; proving quite dexterous in that art after a 26 year furlough.

Afterwards, an open air concert was given by Monahan Post Drum and Bugle Corps. This organization, directed by Drum Major Jack Youngblade, won the state championship for the years 1942-3. They are sons of the Legionaires, ranging in age from 12 to 17, who can really score on the songs of World War I, which have become classics.

Dancing in the club topped off the evening's festivity. Beginning at 2030 until 2300 to the music of our own Sal Carson and his orchestra's hot rhythm.

The appreciation of the Air Base soldiers to Chairman Frank G. Kinney and his Legionaires for a * * * good time.

Legionaires functioning at the affair were Roy Fox, Al Hennington, Glenn Ege, Howard Scott, Tim Murphy, W. Bluitt, Fred Johannson, Geo. D. Lonsberg, ack Duling, T. H. Knudson, Jack Perrine, J. B. Tasker, and Frank G. Kinney, Chairman.

"Forced to Vacate" U. S. O. Party Planned

Forced to leave its present quarters by August 31 because of the expiration of its lease, the downtown U. S. O. will hold a "forced to vacate" party at 8 o'clock Tuesday night.

Dancing to the music of Sol Carson's orchestra, special entertainment, a floor show, door prizes, and dance contests have been planned for soldiers and U. S. O. hostesses.

Shirley Clayton is chairman of the committee in charge and is being assisted by Peggy Guinane, Betty Lou Friend, Edith McArthur and John W. Crowe.

John McEwen, director, has stated that despite the fact that the party is being given August 21, regular activities will continue at the U. S. O. until August 31.

1943 clippings

Betrothal To Sal Carson Of Oakland Revealed By Mr., Mrs. L. V. Glenn

Announcement of the engagement of Miss Kathleen Glenn of Vallejo to Sal Carson of Oakland is being made by Mr. and Mrs. L. V. Glenn, 410 Fourth street, parents of the bride-elect.

Miss Glenn, a graduate of Vallejo High School with the class of 1940, is a sister of Marian, Martin, Norma and Lewis Glenn of Vallejo, and Bill Glenn of Napa. She is a member of Les Amies and is employed in Vallejo.

Mr. Carson is the son of Mr. and Mrs. Joseph Carcione of Oakland, and a brother of Valeria and Gloria Carcione, and Mrs. Sylvia Oppedahl, all of Oakland. He is a graduate of the University High School with the class of 1940, and until enlisting in the Army Air Corps two months ago he led his own orchestra in Oakland.

Wedding plans are indefinite.

NEWEST BRIDE-ELECT

Vallejo's newest bride-elect is Miss Kathleen Glenn, whose engagement to Sal Carson, formerly of Oakland and now a member of the Army Air Corps, was announced today by her parents, Mr. and Mrs. L. V. Glenn. (Photo by "Cap" Crane).

Announcement of the engagement of Kathleen to Sal. Vallejo Times Herald, November 26, 1942.

The Air Force Band. Sal is in the second row. 4th from the left. ca 1940's

Sioux City, Air Force Band. ca 1943

The band playing

Sioux City post card

Buffet Suppers Draw 300 Service Men to U. S. O. Centers

More than 300 service men attended U. S. O. centers in Sioux City Sunday evening, according to estimates by Directors John M'Ewen and Ralph A. Leake of the Nebraska street and Sergeant Bluff centers.

One hundred twenty-five of 200 service men present at the Nebraska street center were served a buffet supper by members of Sioux City chapter, Quota International. A buffet supper also was served at the Sergeant Bluff center by women members of Sioux City's Jewish federation under chairmanship of Mrs. W. C. Slotsky and Mrs. S. H. Shulkin. The federation also sponsored a variety show, attended by more than 100.

Sergeant Sal Carson's tenor band from the Sioux City air base, featured at weekly dances in the downtown U. S. O. center, played for a ball from 8:30 p. m. to 11:30 p. m. in Moose lodge clubrooms Sunday, attended by service men and lodge members. Prior to the ball, a turkey dinner was served members of the orchestra.

USO clipping. 1943

WELCOME
U.S.O. CLUB
SERGEANT BLUFF, IOWA

"THE PROGRAM,
GATHERS SPEED

THURSDAY
JULY 29

DANCE NIGHT
AIR BASE ORCHESTRA
SAL CARSON LEADING—"NUFF SAID"

(THIS ONE YOU CAN'T MISS)

FRIDAY—JULY 30	SATURDAY—JULY 31
DANCING—REFRESHMENTS	"SATURDAY NIGHTER"
PLEASANT GIRLS—ARCHERY—BEST MALTED MILKS	
AND MILK SHAKES YOU EVER TASTED!	

SUNDAY   AUGUST 1

4:30 GOOD MUSIC—ARCHERY
6:30 BUFFET SUPPER
7:30 VARIETY SHOW
8:30 DANCE

USO poster. July, 1943

DANCE!
SATURDAY, NOVEMBER 13
8:30--11:30

•

DOWN-TOWN USO

•

Military Misses

•

TENOR BAND
Sgt. Sal Carson, Directing

USO – Dance. November 13, 1943

MUSICAL VARIETY SHOW!!
Presented by Sioux City Air Base
"SOUND OFF"
RIVERVIEW STADIUM
SUNDAY, AUGUST 1, 1943--8:15 P. M.
Proceeds to Air Base Enlisted Men's Fund

General Admission		
Established Price	50c	
Federal Tax	5c	Nº 1799
State Tax	1c	
Total Admission	56c	

"Sound Off" - musical show, August 1, 1943

HALLOWEEN
FORMAL   In Time of War
Regulation Uniforms
Considered Formal

DANCE!
DOWN-TOWN USO

SATURDAY, OCTOBER 30th
SAL CARSON'S BAND

Military Misses: It's Your Party
Hostesses   Please Come

USO – Halloween poster. October 30, 1943

Old Man Stork paid two visits to the band this week and blessed the Sal Carsons and the Larry Cariells with baby girls.

MERRY CHRISTMAS AND HAPPY NEW YEAR

CARCIONE—In Sioux City, Ia., December 4, 1943, at the Methodist hospital, to Mr. and Mrs. Sal Carcione, 1426 Douglas street, a daughter.

"Old Man Stork". December 4, 1943

Rehear...ns for Air Base Show Begin

Pictured is the air base orchestra which is busily rehearsing for the forthcoming musical revue, Sound Off, The orchestra is under the direction of Corporal Sal Carson. It will be featured in the overture and also will accompany the many and varied acts. The show is written and produced by Staff Sergeant Eddy Joseph and Private John DeVries.

The Sioux City air base is teeming with activity these days as preparation for the coming musical variety revue titled, Sound Off, gets into full swing. The show, whose theme will be the cares and woes that a soldier encounters during the day, promises to be a smash hit and its sponsors say it will keep the audience in an uproar from beginning to end.

Featured in the revue will be military talent from the Sioux City air base and its satellite bases. The performers are all former professionals from the east and west coasts who have appeared in some of the best theaters of the country. Many of the musicians are former members of name bands such as Tommy Dorsey, Jimmy Dorsey, Harry James, Larry Clinton, Claude Thornhill and Tommy Tucker.

Busy days are these for the coauthors Staff Sergeant Eddy Joseph and Private John DeVries, who find themselves not only writing the words and music and various sketches for the revue, but also casting, designing the stage and scenery, handling the publicity and directing the show. The night lights burn long now and if one were to stroll past the music and dramatics building he would hear the tinkling of the piano, the bellowing of lusty baritones and the shuffling of feet as the G. I. entertainers hurry to recapture their "forgotten-for-the-duration" ability.

Highlights of the production will be the original songs written by Eddy and John. They have composed a stirring melody titled, Sound Off, which will be the theme. Also G. I. Dream, At Ease, Soldier, At Ease, A Letter from Mother, are expected to prove to be smash hits.

The show is sponsored by the special service section under the direction of Maj. Aubrey Huston, special service officer of the air base.

The performance is scheduled for Sunday, August 1, at 8:30 p. m. at Riverview park stadium. Tickets are on sale by the Military Misses with Mrs. Gordon Hollan as ticket chairman. For further information about ticket sales the public may call any U. S. O. club room.

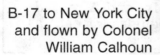

"Sound Off" – rehearsal August 1, 1943

B-17 to New York City and flown by Colonel William Calhoun

Hell's Angels

Quick Search

? ☒☒

303rd Bomb Group (H) Legacy

Clark Gable and
William R. Calhoun

Home • About Us • Contact Us • 303rd BGA • NexGen • Talk Forum • Links • PX • What's New • FAQ • Guest Book
Personnel • Aircraft • Nose Art • B-17 Thunderbird • Ground Support • Uniforms • Journals • More Info • Search
Mission Reports • Combat Crews • Individual Photos • Misc Photos • POWs • KIA • Overseas Graves • TAPS

Colonel William Calhoun. A 1943 photo on a mission to Belgium. Calhoun was
the pilot and Clark Gable flew as the photographer/observer. Front page of Hell's Angels.

–49–

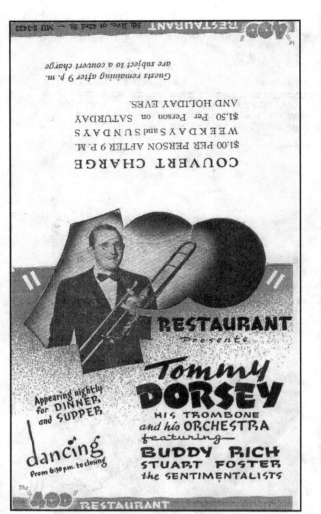

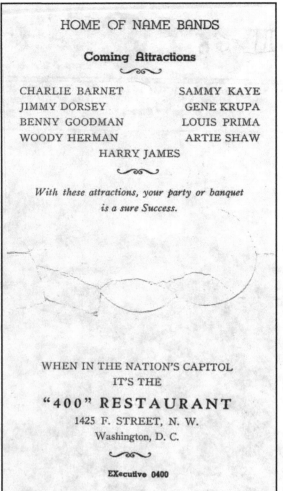

Tent card – "400" Restaurant, 5th Ave. at 43rd St., NYC

Flyer for "400" Restaurant, 1425 F. Street, Washington, D.C. (inside the New York tent card).

Vocal trio. April 1944. Private Robert Jones, Sal and Sergeant Louis Israel

USO Sweetheart Prom. February 13, 1944

February 1944. USO schedule.

(Upper Right)
Melody Pilots, April 8, 1944,
The Bombardier

The Bombardier headline, April 8, 1944

MELODY PILOTS. This trio will be one of the highlights on each Tuesday's program. Reading left to right: Pvt. Robert Jones, Sgt. Carson and Sgt. Louis Israel. WNAX broadcasts have a listening audience in the states of Iowa, South Dakota, North Dakota, Minnesota, Nebraska.

Solo shot of Sal
April 8, 1944. The
Bombardier.
Oops. Sal is right handed.

REHEARSAL. Almost every GI on the base has danced to the music of Sgt. Sal Carson and his tenor band. He's shown above as he rehearses at the WNAX studio in Sioux City for the base-sponsored radio program which starts broadcasting next Tuesday from the base theater at nine p. m. Sal is from San Francisco and had his own orchestra, playing prominent hotels and night spots on the west coast. Just before becoming an EM in October, 1942, he completed a five week engagement at the swank Ahwahnee hotel in Yosemite park—a rendezvous for Hollywood celebrities.
—Photos by S/Sgt. Dallas McKee

Variety Show Starts April 11 From Theater

Aired Each Tuesday Nine P.M.; Features Sal Carson's Band

Starting next Tuesday night GIs will participate in their own radio show to be broadcast over station WNAX from 9:00 to 9:30. Talent for this show will be strictly GI.

The program, which will emanate from the base theater, will have S/Sgt. Frank B. Hobbs as master of ceremonics. S/Sgt. Hobbs, a veteran of service in India with the famous "Flying Cobra" squadron, was a radio announcer in civilian life. He did free lance radio work on the west coast, appearing on programs in Los Angeles, San Francisco and Seattle. Before this he worked with well-known bands as a baritone soloist.

Picked units of the base band will make up the musical portion of the program. The "High Fliers," a swing unit under the direction of Sgt. Sal Carson will be featured. "The Melody Pilots," a trio composed of Sgt. Sal Carson, Sgt. Louis Israel and PFC Robert Jones will also be heard. A short interview with a returned overseas veteran will make up the rest of the program.

The Tuesday night movie scheduled for 6 p. m. will be shown at 6:30. At 8:30 the swing unit and Sgt. Hobbs will take over the stage and entertain all GIs present until 9 p. m. when the show will be aired.

WNAX is a Columbia outlet with studios in Sioux City and Yankton, S. D. It has a listening audience from the five states of Iowa, South Dakota, North Dakota, Minnesota and Nebraska.

Variety Show. April 11, 1944

(Upper Right)
Pre-payday party. The Flying Sioux, March 24, 1945

Air Corp photo

Music, Eats, Dates at Rec Hall Pre-Payday Party Tomorrow

Sal Carson's band, a buffet supper, bingo and the Military Misses head the list of attractions at the Rec hall tomorrow. The occasion is the second monthly pre-payday party, sponsored by special service for the benefit of those GIs who may be afflicted with a slight case of financial embarrassment. It's all for free.

However, you don't have to be broke to gain admittance. And you don't have to come alone, either. Just bring the wife, the girl friend, or somebody else's wife, if you like.

Festivities get underway at 1700, with the supper being served at 1800. The menu consists of shrimp, cold sliced baked ham, cold sliced beef, potato salad, pickles, celery, cake and hot chocolate.

At 1700 Sal Carson and his band will take over and will provide music for dancing until 2200. The Military Misses will be dancing partners for the GIs without dates.

Bingo will be played throughout the evening, and prizes will be given. All this, we repeat, is for free.

Miss Isabel Aufderheide, Rec hall hostess, will be in charge.

Sq. C Anniversary Party Set for Fri.

Next Fri., 30 March, members of Sqs. C and Z, with civilian hostesses, will gather at the Alpine room in Sioux City for Sq. C's anniversary party. Music will be furnished by Sal Carson and his band from 2000 until 2400.

At this time, results of Sq. C's popularity contest will be announced and the winners, "Miss Wac" and "Miss USO" will be honored and presented prizes.

A buffet supper will be served during the evening.

War Fund to Help Prisoners of War

Last chance for base military and civilian personnel to make their contribution toward keeping the Red Cross at the side of the men overseas will be Sat., 31 March, after which the 1945 Red Cross war fund campaign closes.

Contributions so far have reached $3,850, said Capt. James H. Williams, drive officer, this week. Special tables to facilitate last-minute donations will be set up Sat. in each squadron orderly room, the PX, bank, finance office and officers club.

Red Cross war funds pay for packages sent to prisoners of war in Germany and Japan, for blood plasma and whole blood sent to the fronts, for training nurse's aides to help care for returning wounded veterans, for emergency assistance to servicemen and their families and for assistance to disaster victims here in the US.

Aged Strippers in Britain

London (CNS) — The House of Commons is considering a proposal barring women under 50 from the strip-tease stage. One member wanted to know why there were strippers under 50 in view of the shortage of women in factories and on the war fronts.

The Sioux Forum

Question: What New Year's resolutions are you making?

Resolutions for New Year's are pretty much a thing of the past if the answers the inquiring photographer got this week are any indication of a general trend. People just don't make them anymore. They're either being realistic or are disillusioned; they know they'll break them if they make any. And most GIs, having their job already cut out for them, figure making resolutions is just so much wasted effort . . . they just want to go home. Apparently, in a world that is gauging everything by the end of the war, the end of a year doesn't mean much.

The answers:

PFC STEWART — CPL COONEY — W/O BOUND — SGT CARSON

PFC Don Stewart, gunner, combat crew pool: "That I'm going to be home next New Year's—that's all."

Cpl. William Cooney, armorer-gunner, Section 2: "I'm not making any—but I wish Section 2 would resolve to have less PT and more hot water. Also I'd like somebody to figure out how to end the war so I can be home next New Year's."

W/O Joseph E. Bound, personnel officer, unit personnel: "It is my opinion that there isn't much room in the army for New Year's resolutions. But I do believe that GIs can help themselves most by resolving to perform cheerfully and to the best of their ability the duties assigned to them by their superiors."

Sgt. Sal Carson, bandleader, Section A: "I usually make some kind of resolutions—not written out of course. The main one I'm making is the same as I made last year—to keep studying my music. I want to keep improving the new base orchestra, too. I couldn't resolve to treat my wife better because I already treat her fine."

Photographs by T/Sgt. George Sumka.

New Years Resolutions, The Flying Sioux, January 1945

Air Corp photo

New Dance Band Has Opportunities, Money for GIs

Want to pick up a little extra money in your spare time? If you do, and if you can play an instrument, you'll get the opportunity.

Sgt. Sal Carson has organized a dance band to replace the Melody Pilots, a group taken from the military band stationed here recently. The band is coming along well, Sal says, but furloughs, shipping lists and the hospital have a tendency to dig into the band's instrumentation.

Sal needs more musicians, preferably those who can read music. You don't have to be a Glen Gray, Duke Ellington or Bobby Sherwood—there'll be a place for you somewhere. Just call Sgt. Sal Carson, special service office, ext. 219.

New dance band. January 13, 1945

Base Audiences Applaud Songs of Newest Composer

Last week, Sgt. Sal Carson's band introduced a new song, "Dream Road." It made its debut at the Sq. A party and since then has been played at the officers club, the NCO club and the Rec hall.

Written in the romantic vein, the song was well received by all of its audiences.

Another song by the same composer, "Will You or Won't You?" is scheduled for a premiere performance at the officers club party this evening.

The orchestral scores for both songs have been made by Sgt. Carson.

The composer? Lt. Col. William R. Calhoun, Jr., base commander.

New songs by Colonel Calhoun.

The Band at Shore Acres

IN ITS FIRST OUTDOOR appearance of the season, the Sal Carson orchestra provided the music for Sq. A's party at Shore Acres last week. Highlight of the evening was the introduction of a song by Lt. Col. William R. Calhoun, Jr., entitled "Dream Road." Left to right are Cpl. Pete Prestigiacomo and S/Sgt. Frank Grover, saxes; Sgt. Fred Lyman, bass; S/Sgt. Lou Machacek, sax; Sgt. Sal Carson, trumpet; Pvt. Joe Harrington, drums and Cpl. Larry Bonham, piano.

The Band at Shore Acres, ca 1945

Rec Hall Lawn Party Tomorrow To Feature Girls, Food, Music

A picnic lunch, the music of Sal Carson and his band, lawn games and the Military Misses can be entered in your date book for tomorrow at 1800. It's special service's monthly pre-payday party, to be held in and around the Rec hall. Your end-of-the-month poverty need not worry you since it's all for free.

The evening's festivities will get underway at 1800, with a wienie roast on the Rec hall lawn. Athletic-minded GIs will find badminton, croquet and other lawn games for after-dinner entertainment. And they will find the lovely Military Misses on hand to be partners. PT was never like this.

From 1900-2200, Sal Carson

and his popular air base dance orchestra will provide music for dancing.

But it isn't just a stag affair. Married GIs are invited to bring their wives and, if you're not married, you can bring a date.

Miss Isabel Aufderheide, Rec hall hostess, will be in charge.

Rec Hall Lawn Party, 1945?

Page 2 Sept. 1, 1945 The Flying Sioux   THE FLYING

NCO Club Celebrates First Anniversary

NCO Club Celebrates First Anniversary. The Flying Sioux

Local Entertainers, Sal Carson's Band Add to Festivities

With a highly successful party held in the club building last Sun. night, members of the base NCO club and their guests celebrated the first anniversary of the club's founding. Playing to one of the largest crowds in the club's one-year history, Sal Carson and his all-soldier band, civilian talent imported from Sioux City and free beer contributed largely to the success of the evening.

The program started at 2000 with a floor show presented by young ladies from Sioux City. First was the "Ballet Cymbal" dance of Marlis Cooper and Beverly Jean Benson, followed by a group of accordian solos by Jean Russell.

Joyce Kellog, a baton twirler, took the floor next, twirling to a group of military songs.

After the floor show, Sal Carson and his orchestra, with Vocalist Terry Whelan, played for dancing until 2200.

At that time, musical diversion was provided by Lawrence Hawkins and his Knights of Rhythm, a four-piece combination from the Chesterfield lounge in Sioux City.

At the halfway mark in the evening's festivities, T/Sgt. Mario LaBarbera, one of the club's board of governors, spoke briefly on the accomplishments of the club during its year of existence. He paid tribute to the various persons and organizations who had helped make the club a success—financial and otherwise. Among those mentioned were the club's regular civilian employees, the hostesses, Sal Carson's orchestra and the fellows who play the one-armed bandit.

The Sioux City AAB NCO club was organized in July, 1944 as an organization open to the first three grades of EM only. T/Sgt. Charles Dugan, 485th group, (then base sgt. major) was the first president. Building 315, a remodeled mess hall, was opened formally to club members at a housewarming party held on 10 Sept.

In Dec. 1942, revisions in the club charter were made to extend memberhip to buck sergeants, and in Jan. 1943, to corporals, making it a full-fledged NCO club.

LT. COL. DELBERT H. HAHN
Acting Station Commandant

THE FLYING SIOUX

VOLUME 1, NUMBER

Carson's Volunteers

Entertainment at the Rec hall, the Field house, the USOs, the NCO club and the officers club would have suffered a severe setback a few months ago if Sgt. Sal Carson hadn't been left here when the base band was transferred to another station.

Sal, though, will tell you that he deserves only a small part of the credit for preventing base social life from becoming virtually non-existent —he gives it all to the volunteer musicians who make up the combo you've been hearing recently at the places mentioned above.

Here's how it all happened:

The WD moved the local military band to another post, taking with it all the musicians who played the local dances. Foreseeing dire consequences, base officials decided something should be done. Carson stepped up, blew a loud fanfare on his trumpet and said he would do it.

And he did. He combed the base for musicians, found them, assisted them in blowing dust off the instruments that had been tucked away for months, held a few rehearsals, and then the band made its debut.

You've heard the new band. Now step up and meet the musicians.

First we have a tenor man, S/Sgt. Frank Grover, from Rockaway Beach, N. Y. His full-time job is that of maintenance man and instructor in communications. He's well qualified for this job too—was a radio man before joining the army more than three years ago. He plays all the reeds and has seen service with numerous bands along the east coast.

Next is S/Sgt. Lou Machacek, another tenor man who also doubles on clarinet. Lou comes from Baltimore, Md. He graduated from Loyola university in ?—more just before being drafted. He played while in college and with other bands in Baltimore

To the Rescue of GI Social Functions They Came After the Base Band Shipped Out.

before the war. He has 2½ years in Panama as a GI and works in flight line maintenance now. He once studied with Sidney Catlett—and considers him his favorite drummer.

A versatile rhythm man is Sgt. Charles Fulmer, Pottstown, Pa., who doubles on bass and guitar. He works in the tech inspector's section now and played with various bands in Pennsylvania before the war.

At the piano is PFC Jack Buckley, Providence, R. I. Now with the 17th wing statistical section, Jac has more than four years in the army. In civilian life he played with Tommy Dorsey and later had his own band. His teacher was Frankie Carle, who remains his favorite piano man.

Another 88-man is Cpl. Larry Bonham, Cincinnati, Ohio. A gunnery instructor now, Larry worked in several dance bands in the Cincinnati area before entering the army a little over a year ago.

T/Sgt. George Sumka, The Flying Sioux's staff photographer, is Carson's man. Before entering the service over three years ago, George was a student at Morton junior college in his home town, Cicero, Ill., where he was preparing to be a music teacher. Besides dance work, George has also played extensively with symphony orchestras. He has a tour of duty in the European and African theaters to his credit.

Organizer, leader and arranger is Sgt. Sal Carson, from San Francisco. Besides guiding the destinies of the band, Sal is the official base bugler and a supply clerk in Sq. D. He had his own band before entering the service, playing prominent hotels and night spots on the west coast.

Right now he's personnel sergeant major for Sq. M.

Cpl. Pete Prestigiaromo also plays sax and clarinet. His home town is Independence, La. Pete took up music as a pastime, playing with his brothers in the town band. He works in ordnance now but tries to keep up with his music every chance he gets. He says, "I find it's a lot of fun to play with the boys. It's a good way to meet people and make new friends."

Sgt. Jack Fulton, Youngstown, Ohio, plays alto sax. Jack was drafted when attending college in Youngstown—about three years ago. Most of his military career was spent in a military band but he's now assigned to the Sq. A supply room.

One of the drummers, S/Sgt. Lewis B. Crookshank, Leechburg, Pa., uses the spare time from a job at third echelon motor maintenance to beat out the rhythms. He flew 26 missions in the ETO as a tail gunner and now wears the DFC and air medal with three clusters. He worked with Sonny Dunham and other name bands in the east before the war.

Sgt. Joe Sahakian is the other drummer. Joe's from Philadelphia—drummed professionally back there

A REGULAR FEATURE at the Sat. night parties at the officers club is Sal Carson's new band. Sal is the trumpet player at the front. Behind him, in the sax section, left to right, are Cpl. Pete Prestigiaromo, S/Sgt. Lou Machacek and Sgt. Jack Fulton. Sgt. Joe Sahakian is at the drums, T/Sgt. George Sumka is playing bass and the guitarist, Sgt. Charles Fulmer, is at Sumka's left. Cpl. Larry Bonham is seated at the baby grand.

Navy's New SB2C-4 Packs Mighty Wallop

Pacific (CNS)—The SB2C-4—the navy's newest carrier plane which participated in the recent raids on Tokyo—packs the biggest punch ever carried by a single-engined aircraft. In addition to the "more-than-1000-pound" bomb load carried in the belly, as in predecessors of this type, the new plane mounts 20 mm cannon in each wing, carries another 1000 pounds of bombs in wing racks and shoots eight 5-inch rockets from similar positions.

Veteran Soldier, 66, Has Fought in 3 Wars

Auckland, N. Z. (CNS)—Who this is a young man's war? Pvt. Mockford is back home again action in Greece, Crete and Li his gay '90s mustache still erect spite his 66 years. A veteran of South African war and World W Pvt. Mockford was captured by Germans in the second Libyan paign. He escaped three times, each time was recaptured. T wounded sons who enlisted with greeted him on his arrival.

THE FLYING SIOUX is published weekly by and for the personnel of Army Air Base, Sioux City, Iowa. Address all inquiries to THE FLYING SIOUX, headquarters, AAB, Sioux City, Iowa. THE FLYING SIOUX receives Camp Newspaper Service material. Republication of credited matter prohibited without permission of CNS, 205 East 42nd, New York City, USA. Permission is given for the republication of all other matter upon date of issue. Opinions expressed in the newspaper are those of the staff members and individual writers and are not to be considered as expressions of the army air forces. Editor: Cpl. Charles O. Brown, Jr. Associate editors: Sgt. Fred Lyman and Sgt. Jack Sayer. Sports editor: Sgt. William (Tess) Bishop. Photographer: T/Sgt. George Sumka. Staff artist: Cpl. Forney Mumford. Public relations officer: Lt. Patrick J. Cullen. Information and Education officer: Lt. Gordon F. Brown. Printers: Bolstein-Kramer. THE FLYING SIOUX may be mailed outside the base.

Carson's Volunteer. <u>The Flying Sioux</u>, March 24, 1945

Air Corp photo

ENLISTED RECORD AND REPORT OF SEPARATION
HONORABLE DISCHARGE

1. LAST NAME - FIRST NAME - MIDDLE INITIAL		2. ARMY SERIAL NO.	3. GRADE	4. ARM OR SERVICE	5. COMPONENT
Carcione Sal J		19 138 cho	Sgt	AC	AUS
6. ORGANIZATION		7. DATE OF SEPARATION	8. PLACE OF SEPARATION		
556th AAF Band		21 Nov 45	Base Sioux City Iowa AAF Separation		
9. PERMANENT ADDRESS FOR MAILING PURPOSES		10. DATE OF BIRTH	11. PLACE OF BIRTH		
715 35th Ave San Francisco 21 Calif		1 Nov 20	San Francisco Calif		
12. ADDRESS FROM WHICH EMPLOYMENT WILL BE SOUGHT		13. COLOR EYES	14. COLOR HAIR	15. HEIGHT	16. WEIGHT	17. NO. DEPEND.
See 9		Blue	Brown	5' 6"	125 lbs	3
18. RACE	19. MARITAL STATUS	20. U.S. CITIZEN	21. CIVILIAN OCCUPATION AND NO.		
WHITE X NEGRO OTHER (specify)	SINGLE MARRIED X OTHER (specify)		Musical Instrument 0-24.120		

MILITARY HISTORY

22. DATE OF INDUCTION	23. DATE OF ENLISTMENT	24. DATE OF ENTRY INTO ACTIVE SERVICE	25. PLACE OF ENTRY INTO SERVICE
	30 Sep 42	30 Sep 42	San Francisco Calif
SELECTIVE SERVICE DATA ► 26. REGISTERED YES / NO	27. LOCAL S.S. BOARD NO.	28. COUNTY AND STATE	29. HOME ADDRESS AT TIME OF ENTRY INTO SERVICE
Not X	Available	Alameda Calif	370 63d St Oakland Calif

30. MILITARY OCCUPATIONAL SPECIALTY AND NO.	31. MILITARY QUALIFICATION AND DATE
Supply Clerk 835	Gnr Cal 30 M-1 16m 44

32. BATTLES AND CAMPAIGNS

None

33. DECORATIONS AND CITATIONS   American Theater Service Medal Good Conduct Medal SO 31 Hq 393 GCFB
AAB Sioux City Iowa 44 World War II Victory Medal 1 Service Stripe

34. WOUNDS RECEIVED IN ACTION

None

35. LATEST IMMUNIZATION DATES				36. SERVICE OUTSIDE CONTINENTAL U.S. AND RETURN		
SMALLPOX	TYPHOID	TETANUS	OTHER (specify)	DATE OF DEPARTURE	DESTINATION	DATE OF ARRIVAL
28 Mar 44	26 Mar 45	7 Oct 43	(See 55)	None	None	None

37. TOTAL LENGTH OF SERVICE						38. HIGHEST GRADE HELD
CONTINENTAL SERVICE			FOREIGN SERVICE			
YEARS	MONTHS	DAYS	YEARS	MONTHS	DAYS	
3	1	22	N O N E			Sgt

39. PRIOR SERVICE

None

40. REASON AND AUTHORITY FOR SEPARATION Convenience of the Government AR 615-365 15 Dec 44 and WD Ltr
WDGAP 220.8, Subj: "Discharge of Surplus Enl Pers in ZI" 22 Sep 45

41. SERVICE SCHOOLS ATTENDED	42. EDUCATION (Years)		
None	Grammar 8	High School 4	College 0

PAY DATA

43. LONGEVITY FOR PAY PURPOSES			44. MUSTERING OUT PAY		45. SOLDIER DEPOSITS	46. TRAVEL PAY	47. TOTAL AMOUNT, NAME OF DISBURSING OFFICER	
YEARS	MONTHS	DAYS	TOTAL	THIS PAYMENT				
3	1	22	$ 200	$ 100	None	$ 99.50	$ 234.9	W H Hutchinson Maj FD

INSURANCE NOTICE

IMPORTANT IF PREMIUM IS NOT PAID WHEN DUE OR WITHIN THIRTY-ONE DAYS THEREAFTER, INSURANCE WILL LAPSE. MAKE CHECKS OR MONEY ORDERS PAYABLE TO THE TREASURER OF THE U.S. AND FORWARD TO COLLECTIONS SUBDIVISION, VETERANS ADMINISTRATION, WASHINGTON 25, D.C.

48. KIND OF INSURANCE			49. HOW PAID		50. Effective Date of Allotment Discontinuance	51. Date of Next Premium Due (One month after 50)	52. PREMIUM DUE EACH MONTH	53. INTENTION OF VETERAN TO		
Nat. Serv.	U.S. Govt.	None	Allotment	Direct to V.A.				Continue	Continue Only	Discontinue
X			X		30 Nov 45	31 Dec 45	$ 3.30	X		

55. REMARKS (This space for completion of above items or entry of other items specified in W.D. Directives)

Lapel Button Issued   ASR Score (2 Sep 45)-47
(35) Typhus 17 Apr 44 Cholera 28 Mar 44 Yellow Fever 21 Mar 44

54. RIGHT THUMB PRINT	

56. SIGNATURE OF PERSON BEING SEPARATED	57. PERSONNEL OFFICER (Type name, grade and organization - signature)
	VICTOR D WALKER

Enlisted Record and Report of Separation

Army of the United States

Honorable Discharge

This is to certify that

SAL J CARCIONE 1o 136 cho Sergeant

556th Army Air Force Band

Army of the United States

is hereby Honorably Discharged from the military service of the United States of America.

This certificate is awarded as a testimonial of Honest and Faithful Service to this country.

Given at ARMY AIR FORCES SEPARATION BASE
SIOUX CITY IOWA

Date 21 November 1945

LEWIS N MILLER
Major Air Corps

Honorable Discharge

Hoberg's flyer

Entrance sign in 1962

1940's ad

Clear Lake Area post card

Chapter 4
Hoberg's Lake County

Sal Carson's Band from 1947 to 1967 was the Hoberg's house band for the summer except for the summers of 1952 (Spokane) and 1957 (Las Vegas). Hoberg's was a very popular Lake County resort and many people came by bus where they were greeted by Sal's band and the unforgettable Ozzie Coulthart.

Bill Bardin, a jazz trombone player, told me he was once in a small pick-up band at Lou Rosenaur's Lovchen Gardens. The drummer in that group was Ozzie Coulthart and the band leader was Burt Bales.

Hoberg's did everything possible for their guests including very good food, dancing, nightly swimming and just about everything that one would want at a resort. If Ozzie found a shy single person he would introduce that person to another shy person with often good results. The Hoberg family and staff must have done things just right because a high percentage of guests came back year after year.

Some well-known orchestras played at Hoberg's and in Tommy Dorsey's case they even challenged Sal's soft ball team to a game...(they lost)

Freddy Martin and Xavier Cugat are examples of other name bands that came to Hoberg's for one-nighters.

Vacationers paid for a week's stay and received, at no additional cost, three meals a day. No wonder the resort was sold out in the summer and fall.

For those of you that enjoy history as I do, there are some interesting articles about Hoberg's at the end of this chapter.

It was at Hoberg's that Sal first met Mel Pleasant who became a good friend and number one fan. Pleasant was impressed with the band and often wrote news items with many appearing in columns such as Herb Caen's.

The Hoberg family and Sal became good friends and because of the Hobergs' many other gigs came along. There was a real love relationship between the Hobergs' and Sal. It is just a shame the wonderful Hoberg's Resort no longer exits.

Early ginger ale bottle (green)

Green glass ash tray   1940's

Grandma and Pa Hoberg

Resort
dining room

Guest cabins

Post card.   ca 1910
bowling alley

Frank and George Hoberg

George Hoberg, Jr. and Eileen

The band waiting for a bus load of guests.   Photo by Bud Taylor.   August 1, 1947.
That's Sal on the far left.

Beverlee Foster, 1947

1947 photo of Beverlee by Romaine

1947 photo of the band.   In front, Beverlee Foster, Gene Ortet (p), Harry Bartlet (d) Burt Silver is next to Beverlee, Sal on the far right.   Names of the others not known.

Beverlee Foster, 1947.
Photo by Romaine

Miss Lake County, Hoberg pilot and Sal at the Hoberg airport.   1948 photo by Bud Taylor.

* * *
Hoberg's in Lake County will stage a huge professional all-star show on September 5, to celebrate Labor Day weekend. There will be four star acts, supported by Hoberg's new singing sensation, Gloria Craig, and Sal ("Borrego") Carson's orchestra, with Ozzie doing the emceeing chores. Incidentally, "Borrego," the hit tune of the summer season, will be released nationally early next month . . .

Hoberg's has a new singing sensation, Gloria Craig. The resort had a big pro all-star stage show on September 4th. By the way, Sal Carson's new tune, "Borrego' is expected to hit the big ten hit parade. It will be recorded and released soon.

Clippings, 1947

Ad in Travel
Treasure, 1948

MOTORISTS COME BY THE THOUSANDS--
. . . but the BEST way to Hoberg's is to FLY !

's so easy — it's so quick, you can come often when you fly! hour by lightplane from San Francisco Bay Area and an hour om such cities as Sacramento, Auburn, Nevada City, Marysville, Chico, Red Bluff, Garberville, Willits, Ukiah, Santa Rosa and If you don't have a plane of your own, you can rent or charter any airport.

The mile long, paved runway on the Hoberg Airport is a pleasure for any pilot. Elevation at the field is only 2100 ft. (Hoberg's RESORT has an elevation of 3500). There is a telephone on the field, and free ground transportation is supplied to registering guests.

•

No overnight tiedown fee

No landing fee

*By flying in, you have
more time for*
Swimming
   Riding
       Hiking
            Dancing
and many other sports

•

Enjoy the "big time" dance music of Sal Carsons and his orchestra 'Ozzie, the good natured, chubby little M. C. will blast your birthdays and anniversaries. Conventions and large and small groups find Hoberg's *unsurpassed* for good food, beautiful surroundings, congenial help and good clean fun for everyone.

•

HOBERG'S AMONG
THE PINES

(10 miles South of Clear Lake) is a real *pleasure* resort— enjoyed by young and old.

P. O. ADDRESS:
Lake County, California

Band photo by Bud Taylor, 1947. (l to r) In front: first two, not known, Fay McNalley (far right), In back: Burt Silver, not known, Sal, Gloria Craig, Jack Taylor, Don Smith and Harry Walker.

Post 8/20 . Sal Carson, the popular maestro at Hoberg's Lake County whose picture appeared in this column last week with Tommy Dorsey looking over Sal's new original "Borrego," may have a song-hit on his hands. Dorsey likes it. Sal wrote the song honoring the Hoberg Southern California resort of the same name, and has hundreds of re-

Clipping, 1947

Publicity photo of Donna Craig. 1948

Sal, Jack Taylor, Burt Silver. In front: Gloria Craig and Mr. Unknown on violin

Bud Taylor photo 1948 or 1949 outside the dining room.   Far right in back is Bob Ferreira. In front holding a trumpet is Ozzie Coulthart.

August 12, 1950

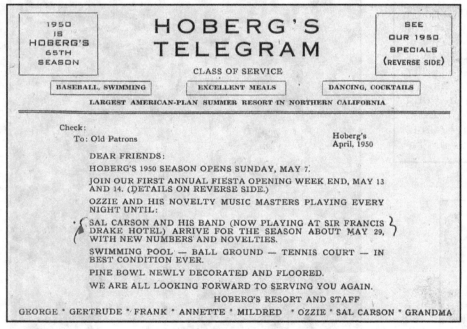

Telegram from Hoberg's.

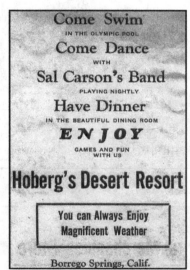

Borrego Springs flyer, 1950

Photographs of Vacation Moments by C. L. "Bud" Taylor

Brochure used in the 50's (cover)

Meet "Ozzie"

MASTER OF CEREMONIES, HOBERG'S

This remarkable character, who got his start on the trumpet as a Boy Scout in Canada, makes sure there is never a dull moment "Among the Pines." He was once presented with a gold trumpet by the Prince of Wales, and never got over the shock! He has since played with bands all over the United States, made stunt dives in the movies and displayed his versatility on the drums in stage shows. Don't be surprised at anything he may dream up!

You can't miss having a good time with "Ozzie"

First page of brochure

Your Congenial Maestro - - - SAL CARSON
HIS TRUMPET AND ORCHESTRA

Sal, besides arranging and singing, has composed several tunes, one being that catchy little closing number he entitled "Hoberg's." His orchestra first gained fame at Cal and Stanford Universities, but Sal was then called for a three-year "engagement" with the Army Air Corps. He later reorganized his band, and has since played at the Normandy Manor in Oregon, the Empire Room of Hotel Utah in Salt Lake, Forest Lake Resort, the Ahwahnee Hotel at Yosemite, the New Town House, and Leon & Eddie's, Oakland, besides several radio engagements. This is the band's second season at Hoberg's "Pine Bowl" Ballroom. Sal will resume nightly appearances here commencing July 3d.

Featuring Beverlee Foster *Vocalist*

Second page of brochure

Hoberg's Resort

The largest privately owned summer resort in California today, Hoberg's dates back to 1885, when Gustav Hoberg, veteran of the Civil War, arrived in Lake County with his wife and family of five children (oldest 12), to begin life in California. No roads at that time touched the land that is now Hoberg's. Lumber for the first house was brought in by pack-horses; trees were felled and land cleared and fenced for a stock, fruit, vegetable, poultry and dairy farm.

In 1895 Gustav Hoberg passed on, leaving Mrs. Hoberg and five children to carry on. What to do! There was lots of fruit, vegetables, butter, eggs and poultry, but no money. Mrs. Hoberg, who was a wonderful cook, met the emergency by taking in a few boarders at $7 a week. Soon many more than could be accommodated wanted to come, and to meet the demand more accommodations were provided. At one time there were more than 40 guests sleeping in tents "Among the Pines." In 1902 Max Hoberg married "Grandma," as she is lovingly called by thousands, and she did much to build Hoberg's and help the then aging Mrs. Hoberg Sr. George, Paul and Frank were born to Max and Theresa, and from childhood each boy did his share in promoting and building the resort. In 1918 Mrs. Hoberg Sr. passed on, and in 1928 Max and Theresa retired, leaving the place to the boys (the third generation). To their energy, aided by their wives—everybody works—is credited the HOBERG'S RESORT of today.

Photo Number Appears on Back of Prints. For Reordering, Use That Number. Address Bud Taylor, Hoberg's, Lake County, Calif.

Back cover of brochure

Oswald "Ozzie" Jonah Coulthart
and Sal.

Ozzie and Sal

"OZZIE"
Your Master of Ceremonies at
HOBERG'S

Ozzie was very popular

Master of Ceremonies
'Ozzie' Coulthart Dies

Many long time residents of Lake County together with thousands of people throughout California were saddened recently by the death of Oswald Jonah Coulthart. "Ozzie",

OSWALD JONAH [OZZIE] COULTHART

as he was known to one and all, was the master of ceremonies and unoffical greeter for Hoberg's Resort on Cobb Mountain for nearly half a century. His cherubic face, sparkling personality, endless energy and musical ability made him a favorite of people of all ages. Chrildren especially were attracted to him and he in turn, showered his

affection and attention on them. From the time the sun came up in the morning until stars twinkled through the towering pines he was up and about, organizing games, calling Bingo, setting up amateur hours, getting the softball tournaments going and distributing friendship and good cheer.

Everybody was somebody special to Ozzie. Governors, senators, mayors and other officials were greeted with warmth and affection but so were children, teenagers and the ordinary Hoberg guests. From the depression years right through the 60's a lot of people who never heard of Lake County knew about Hoberg's and that meant they knew about Ozzie. He was probably the most popular individual in Lake County for decades. He meant a lot to Hoberg's and Hoberg's meant a lot to him. So much so that he was married in a plane while flying over Hoberg's Resort making sure that when he said, "I do", he was directly over the place that he loved for so many years.

When Hoberg's was sold in the 70's, Ozzie moved to a retirement home in nearby Middletown. Although his beloved Hoberg's was gone, Ozzie still kept doing what he had done for so long, bringing happiness and a smile to his new neighbors. Many times the residents of Middletown would hear a trumpet blowing its greeting and everyone would know that Ozzie was on the job. He is probably still on the job somewhere else, and Gabriel might well be looking for a new job. Move over Gabe, here comes Ozzie.

Article about Ozzie. He was born November 27, 1904. Died
December 17 1983 In Santa Clara, CA

Lake County ad, 1950's

Poster for June 10, 1951.

Sal's boat on Clear Lake, 1950's. Had the 26 foot Criss Craft for years. It had a 225 horse power engine.

Julie Mason
At Hoberg's

Julie Mason, frequent vocalist on the Sherwood TV show will join up with Sal Carson and his orchestra, at Hoberg's Resort for the next few weeks.

Sal reports biz is zooming at this Lake County vacation retreat and invites all his pals to drop by for a swim, fizz and eats.

Clipping about Julie Mason, ca 1950's

Fay McNalley, ca 1950's . Photo by Bud Taylor

Costume night at Hoberg's.   Photo by Bud Taylor.   ca 1950's.   (l to r)   Fay McNalley, Beverlee Foster, Dick Keegan, Sal, Jack Taylor, not known sax player next to Sal, Burt Silver, Harry Walker. The cute little girl is Sal's daughter JoAnne.

The Tommy Dorsey Orchestra.   Charlie Shavers at the mike. Standing is Tommy Dorsey.   1958

BANDLEADER SAL CARSON of Hoberg's in Lake County has turned composer. Sal now has over 1,000 orders for his new tune, "Borrego." The title is drawn from George Hoberg's new southern California desert resort of the same name. Many critics have given the number the go-ahead and predict that it will hit the top before the year is out. The "Sentimental Gentleman," Tommy Dorsey, picked up the tune when he played at Hoberg's recently and will probably be featuring it in the near future.

Baseball game at Hoberg's. The umpire is Frank Hoberg, Sal is the catcher and at bat is Tommy Dorsey, 1958

(Sent by Ozzie, the m. c. and Mel Pleasant at Hoberg's.)

"Here's an item for your paper. The hit tune of the season here is "Borrego" written by Oakland's and our own Sal Carson. When Tommy Dorsey was here recently he took the tune with him and predicted a bright future for it. The tune will be recorded and released in the very near future."

* * *

Hoberg's in Lake County will stage a huge professional all-star show on September 5, to celebrate Labor Day weekend. There will be four star acts, supported by Hoberg's new singing sensation, Gloria Craig, and Sal ("Borrego") Carson's orchestra, with Ozzie doing the emceeing chores. Incidentally, "Borrego," the hit tune of the summer season, will be released nationally early next month . . .

Sal with Tommy Dorsey, 1958

Three clippings.

Charlie Shavers. Vogue picture record. Shavers (trumpet); Buddy De Franco (clarinet); Alvin Stoller (drums); John Potaker (piano); Sidney Block (bass). 1958

SAL CARSON and TOMMY DORSEY
At Hoberg's

Article and photo of Tommy Dorsey, 1958

"Borrego"

Dorsey and Sal, 1958

Hoberg's Shutout Oakland Ramblers

Hoberg's Resort in Lake county closed its baseball season during the past week with a 3-0 shutout win over the Oakland Ramblers. Salcarson did the heavy hitting for the winners, with three for three.

Walden, p	4	1	2	Graham,p	4	0
Gonsalves,c	4	1	2	Suppe,c	4	0
C.Hoberg, 1b	4	1	2	Hanson,1b	4	0
Mageson,2b	4	0	1	Mondini,2b	4	0
G.Hoberg,3b	4	0	1	Thomas,3b	4	0
Pleasant,s	4	0	1	Peterson,s	4	0
Olson,lf	4	0	1	Simmons,lf	4	0
Angelly,lf	4	0	0	Parrot,cf	4	0
Silver,cf	4	0	0	Hipse,lf	4	0
Salcarson,rf	3	0	3	Jorgeson,p	4	0
Totals	39	3	12	Totals	40	0

(l to r) Ozzie Coulthart, Dick Keegan, Sal, Hazel Mack, Mr. Unknown on clarinet and Jack Taylor. Photo by Bud Taylor and courtesy of Vince Emerson. Ca 1950's

Piedmont Lounge softball team of Oakland beat Hoberg's Sunday 7 to 4. Joe Donohue, 64, ex-New York Giant hurler, pitched the win and also got two hits. It was a very warm day but Donohue was good for the full nine innings— and don't think Hoberg's wasn't trying to win! Bill Welch and Louie Navonni stared for the Hoberg team, each getting two hits. There were so many Oaklanders there it looked like 20th and Broadway. Sal Carson and his band are drawing great crowds, and the Doug Strand Trio at Forest Lake is doing great. All of which news comes on a card that is signed "Ozzie, MC and Mel Pleasant."

Sal and two talent show participants, 1953. There was a contest once a week.

Hoberg's mailer. ca 1952

Hoberg's Resort Will Open Friday, Free Show Sun.

SAL CARSON

At the grand opening of Hoberg's Resort on Friday, May 27, Sal Carson will present his 11-piece orchestra featuring lovely vocalist Beverlee Foster.

One of the highlights of the band will be a five-violin ensemble to play for the first time in Lake County. Added attractions of the band will be renditions of vocal duets by Beverlee Foster and Maestro Sal Carson, and novelty numbers featuring individuals of the band.

Previous to a three-year engagement at Hobergs, this popular band appeared at Forest Lake for three years. Appearing for their seventh season in Lake County, the band has just completed the winter season with Hobergs at their Borrego Desert Resort in southern California.

Dancing will be nightly commencing at 9 o'clock at Hobergs new and lovely Pine Bowl, one of Lake County's favorite dance pots.

A show will be presented without charge at Hobergs Sunday night, May 29, beginning at 8:00 o'clock. In presenting the program and entertainment, the management of Lake County's famous resort extends a cordial invitation to everyone to attend. Dancing will follow the show.

Success note: Sal Carson, ex-California athlete, has written a tune entitled "Borrego," which is now all the rage at Hoberg's, where Sal conducts the resort's dance band. . . . Mel Pleasant predicts the tune will eventually make the Hit Parade. . . .

Desert tan: The Seals, who have sunned themselves in Hawaii in the past, may try Borrego's desert rays next spring. Anyway, that's what SAL CARSON musicmaker at Hoberg's is rumoring. Sal has written a tune, "Borrego," all about the resort near San Diego, and if the Seals train there he might even arrange for a stanza about the O'Doul-brood in the recording.

The champ: Hey, want National Open Champ CARY MIDDLECOFF to exhibit his strokes at your golf club in the last two weeks of October? Write him at 165 Union in the Peabody, Memphis 3, Tenn. He'll come a-swinging, he will.

Private eyeball: Cal's football team has a high powered line, but can you guess the one man pro scouts have eyed lovingly. The name's GEORGE SOUZA, second string end.

Newspapers as a rule generally run the last names of all players appearing in box scores — that is unless two similar names appear; then the initial is used. But very seldom is the first name used. But you have to hand it to Mel Pleasant of Hoberg's. They have a ball team. One of the star players is Sal Carson, the bandleader. To gain the best advantage out of the publicity, clever Mel sent in this box score to a paper, Salcarson. Get it! And who is this Borrego, who plays one of the outfield spots? I thought "Borrego" was the name of a tune Carson composed, and which soon will be on records!

Our own trumpeter, Sal Carson, has just had his great new song, "Borrego," published and recorded. It was the hit tune at Hoberg's all summer, and Sal already has several hundred orders for "Borrego," which we trust will be on the "Hit Parade" shortly.

Play "Borrego," and help yourself and Sal!
* * *

* * *
Hoberg's in Lake County will stage a huge professional all-star show on September 5, to celebrate Labor Day weekend. There will be four star acts, supported by Hoberg's new singing sensation, Gloria Craig, and Sal ("Borrego") Carson's orchestra, with Ozzie doing the emceeing chores. Incidentally, "Borrego," the hit tune of the summer season, will be released nationally early next month . . .

Grand opening article and advance notice of Borrego Resort.   ca 1950's

Five more clippings.

July 76

Sal Carson Band Beats Dorsey Nine

The Sal Carson Orchestra of Hobergs outdid Tommy Dorsey's Band on the ballfield during the past week end, winning 9-4, while in the regular weekly action the Hoberg nine turned back Montclair Post of the Legion, 7-4.

SAL CARSON ORCH. 9, TOMMY DORSEY

Taylor,c	3	1	1	Duffl,c	3	1	
Gene,p	3	0	0	Radsliff,p	3	1	0
Delenikos,1b	3	1	2	Thompson,1b	3	1	1
Wally,2b	3	1	2	Schlinger,2b	3	1	0
Hoberg,3b	3	1	1	Callelo,3b	3	0	1
Pleasant,s	2	1	0	Amoroso,s	3	0	1
Paul,lf	3	1	1	Stout,rf	3	0	1
Silvers,cf	3	1	1	DeMaio,lf	3	0	1
Bert,rf	3	0	0	Levin,cf	3	0	1
Sal Carson,rf	3	2	2	Caloro,lf	3	0	1
Toff,s	3	0	1	Rkhamar,rf	3	0	0
				Dorsey,p	1	0	1
Total	31	9	11	Total	34	4	9

HOBERGS 7, MONTCLAIR POST 638, 4

Lofay,3b	3	1	1	Robinson,c-1b	3	1	1
Seigler,s	3	0	0	Flagg,c	3	0	0
LaMott,c	4	1	1	Fletcher,2b	3	0	0
Clar,p	4	1	1	Robinson,f-s	3	1	1
Pete,lf	3	1	1	Stuckert,lf	3	1	1
Clark,rf	4	0	1	Bird,cf	3	0	1
Lico,lf	3	1	1	Sonntag,rf	3	0	1
Andrini,1b	3	1	2	Porter,lf	3	0	0
Pleasant,2b	1	0	0	Souza,3b	3	1	1
Toff,lf	2	0	0	Lee,cf	3	0	0
Paul,cf	3	1	0	Degler,lf	3	0	0
Sal Carson,rf	1	0	0				
Hunn,c	2	0	1	Total	33	4	6

Hobergs Softballers Trim S. F. Club, 9-0

HOBERGS RESORT, July 25.— The Hobergs softball team defeated Mindy's Lounge of San Francisco, 9 to 0, Saturday as Pitcher Phil Ellis worked a two-hitter.

Sal Carson, Oakland bandsman, and Captain Mel Pleasant featured the winners attack, each collecting two hits.

Cover of brochure

Still another reason why Hoberg's guests are Happy is the proximity to many other fine establishments in the natural playground area. Hoberg's guests may also enjoy the privileges of Seigler's Hot Springs at no additional expense.

Thousands of acres of Pine Scented Forest.

One of Several Comfortable Lobbies.

One of our Cocktail Lounges

Inside brochure (1)

BECAUSE OF ITS CEN- TRAL LOCATION AND MANY DESIRABLE TRAVEL FEATURES, HOBERG'S ATTRACTS ITS GUESTS from the entire coast, from BORDER TO BORDER

The Outdoor Theatre provides Fun in the balmy evenings.

SOMETHING NEW
has been added to our recreational facilities!

ALL GRASS NINE-HOLE GOLF COURSE
Excellent playing condition. Located on main highway four minutes from resort. .New Club House and Lounge.

Friendly, congenial atmosphere.

Inside brochure (2)

Costume night, ca 1953. That's Sal in front and behind him on sax is Danny Peteras who became a member of a New York City pit band. Very good musician. I don't know the names of anyone else in the parade.

Betty Decker
a.ween for the day
Hoberg
mid 50's

Betty Decker and Sal. She was Hoberg's Queen for the Day., ca. mid 1950's

(Left Middle)
(l to r) Freddy Martin, George and Gertrude Hoberg and Sal. Mid 1950's.

(Left bottom)
Dressed-up band at Hoberg's. (l to r) In front: Gus Gustavson, Sal, Bob Sulpizia (possibly) Jack Reese, Darrel Parker, "Howie" Segerson. In back: Shelly Denny, Bill McCubblen, Fred Radke. ca 1950's

Band photo (l to r) in front: Bill?, "Howie" Segerson, Sal, Earl Richardson, Bob Ferreira.
In back: Fran Ashman, the drummer is not known, Bill Catalano, not known.   Hoberg's
in the 1950's.

Cugat drawing on one of his LP's.   He was a
newspaper cartoonist before he had a band.
Had a strong influence in popularizing Latin
music.

Xavier Cugat was another big name band
leader who came to Hoberg's.   He was born
January 1, 1900 in Gerona, Spain.   He died
October 27, 1990 in Barcelona, Spain.

Promotion truck in Lakeport, 1958. Trombone player is Dick Maloff who went to Lawrence Welk's Ork., Sal. The other two are not known.

Poster for stained glass. Sal was the contractor. 1966-67

Two bands: Sal's and The Marlins. August 12, 1967

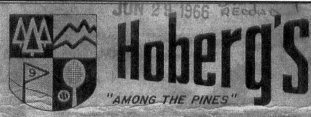
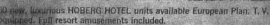

(Top)
June 29, 1966 ad
and article.

(Middle)
August 12, 1967 ad.

(Bottom
San Mateo Times article.
August 11, 1967

–81–

Gina and Patricia D'Arezzo holding the August 12, 1967 poster. Photo by their "papa" Jim Goggin. 2005

(Opposite Page) Article by David Caraccio in 1970's or 1980's. The clipping, unfortunately, did not include the newspaper's name or date.

Obituaries

George Hoberg, Resort Operator

Special to The Examiner

CLEAR LAKE — George G. Hoberg, owner of the 85 year old Hoberg's resort at Cobb Mountain here, died early yesterday after suffering a heart attack.

Mr. Hoberg, 66, and his two brothers developed the well-known resort here on land their grandfather homesteaded shortly after the Civil War. The resort, which started with minor beginnings in 1885, has been popular with generations of vacationing Bay Area residents.

Mr. Hoberg, one of the original investors of the Palm Springs Borrego Desert, was past president of the Redwood Empire Association, Lake County Chamber of Commerce and Western America Convention and Travel Institute. He was a longtime director of the California Hotel-Motel Association.

Survivors include a son, George Jr., and a daughter, Mrs. Marilyn Angelley, both of whom are connected with the resort's operation.

Funeral services will be held 2 p.m. tomorrow at the Hoberg's Lutheran Church at Cobb Mountain. Interment will follow at the adjacent cemetery.

George Hoberg's obituary, July 20, 1970. San Francisco Examiner

NOSTALGIA: Bandleader Sal Carson was reminiscing about his many years at Hoberg's, the Lake County resort that catered for 85 years to families, and the romantically inclined, until Tahoe gambling and skiing took the play away. Hoberg's had one policy, "Keep everybody busy and feed well." Thousands of married couples first met there. If you overslept, pint-size Ozzie, the director of entertainment, was there with a drum and bugle corps. In the evening no girl sat alone for long. Ozzie would bring up an equally shy guy and nature took its course among the pines and firs.

1980's article.

Hoberg's Employees Reunion

September 16, 1995

Old Red School House
Cobb Valley

Lake County, California

Employee reunion, September 16, 1995.

Hobergs resort circa 1942.

The boom and retreat at Hobergs

By David Caraccio
Staff writer

The former dining room at Hobergs resort was burned out by fire in the late '70s while it was owned by the Maharishi. It still stands as a reminder of what once was.
Photo by David Caraccio

HOBERGS — Where the big bands used to play under the stars, and busloads of people arrived every week for recreation, dancing and partying, a person or a peep is rarely heard now.

That's the irony of the rise and fall of Hoberg's resort, once Lake County's premiere vacation spot, located among the pine trees of Cobb Mountain.

The former resort that hosted California statesmen and booked big bands, such as Tommy Dorsey's group, once or twice a year is now the quiet home of the Northern California Maharishi Capital of New Age Enlightenment, which is a private organization for people practicing Transcendental Meditation.

Times have changed; more cars pass by the site in a day than went by in a week during the crest of the resort's popularity in the '40s, '50s and '60s; and people have settled to form a community where a string of mostly popular resorts had existed earlier.

In front of the buildings that once accommodated more than 500 people at a time, parked cars still fill the parking lot during most weekends, but you would hardly ever know people were there.

Certainly that was not the case during the big band era, when they hung in effigy a facticious night guard that wanted the place quiet.

"There was nothing like it around," said Cyril Saviez, a Napa Valley grape grower who frequented the place nearly every weekend in the '40s. "They had everything up there in those days. It was the opposite of what it is now."

Saviez spoke of the days of dancing underneath the stars

See Hobergs, back page

Cont. from front page

in the big open air dance hall to the sounds of a six-, eight-, or 12-piece orchestra.

"A group of us would go up," he said. "It was a great place for singles. There were other places but they didn't impress me like that place."

Evidently, Saviez wasn't the only one. Operating mostly on the popular American Plan, where vacationers paid for a week's stay and received three meals a day and access to myriad activities, the resort filled to capacity in the summer and fall.

"July and August were the big months," said George Hoberg Jr., who grew up in the Disneyland-type atmosphere and later helped run the place. "We probably had more people than we could handle."

Lake County's official chronicler, Marion Goeble, writes in her historical account of the resort that it was the "largest privately run resort in the state for many years and was run as a family enterprise."

"If it had been part of a chain, it might have survived," said Hoberg.

It had always been a family affair from its modest beginnings in 1895. A pioneer story from "The Grizzly Bear" in 1946 said: "On Thanksgiving 1885, Gustav Hoberg came to Lake County with his wife and five children and settled in the mountains in the very middle of a pine forest wilderness. Since Lake County was good for growing fruit, the Hobergs planted like the neighbors and supply soon exceeded demand."

Goeble picks up the story later after Gustav's death in 1895, writing about horseback travelers who would stop at the nascent resort to "eat bountiful home-cooked dinners prepared by Mathilda from her fruit and vegetable gardens and livestock (and) poultry.

"As (her) fame of hospitality spread more and more people visited, (and were) put up in tents . . . Eventually a canvas was stretched around four trees in the grove to accommodate (the guests)," the account continued.

By 1914, the resort had grown modestly to accommodate 80 people. By 1961, it was capable of handling more than 1,000 guests. Around the time Saviez swirled on the dance floor under the stars, Hoberg's boasted of a staff of 30 waitresses, 15 maids, 10 bartenders, Sal Carson's band (he still plays around the county), a 12-piece orchestra, 20 coffee shop employees, a swim instructor for three tile-heated pools, a resident physician, a barber, and personnel for the beauty shop and general store.

"It was a wonderful atomosphere," Hoberg said during an interview at his house in the small town of Hobergs. "It was very informal. Back then you didn't have television and videos. You made your own entertainment. It was very convivial. People sat together, ate together, and came to meet people."

At night there were cocktail parties in rooms with its doors open, where passers-by would automatically be invited inside, he recalled. During the day guests would play softball, swim, go down to Clear Lake to aqua-plane, ride horses or go to Siegler's Resort, also co-owned by the Hobergs, and take a hot springs bath.

On some nights there were cars parked 1/2 mile up and down the road, but most people stayed from Sunday to Sunday. Busses dropped them off and the next morning the drivers would leave, returning for their human cargo six days later.

Most clientele were regulars from the Bay area.

Hoberg's was profitable, he said, but as a child growing up in that atmosphere he might as well have been a prince. He was 18 years old when Dorsey played there, as well as when Dorsey's band played the resort's band in softball games.

"The oldest days were the greatest of my life," he said. He now owns and operates the Hoberg's Golf and Country Club in Cobb. "It was like living at Disneyland, like a big playground for us."

However, times change and people's ideas of entertainment change. People don't socialize on vacations like they once did, and the cabins of the resort may be too austere for the tastes of today's tourists, Hoberg said.

Also, he noted, transportation has simplified and vacations to Mexico and Hawaii are as easy and are a farther escape than a trip to Cobb. Futhermore, Cobb and its surrounding hamlets, although still scenic, are no longer remote. A shopping center and video store are the signs of a growing community.

"You can't imagine how Cobb Mountain was in those days," Hoberg said. "Once it changed, it changed relatively quickly."

The state's Chamber of Commerce statistics show that in 1967, 155 employees still worked at Hoberg's Resort. Yet, the doors shut in 1971. From 1971-74, ideas for the place included a school for special children, or a sports camp, but didn't come to fruition. Subsequently, the Maharishi bought the facilities and an estimated 60 acres.

However, there are those who remember the bloom of Hoberg's Resort.

Hoberg's in the Pines, Northern California's Largest. Circa 1940

A SAN FRANCISCO LAWYER named William Winter is planning a resort in Lake County, north of Middletown. He told reporter Carolyn Lund he remembered the good times he had in his youth at a place just down the road from his site called Hoberg's Resort. If you've been watching the papers this past week you'll catch the irony in the timing of his announcement.

You see, Gertrude Hoberg, the last owner of "the largest privately owned resort in Northern California," died last week. Renewal of life, the theologians call it. One dies, one is born. If Winter's resort can be half the success that Hoberg's was, for half the time, Winter is home free.

Gertrude Hoberg was the last of three generations of the Hoberg family whose customers were "guests" and whose guests became old friends. Likewise, a stay at Hoberg's was a summertime way of life for three generations of Bay Area visitors who came year after year to sit in the sun, swim, eat good food and dance the night away. They expected to find a Hoberg behind the desk, a Hoberg in the dining room, a Hoberg in the kitchen and, mostly certainly, a couple of Hobergs on the dance floor. In 69 years, they were never disappointed.

THE NEW RESORT (You will notice I have not used its name, which is proposed to be "Club Chardonnay." I have not used that title because I hate it. I wish Winter all the best but I hope he finds another name.) will cost $8 million. Hoberg's Resort, while it ultimately represented a substantial investment, like Topsy, "jes' grew."

When Gustav Hoberg, a German immigrant, came to Lake County in 1885 he came to be a farmer. He and his wife Mathilda and their five children bought a small ranch called "The Pasture" — 20 acres of meadow land, three acres of orchard and vineyard and some dilapidated buildings — and

way from San Francisco had to spend the night and tent cabins were added. As many as 50 guests at a time slept in the pine grove, before the first cabins were constructed.

By the time Max's sons George and Paul and Frank took over in 1928 there was a hotel, a social hall for dancing, a bowling alley and a "modern" cement swimming tank (later to be replaced with a tiled, Olympic-size pool.) Paul had learned his mother's and grandmother's art and became the resort's chef. The trio bought Siegler Springs and Frank managed that resort until he opened Hoberg's Desert Resort near Borrego. They added housekeeping cabins at Pine Summit, a quarter of a mile from the hotel, opened a store and a service station, built an airstrip and a golf course and brought in big name bands, like Freddy Martin, Tommy Dorsey and Xavier Cugat, to play for the dancing under the stars in the Pine Bowl.

IF HOBERG'S was THE Lake County resort in those years, it was because the Hoberg family worked at it. And loved doing it. Gertrude Hoberg, who came to the resort as a teenager with her family, married the family tradition when she and George were wed. She was, as Catherine Barnett wrote in her obituary, "the friendly face behind the desk who could remember everyone who came back more than once." She was also the postmaster at Hoberg's, Calif., an official mailing address.

Family memories are all tied up in the resort. Marilyn Hoberg Angelley recalled that, in the rush of the summer season, her parents "dressed" every night, had a couple of cocktails, dined and then went to the dance floor to "mingle with the guests," which was hosting in the grand style. George Jr. said last week that "at least 50 men have told me what a great dancer my mother was. 'Once you've danced with Gertrude Hoberg,' they said, 'nobody

An article by Gaye LeBaron. January 22, 1984 in The Press Democrat.

of life for three generations of Bay Area visitors who came year after year to sit in the sun, swim, eat good food and dance the night away. They expected to find a Hoberg behind the desk, a Hoberg in the dining room, a Hoberg in the kitchen and, mostly certainly, a couple of Hobergs on the dance floor. In 69 years, they were never disappointed.

THE NEW RESORT (You will notice I have not used its name, which is proposed to be "Club Chardonnay." I have not used that title because I hate it. I wish Winter all the best but I hope he finds another name.) will cost $8 million. Hoberg's Resort, while it ultimately represented a substantial investment, like Topsy, "jes' grew."

When Gustav Hoberg, a German immigrant, came to Lake County in 1885 he came to be a farmer. He and his wife Mathilda and their five children bought a small ranch called "The Pasture" — 20 acres of meadow land, three acres of orchard and vineyard and some dilapidated buildings — and homesteaded 160 acres of adjoining government land. Ten years later, after his work produced a model farm yielding an abundance of fruit, berries, vegetables, milk, cream, butter, eggs, poultry and meat, Gustav Hoberg died suddenly. Mathilda, who had six children by this time, called on her reputation as a first-rate cook and started serving meals to travelers. According to a small history of the resort, published by the family in 1950, these meals included soup, salad, vegetables from the garden, fresh-killed spring chicken, homemade pies and relishes and jellies — and a bottle of wine at every fourth place — for 50 cents.

When Max, the oldest son, married Theresa Bleuss, she, as the family history says, "fell in with the general idea." Soon she was canning an astonishing 4,000 two-quart jars of applesauce, berries and vegetables each season to feed the hungry hordes who came now by horse stage from the railhead at Calistoga. The ones who came all the

dancing under the stars in the Pine Bowl.

IF HOBERG'S was THE Lake County resort in those years, it was because the Hoberg family worked at it. And loved doing it. Gertrude Hoberg, who came to the resort as a teenager with her family, married the family tradition when she and George were wed. She was, as Catherine Barnett wrote in her obituary, "the friendly face behind the desk who could remember everyone who came back more than once." She was also the postmaster at Hoberg's, Calif., an official mailing address.

Family memories are all tied up in the resort. Marilyn Hoberg Angelley recalled that, in the rush of the summer season, her parents "dressed" every night, had a couple of cocktails, dined and then went to the dance floor to "mingle with the guests," which was hosting in the grand style. George Jr. said last week that "at least 50 men have told me what a great dancer my mother was. 'Once you've danced with Gertrude Hoberg,' they said, 'nobody else will do.'"

George Hoberg Sr. died in 1970. In 1971, the resort sold. It was a home for retarded children for a time and now is a Transcendental Meditation center.

HOBERG'S MAY BE GONE forever but the destination resort is coming back. Whether it's rising gasoline prices or a cooling in America's "on the road" love affair with the recreational vehicle, more people seem to be looking for the kind of place that Hoberg's was — a place where you actually "spend" your vacation.

So maybe this guy Winter has the right idea. Maybe it's time again. I was interested in one of the things he told reporter Lund. He said "I'm going to spend the next 26 (years) having a good time and making people happy." Nothing wrong with that. That's how the Hobergs spent their whole lives.

George and Gertrude Hoberg (center) flanked by bandleaders Freddy Martin and Sal Carson

HISTORY OF HOBERG'S

By Diana Gallagher

Amid all the social functions, births and deaths, showers, weddings and weather and all the "corn," Cobb has also set its mark in history. Memories of the "good old days" linger on. Cobb in its "heyday" was Hobergs, Sieglers and Adam Springs resorts, Whispering Pines, Loch Lomond, Howard's Hot Springs, and Calistoga. An "advertisement" from this era is framed at the home of Frank Bleuss, Sr., who lives adjacent to the property formerly known as Hobergs Resort on Hwy. 175, now the Age of Enlightenment.

I recently fell "privy" to a booklet entitled "How Come Hoberg's: the Hsitory of Hoberg's Resort, 1885-1950." It was written by Oscar Hoberg in the '50s in an effort to preserve the record.

According to the pamphlet, the Hoberg family arrived in Lake County in the fall of 1885 and settled on a 360-acre parcel of land a quarter-mile south of resort's location during its later heydey. This parcel was referred to as "the pasture," formerly used to keep horses and cattle, and was to serve as the scene of the early struggles and efforts of the family.

Gustave Hoberg came from Germany at age 16 in 1860, enlisted with the Yanks in the Civil War, and marched with Sherman from "Atlanta to the Sea." He was later recruited with a detachment of soldiers to Montana, Idaho, Nevada and California in the surpression of Indian uprisings, and also accompanied the soldiers to Alaska to plant the American flag there when the territory was purchased from Russia. He was mustered out of the army in 1868 in Chicago and moved to New Holstein, Wis., where he met and married Mathilda Stolzenwald.

Then the yen for the west began tugging at his heart. Letters from his wife's brothers and sisters living in San Francisco augmented this desire and at the first opportunity he made the journey with Mathilda and five children, aged 12 years to 18 months. The Southern Pacific railroad had completed its line to a terminal in Calistoga and the Northern Pacific had pushed through Santa Rosa valley to a terminal in Ukiah - a survey was being made through Lake County to unite the two terminals by rail.

Gustave purchased "the pasture," originally a 3-acre orchard and vineyard and 20 acres of meadow land, a two-room cabin, outhouses and a delapidated barn. This parcel soon proved inadequate, but 160 acres of fairly level government land with good springs, but no roads or no trails, could be had for the taking. Hoberg wasted no time cutting a trail to the new homestead.

Lumber was transported, land was cleared for a garden and orchard; a barn built for horses and cattle, hay and farm implements. Hoberg built the first road connecting the farm with the highway at Cobb, some two miles away, and Hoberg's resort was on its way to becoming a landmark.

Things weren't easy. The family worked hard planting and caring for livestock and the older boys took outside work to bring in extra money. Friends tried to convince them to return to Wisconsin and take life easy, but Gustave refused. He planned to start taking it easy on his now-abundant farm, but a stroke ended his life just after the birth of his sixth child, Karl.

The Hoberg's had plenty of everything but money. Travelers often stopped by for one of Mrs. Hoberg's famous dinners and an idea began to form. When requests began coming in for room and board for summer friends, Hoberg's Resort was born.

Great-Grandma Hoberg did all the washing, cooking and canning; the boys helped with the farm chores. The resort was a great success from the beginning and demand always exceeded accomodations; many visitors slept under the stars. In 1902, Max Hoberg married Theresa Bleuss, who immediately took on the work at the resort. "Grandmother" Hoberg died in 1917, then a great-grandmother to George, Paul, Frank and Matilda.

George went on to Cogswell College in San Francisco and returned in 1928 to take over the resort with his brother, Paul. Shortly thereafter, with financial help from a Captain Olsen, the family purchased Seigler Springs - then in a sorry state. They spruced the place up and brother Frank managed it until he sold to invest in a half-million dollar project in the Borrego Desert, Hoberg's Desert Resort.

Hoberg's developed into what was the largest privately-owned resort in northern California in the 1950's, sporting an airstrip for transporting guests, a 12-piece orchestra and the Pine Bowl for dancing under the stars, a ball park, swimming pool, general store, barber, beauty parlor, saddle horses and all the games vacationers could dream up.

Slick brochures advertised its many attractions and lured vacationers to "the hill." An old advertisement boasts board for $8 per week with "unsurpassed" surroundings. Round-trip tickets were only $10 and included a train ride leaving from Market Street in San Francisco at 7:30 a.m. and arrival by stage at 5 p.m. In the '40s and '50s the prices were higher, of course, but many still considered Hoberg's a bargain vacation.

Today, things have changed and resorts are, for the most part, things of the past. Hoberg's Country Club and Golf Course remains an important part of life on Cobb, however, and the Hoberg family keeps up the tradition of hard work and abiding love for this area.

Diana Gallagher's "History of Hoberg's" is interesting

Good friends Don and Dorothy Emerson

Borrego Springs Resort post card

(Top)
Letter head, ca 50's

"I'll Be Around" was one
of many hits by The
Mills Brothers

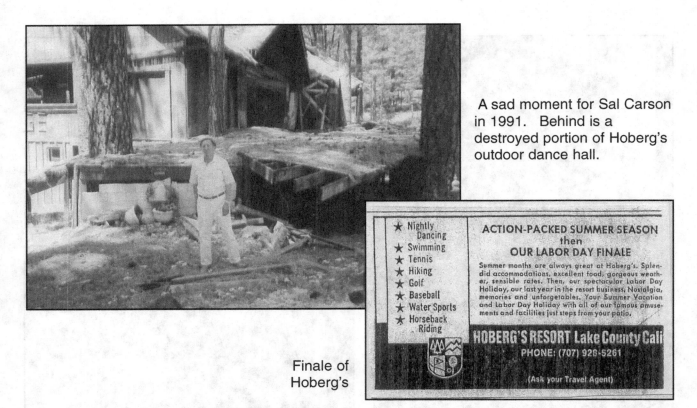

A sad moment for Sal Carson in 1991. Behind is a destroyed portion of Hoberg's outdoor dance hall.

Finale of Hoberg's

Let's end this chapter with a more pleasant photo.   In front is Marilyn Hoberg Angelley and Kathleen Carcione.

Chapter 5
The 50's

Early in 1950 the Hoberg family joined with some people from San Diego to build a resort in the California desert. "They built a really pretty resort and put a lot of money into it". Sal played there with a smaller band at the Borrego Springs resort and wrote the tune "Borrego", a nice ballad.

It was a typical Hoberg family effort. The whole family went down there for the winter and worked hard to make it work. The week-ends did quite well, but it "never seemed to take off". They hoped to get gambling down there, but they were ahead of time. Now there seems to be legalized gambling everywhere. After about four or five years they sold out leaving the beautiful place that is still there.

March 25, 1950 Sal opened at the Persian Room where he was well received and came back in 1951 for a long engagement plus 1952. The same band personnel had a three to four month gig at the El Rancho in Sacramento which kept them busy before going to Hoberg's for the summer months. Sal has always done well in the Sacramento area; consequently, he had long lasting gigs there.

The Mills Bros. Twice in the 1950's Sal had month long gigs at the Top of the Windmill in Billings, Montana and a club in Casper, Wyoming. At one of the clubs they backed the Mills Bros.. Sal is not sure which one, but he is sure that their singing was superb.

In the late 50's Sal worked with Mel Torme at Fack's II for about three weeks. "I had always heard that Mel Torme was really tough to work with. Ridiculous. He was a nice gentleman and very professional. The rehearsals went perfect. It was a show also. Tough job, but we got along well with him. At the bar he complemented me and bought me a drink".

Sal also shared the entertainment with Cab Calloway at Fack's II.

In December 1957 Sal was back at the El Mirador in Sacramento. From there he went to North Shore in Tahoe for one month in 1959. "It was a very popular place and difficult to get in there". Later he was at Harvey's.

Frank Judnich did casuals at the Forest
Lake Resort, 1950-1960

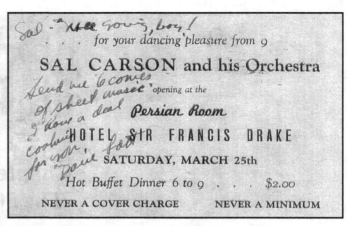

Flyer for March 25, 1950 opening at the Persian
Room. "I have a deal cooking for you". How
often musicians hear that.

Sal and his father at the Persian Room. Ca
1950. Guiseppe Carcione sang a few songs
with the band.

Sir Francis Drake Hotel post card

SIR FRANCIS DRAKE

Check Hotel Rates

Address
450 Powell St.
San Francisco, CA 94102
United States (USA)   Map
(Downtown-City Center)

HOTEL SIR FRANCIS DRAKE

E. B. DeGOLIA, President   WILLARD E. ABEL, Manager

EXECUTIVE OFFICE   SAN FRANCISCO, 1

May 3, 1951

Mr. Sal Carson
Hotel Sir Francis Drake
San Francisco, California

Dear Sal:

Pursuant to our conversation a few days ago, please consider this your two weeks' notice, terminating your engagement in the Persian Room, Hotel Sir Francis Drake on May 30.

I wish to extend to you and all members of your band my sincere appreciation for the fine music you have provided in the Persian Room.

Sincerely,

HOTEL SIR FRANCIS DRAKE

Willard E. Abel
Manager

WEA/m

Letter from the manager

Kathleen and Sal at the Persian Room
ca 1950

INLAND EMPIRE
EARLY BIRDS BREAKFAST CLUB
Incorporated
SPOKANE, WASHINGTON
April 22, 1952

Mr. Sal Carson
Early Birds Club
Spokane, Washington

Dear Mr. Carson:

In accordance with our recent conversation, this is to advise that am picking up option on your band up to and including Saturday night, May 24th.

I wish to commend you and your men on the fine job you have done and hope that we can have you with us again next fall.

Yours very truly,

G. S. SWARTOUT,
Manager.

GSS:g

Early Birds Breakfast Club's manager regarding the picking up of an option

Jeanne Stone (gulp) was with the band
at Eureka in 1955

Sal's Dad

Eureka post card

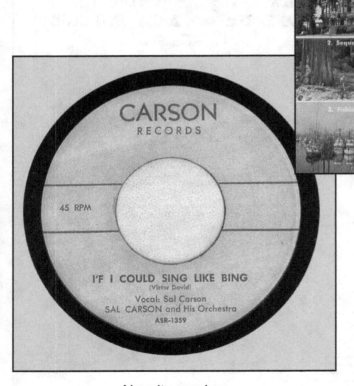

Novelty number

The Call Bulletin

☆☆   TUESDAY, MAY 7, 1957   13

PAUL *not true*
SPEEGLE

He Couldn't Even Yell

Outa' Th' Way;: Sal Carson, the perennial bandleader at Hoberg's, underwent throat surgery at S. F. Polyclinic recently, and just before going into the cutting room the nurse strapped him to the gurney. "Why?" asked Sal. Said the nurse, slyly: " 'Cause you've got a woman driver!"

Paul Speegle article in The Call Bulletin, May 7, 1957. "Nice story, but not true. It never happened".

El Mirador, Sacramento, ca 1957. The band played for the opening and had a long gig.

El Mirador Hotel

features

CONTINENTAL ROOM

► Superb cuisine prepared by Internationally famous **Chef Helmut Nittka.**

► Dancing with **Sal Carson**—your singing maestro, his trumpet and orchestra.

SKY ROOM

► Fast becoming known as the **most beautiful** room on the West Coast.

► Dancing every night to the lilting rhythms of the **Sophisticats.**

TERRACE and ESQUIRE LOUNGES

► El Mirador's lovely **"Mir-a-Maid"** performs for your delight in our glass framed pool.

► **"Biggie Kanae"**—Hawaii's versatile entertainer fascinates you with his rhythmic guitar.

El Mirador flyer, 1957

The vocalist at the El Mirador was Jackie Martinia

The San Matean

Official Student Paper, College of San Mateo, issued twice weekly

Volume 71 (Fall Semester)   San Mateo, California, October 4, 1957   Number 6

'Beachcombers' Dance Tonight

167 Students Awarded Membership To Honor Society for Fall Term

As a result of grades earned during the spring semester, 167 students were awarded membership in Eta Chapter of Alpha Gamma Sigma, the California State Junior College Honor Society.

According to Miss Jeannette Jennings, Dean of Women, this number represents 8.1 per cent of the total number of students enrolled last Spring and includes 56 June graduates.

To have earned membership in the local chapter, students must have had at least 30 grade-points in no less than 12 units (not counting work experience or P. E.), with no grade below a C. Grade-points were based on the 3-point scale. Starting this semester grade-points are based on the 4-point scale, thus raising the required grade-points from 30 to 45.

Mr. Robert Olson is the new adviser for the group.

Those awarded membership were Ronald Abrams, James Alcox, Donald Alves, S. Tilve, Anderson, Arthur

Girls Needed for Homecoming Dinner

Girls are needed to serve at the Homecoming Dinner on October 26. Anyone interested is urged to leave her name at the student activities office or contact an AWS board member.

Congressman Talks Here

"In 1960 California will gain seven

And this, all you casual beachcombers, is Julie Mason who will make your heart pound like surf smashing sand at tonight's dance.

Many Plans Slated As AWS Names Heads

The Associated Women Students of CSM meet every Wednesday at 12:15 in the student council room. All students (women students, that is) are eligible and welcome. The purpose of AWS is to represent all the co-eds at CSM. The larger the attendance is at the meetings, the larger representation will be.

At a recent meeting, heads of committees were chosen, plans were made for the semester, and Sophie Michalski was selected as queen candidate. Coming activities include the annual Christmas semi-formal dance, participation in homecoming, the annual AWS-WRA ski trip and the annual AWS-WRA awards dinner. Co-eds are urged to support the AWS by attending the meetings and working to make the activities a success.

Gala Costumes Are Featured

Nine to twelve tonight are the hours that beachcomber couples will be dancing in the cafeteria to the music of Sal Carson. The boys can wear anything from denims to bermudas and the girls, sarongs or bermudas.

Socials co-chairmen Jean Britton and Duncan Webb are working hard to make this a very successful dance.

Admission is free to Student Activity card holders and $1.00 for non-holders.

All the nominated queens who are at the dance will be presented to the students during intermission. Queen candidates should contact Duncan Webb, socials Co-chairman, at the beginning of the dance at the ticket booth.

Alumnus To Talk on Pre-Med Schools

Dr. John Tocchini, alumnus of CSM and head of the College of Physicians and Surgeons, a dental school in San Francisco, will give a talk at the College House, about "The Problems of Gaining Admission to Dental and Medical Schools." This 8 p.m. program on October 10th will be sponsored by the Pre-Med Club.

Mr. Sam Elkins, the Pre-Med adviser, cordially invites everyone to attend this meeting.

Tryouts Tonight For Term Play

Tryouts for the term play, "Joan of Lorraine," started Wednesday and will continue tonight from 7 to 9 o'clock. There are 18 male parts and 6 female parts to be cast. You need not be in the acting class or Players' Club to try out for the play. Anyone is eligible for an audition. The tryouts will be in the Speech and Drama room 11B.

o o o o

Fack's II has Cab Calloway at their new spot on Bush St. starting Wednesday. The dance music is by Sal Carson . . . Alan Carney at 365 with the DeMarlos and Ann Mason.

SAL CARSON
Musician at Fack's II

The San Matean periodical, October 4, 1957. Julie Mason was the vocalist.

Fack's II, ca late 1957. The band backed Mel Torme, Four Freshmen and the Hi-Lo's. Sal closed Fack's I and opened Fack's II.

Your Dance is as Good as Your Band

SAL CARSON ORCHESTRAS and COMBOS
Phone: BAyview 1-6194 — SKyline 2-6942
715 35th Avenue, San Francisco 21, Calif.

SAL CARSON . . .
Direct from these Extended Engagements

Sir Francis Drake Hotel .... San Francisco
Fack's No. 2 .... San Francisco
Hoberg's Resort .... Lake County
New Frontier Hotel .... Las Vegas
Stateline .... Lake Tahoe
El Dorado Hotel .... Sacramento
El Rancho Hotel .... Sacramento

SAL CARSON has acted . . .
As Musical Director for Such Stars as:
HI-LO'S, MEL TORME, JUNE CHRISTY and FOUR FRESHMAN. His Orchestra's and Combo's are being continually booked by Colleges, High Schools, Society Parties, Weddings, Club Dances, Conventions or for any occasion that calls for Danceable Music.

SAL CARSON assures you . . .
1 — DANCEABLE MUSIC — Any style presented in his own inimitable manner.
2 — EXPERIENCE — Suggestions to help make your next party or dance an outstanding event.
3 — FAIR PRICES — By furnishing a group to fit your budget from Trios to Full Orchestras.

— PHONE OR WRITE —
SAL CARSON
Orchestras and Combos
BAyview 1-6194 or SKyline 2-6942
(Out-of-Town, Call Collect)
715 35th Avenue, San Francisco 21, Calif.

EXCERPTS OF JUST A FEW LETTERS RELATIVE TO
SAL CARSON ORCHESTRA

(Two six months engagements)
Dear Sal:
I wish to extend to you and all members of your band my sincere appreciation for the fine music you have provided in the Persian Room.
> Sincerely, WILLARD E. ABEL
> HOTEL SIR FRANCIS DRAKE, San Francisco

Dear Sirs:
I want to go a little farther on recommending Sal Carson. He really has a splendid band — one of the best that has played our room in two or three years.
> Sincerely, GUY TOOMBES, Manager
> HOTEL UTAH, Salt Lake City, Utah

(Following a one year steady engagement)
Dear Sal:
Greetings for a successful season for a great band and a great band leader.
> EARL IRWIN, Owner and Manager
> CAPITOL INN and HOTEL, Sacramento

(3 Winter Engagements)
Dear Ray:
. . . Sal Carson has just concluded a very successful engagement at The Ahwahnee.
. . . The music furnished by this group has been received very favorably by guests.
> Sincerely yours, GEORGE W. GOLDSWORTHY
> Supt., Hotel Division
> YOSEMITE PARK and CURRY Co.

Sal Carson flyer in 1958

The band at the El Mirador, 1958. Names not known

SAL CARSON
El Mirador, Sacramento.

Pool on Roof And Music by Sal Carson

Sal Carson and his grand band are now firmly entrenched at the New El Mirador Hotel in downtown Sacramento. Sal writes that the place has a swimming pool on the roof—sort of a Top Of The Mark Skyroom.

"This hotel is a real classic and a "must visit" whenever you're in Sacramento," concluded Sal.

Joan Blackman also sang with the band in 1957

El Mirador article in the San Francisco News, December 21, 1957. This was a two year gig., six nights a week

Square, el público pudo adquirir la nueva estampilla con el diseño de un antiguo carrito de cable. Ese día la venta del sello postal de 20 centavos fue exclusiva para San Francisco, al día siguiente fue puesta a la venta al público, simultáneamente, en las 40.000 oficinas de Correos a través de los Estados Unidos.

Una colección de sellos postales dedicada a los Carritos de Cable de San Francisco fue enviada al Presidente Ronald Reagan, en recuerdo de esta emotiva y trascendental fiesta.

Carl Payne, quien durante los últimos 11 años ha ganado el Concurso Mundial de Música con Campana de Carritos de Cable, demostró su extraordinaria habilidad al interpretar una armoniosa melodía valiéndose únicamente de la campana de un carrito de cable, que fue subido para tal fin a Union Square. Carl Payne fue muy aplaudido.

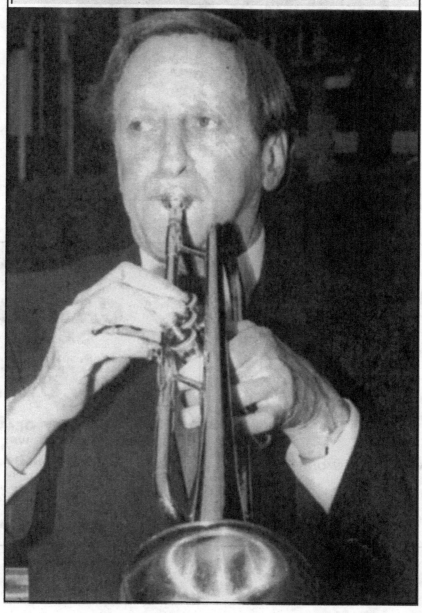

A nice article in the <u>El Bohemio News</u>, November 2, 1958.
I hope it was nice.

Chapter 6
The 60 s

The 1960's was a good year perhaps for wine, but a solid working year for Sal Carson. His reputation was highly considered so, as a result, he was very active. This activity led to more publicity for him which led to even more gigs. One 1960 highlight was the Big Game Dance in the Harmon Gymnasium at the University of California. There was some 4,000 people there. That's right, 4,000.

Another highlight was getting to know Harry James when he was staying at the Holiday Lodge in Reno and Sal was the house band. James was booked at Harrah's in Reno. The two met one afternoon at the bar in the Holiday Lodge where they talked and drank martinis. The bartender told him the next day they had 19 (gulp!) martinis. In any event they consumed quite a lot and James asked him to join him for dinner. Fortunately it was Sal's night off.

"I will never forget sitting there at Harrah's and the James Band started at Midnight. The band played about two tunes and Harry James came out from behind the curtain and started playing very well as always and then he introduced me which made me feel pretty good".

Here's another Harry James true story that you might find interesting. "On another day at the Holiday Inn bar Harry James told me he needed another trumpet player. It just so happened that a friend of mine, Fred Radke, was playing at the Riverside Hotel. He was a young trumpet player that had often played in my band at Hobergs. I knew Fred was a big fan of James and that he was a superb musician. "I called him that afternoon and he came over to the Holiday Lodge where I introduced him to Harry James and gave Fred a big buildup. Harry hired him and he stayed with James for many years and when Harry James died, Fred took over the Harry James Band.

"Fred Radke is a wonderful guy and he really appreciated what I did to help him get the job". One of his singers, Mackie Brooks, was a vocalist on Reno gigs and a one-nighters. "She was just as sweet as she looks. A very good singer and she eventually married a nice guy. He was a musician, but he never went into the business. We played at their wedding and they moved to San Diego".

Sal recorded an LP "Honey Dear" and the liner notes were by Jack Carney who, at that time, was with KSFO radio and very popular. His liner notes are worth reading.

On March 23, 1968, The Cow Palace had a group of headliners including Carol Channing who I always enjoyed. I asked how did the show go and particularly what was his opinion of Carol Channing's performance. "The show was terrific. I got the job through Jack Carney who was the MC. We had a big band. I really liked Carol who was a sweetheart and a delightful performer. I worked with her at a couple of other jobs". In April 1968 there was a benefit for the 7th Step Foundation with a top notch list of entertainers including, once again, Carol Channing.

Duke Ellington was a guest on the Jack Carney Show January 28, 1969. Sal and other members of his band got to chat with Ellington in a back room while waiting to go on. "I was really impressed with the man. He went on and started with 'Take the A Train'. We backed him with our rhythm section. He was a nice guy".

The last part of 1969 Sal was at the Konocti Harbor Inn and the North Shore Club Hotel. 1969 was another special year for Sal. He provided the music for the Jack Carney Show, backed entertainers such as Ed Ames, Duke Ellington, Louie Prima, Frankie Laine and others.

A Santa Claus gig, ca 60's (l to r) In front: Bill Perkins, Sal, Stefame Teel.
In back: Dick Clark, last two not known.

Robert "Skinnay" Ennis offered the lead trumpet chair to Sal who declined because he wanted to stay in the Bay Area. Ennis was born August 13, 1909, Salisbury, NC. He died June 3, 1963 in Beverly Hills, CA Ennis choked to death in a restaurant.

Dinner dance at the San Francisco Hilton. The Forester Fraternal Group, Ed Cohen, Head Guide. Photo by Don Lorenzo. Ca 1960's

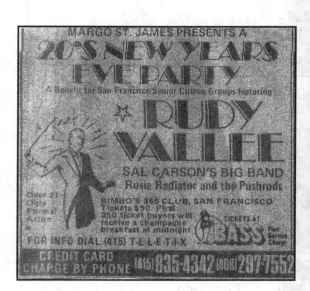

New Years Eve Party. Rudy Vallee and Rosie Radiator and the Pushrods (what?) ca 1960's.

Vallee photo on sheet music cover.

At the Firehouse. October 8, 1960. (l to r) Bill Nawrocki, Sammy Blank, Sal, Al Walcott and Howard Fredric who was once a band leader and with MCA.

NELLO FALASCHI, All-American half back for ta Clara in the late 30's, and family held a bir dinner party recently at Jovanelo's. . . A complime glass of wine is served with complete seafood or dinners on the early bird speci pm) — $6.95 at the Ocean Breeze r rant on Van Ness. . . Luncheon pa at the Four Seas can opt for Ch combination lunches, or select carte. . . Bandleader Sal Carson w guest speaker today at the Over Hill Gang's luncheon at Bruno's. works of Yang Jin-tien are at the ican California Bank at 250 Sut When Delta Sigma Delta Zeta, a fraternity, held their dinner a Gold Mirror, Chef DiGrande mad tain that the pasta was served al dente. . . The Seafood restaurant on Ocean has a coupon off these pages. . . Seafood lovers are discovering th

Yang Jin-tien

Over the Hill Gang luncheon. ca 1960's.

Dance to Be Held Tonight

Sal Carson's orchestra and combo will provide the music at the 1960 Big Game Dance in Harmon Gymnasium after the rally tonight. The orchestra and combo will play alternating periods, providing continuous music throughout the evening.

Carson and his band have played at Stateline, Las Vegas, and San Francisco audiences.

They have also played to dance crowds at several colleges in this area.

The California Marching Band will lead the crowds from the rally to the dance, doing the bunny hop all the way from the Greek Theater to the gym. The Big Game Queen and her attendants will be present at the dance, adding to the general gaiety.

Dailey Cal--November 14, 1960
This is the biggest College Dance of the year. A tremendous success.
4000 people.

Big Game dance. November 1960.

HERB CAEN

tors in the West!" . . . "And Bandleader Sal Carson has already composed, bless him, a theme song for the '61 baseball season: "It's Dark at Candlestick Park."

Herb Caen, in 1960's. San Francisco Chronicle. It was a joke.

Howard Fredric, ca 1960's. Photo by Romaine. Sal was a sideman on some of his gigs and Fredric was often with Sal's band.

DICK NOLAN
THE CITY

JOTS & TITTLES — Word from Washington that Frank Prendergast, career FHA man who is now an assistant field director, will be named FHA boss for this area. . . . Builder Joe Eichler, the man often mentioned for the job, has okayed the Prendergast appointment as jake with him. . . . Ted Shafer, a San Carlos contractor, heads a group which is taking over the Black Sheep on Sacramento, which became a $150,000 nuttin' mutton when the liquor laws prevented that "key club" gimmick. . . . Sal Carson, musician, wit & hepatitis victim, groans from his Polyclinic bed: "The anti-Castro invasion failed because there were just too many of them Cuban heels." . . . Quick, nurse! The thermometer.

•

LLOYD DOWNTON says his Mike's Pool Room Sandwich & Billiards Emporium is in the Board of Trade for $11,000 worth of debts, which will all be paid off only if people eat well. With this in mind he has posted a sign, a big one: "Help Stamp Out Metrecal." Also a smaller one: "Help Stamp Out 'Help Stamp Out' Signs." . . . I'll buy Sign No. 2. . . . Barkeep Dennis O'Connor reports that Maiden Lane's In Between is in the midst of a big refurbishing project. "We just bought a vacuum cleaner."

Examiner   April 14, 1961

DICK NOLAN
THE CITY

SHORT STUFF—Would Barbara Hutton leave town without shopping at Shreve's? She wouldn't and didn't, and among her new jools, my dearies, is a pair of black pearl earrings. Of course they're unique. . . . Artie Samish was perhaps the most vocal fan of the Pirates on Opening Day, and the word among the Tenderloin bettors, a notoriously gossipy bunch, is that Large Arthur won a bundle. . . . John Barth, who fled Publicity Row here last summer, postcards from the Riviera a further report on W. Somerset Maugham, the Old Party: "Willy looks fine." . . . Barth was never that terse in his sales copy.

•

THE CHRYSLER CORPORATION has put the old Dodge plant in San Leandro on the market, and if you're interested in making old Dodges the whole thing won't cost you a cent more than $6,500,000. Coldwell Banker & Co. got the sell order only the other day. . . . Hepatitis, which seems to be sweeping the country, has felled Sal Carson, the band leader, who is in Polyclinic Hospital for treatment. . . . The Canterbury hotel must have mixed emotions about Our Athletes. I deduce this from the bar concoction the Canterbury is selling — well, offering — at $1.25 these days. It is called a Giants Special, and it consists of a scoop of vanilla ice cream blended with a bottle of stout. Graack? And do the Giants deserve it?

•

NEW LAWS DEPARTMENT—Sam Cohen, the saloon keeper, still owns some Giants stock. This, he figures, gives him the right to propose a rules change for gale-swept Candlestick. To the management, in a letter writ by hand, Sam has suggested issuance of a "wind check" with each ticket, to the same effect of a rain check. When the winds hit 30 knots, the game would be called off. . . . I do not care much one way or the other about Sam's plan, but I plump very seriously for my own suggested law change. I would like to see Congress make it a jail offense to capitalize on the President's family in commercial ventures. At least without their consent. Latest such scheme is the plan of Chancellor Records to issue an album, with Mrs. Kennedy's profile on the cover, called "Theme for Jacqueline." . . . Maybe it's all a Republican plot, and I'd really guess that it was, only I never met a Republican yet with that much subtlety.

Dick Nolan's column in the <u>San Francisco Examiner</u>, April 14, 1961.

Another Dick Nolan column. April 27, 1961. Just for the record: Notice the reference to Mike's Pool Room. Entertainers such as Pat Yankee had worked there and the food was good.

HI-TIMES

By

Pat Lacky

Plans are now in full swing for the Senior Class Graduation Party. Senior parents met for the first time about two weeks ago to discuss initial plans for the party. A committee was chosen to meet with the Senior students and find out what their wishes were for the party.

Last Monday night, the parents held their second meeting and the interested Senior students were invited to come. Mr. and Mrs. James Leathers, co-chairmen of the party conducted the meeting. Suggestions for planning were asked of the students and parents, and some definite plans were made.

The graduation party will be held at the Home Arts Building on the Yolo County fair grounds. All students who are planning to attend the party must be inside the building before 11 p.m. on the night of graduation.

★   ★   ★

There will be no show this year but dancing will continue until 4 o'clock in the morning. Sal Carston and his band will provide the music for the occassion. Carston is from San Francisco and is very popular in the Bay Area. This year he's playing many repeat performances at commencement dances in Menlo, Atherton, and cities in that vicinity. Each summer his band plays at Hobergs.

The band, consisting of eight pieces and a singer will begin playing at 10:30. At 2 a.m. a combo will take over for the rest of the evening.

Soft drinks and cookies will be served through the evening and starting around 2 o'clock a breakfast will be served. This will be served in shifts so the large number of students can be accommodated easily. The main course of the breakfast will be steaks and what ever else the Food Committee decides.

Other activities besides dancing are being planned for the evening. Card tables will be set up in convenient places around the room. (You have to bring your own cards) Ping-pong tables will be set up if possible and other games will be on hand for any interested students. The parents want to get an artist to do sketches of the students if he is available on that evening.

There were two other suggestions for entertainment for the evening; either entertainment from the students or some sort of entertainment that the parents would put on themselves.

Hi-Times by Pat Lacky, <u>Daily Democrat.</u>. May 1, 1961.

(Top right) A Reno gig in 1963. Mackie Brooks did the vocal.

(Bottom right) At the Cloverleaf Lounge, Contra Costa County, ca 1963. A tent card with a photo of Donna Theodore.

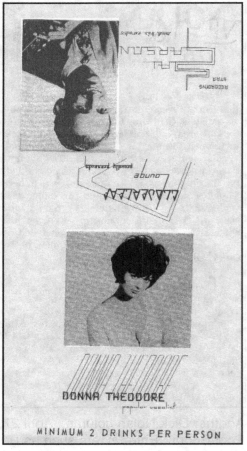

Another photo of James on a CD. A wonderful jazz player as well.

Harry James was one of Sal's favorite musicians.

SAN FRANCISCO CHRONICLE

Trumpeter Sal Carson, "Mr. Music" of Hoberg's for many summers, is being held over at Mariani's in Santa Clara, which has had their busiest week of business. Sal has had two offers this week, one from Reno and one from Las Vegas, and it's easy to see why, as besides being one of the finest trumpeters in show business today, Sal is equally as popular for his singing ability.

San Francisco Chronicle clipping. ca. early 1963

Fred Radke's CD. Sal recommended Radke to Harry James who was looking for another horn player. He was with James for quite some time and has been the leader of the Harry James Orchestra on numerous tours.

Dick Nolan

Short Stuff,
With Dots . . .

shell, of course.

▼

MICHAEL JACKSON, KEWB's midnight-to-dawn talksmith, spent last weekend in Hollywood making good in an audition for the NBC show, "Your First Impression." Michael will start filming as a panelist on the show this month, with the first of his appearances going out on the NBC network March 4. . . . His contract with KEWB is up for renewal in two months, so he and the station management have been dickering. He's happy enough at KEWB, but has at least two attractive offers from other stations. Indications are he'll stay with KEWB, provided his contract is flexible enough to let him do occasional outside stints, like that NBC panel show.

▼

CABLEGRAM from Tokyo advised KSFO's Al Collins: "Talk louder, we can't hear you." (Signed, Walter Keane.) . . . Bandido Collins don' need no steenking bodge. He needs shorter waves, senor. . . . Jim Leary, City Purchaser's man in charge of everything else, is selling off 30 retired police sedans next Wednesday. "Driven only by little old policemen to and from their assignments at school crossings," says Jim. . . . The Mark is keeping its holiday lights on all year, they made such a hit during the Yuletide. And they reflect so nicely in the windows of the Fairmont's Crown Room. . . . Sal Carson's orchestra, playing a dance at the Rinconada Country Club, turned up short a drummer. (He got sick.) An obliging guest, former drummer with George Shearing, filled in nicely. Our Real Estate Editor, Brian Taylor.

Dick Nolan column. Ca 1963

ORCHESTRA Leader Sal Carson, who plays for dancing at the Holiday Lodge every night, looks over a new number for the band. When he isn't leading the band, the enterprising Carson keeps followers in the Bay Area and Sacramento up to date on the new resort west of Reno by way of his own mailing list.

Two clippings about The Holiday Lodge. Ca 1963

Peach of an Item.—

RENO — This [meaning Holiday Lodge] is a beautiful spot. Sal Carson with his new record, "That's My Baby," is doing great. "That's My Baby" should do well in San Jose. . . . The golf course here is new but a dandy. Drop up sometime. . . . Cocktail time here is where many a luscious peach turns into a stewed tomato.—MEL PLEASANT. . . . (Remind me some time to take advantage of a fringe benefit Mel enclosed, specifically to be at Holiday Lodge some Wed. between 2 a.m. & 6 a.m. as a "complimentary guest" of the lodge's Bud Ruppert.)

★ ★ ★

Holiday Lodge Accents Carson's Dance Music

Veteran dance band leader Sal Carson, now head of the dancing and entertainment program at the Holiday Lodge, says dance crowds at the new resort on the Truckee River have been "unbelievably large."

"And many of the people in the crowd tell us how much they enjoy the dancing and the music," he added. "Not a few of them point out that there aren't many spots in the Reno-Carson-Lake Tahoe area that offer dancing."

The Sal Carson Show at the Holiday Lodge currently features star pianist Rosa Linda and a combo, and an exciting new singing discovery named Gene Scott.

"This young fellow has a very beautiful tenor quality voice, and does all the show tunes exceptionally well," says Carson who has heard many good singers in his years fronting dance orchestras.

Carson himself is featured on vocals and trumpet. He is in a familiar role as emcee of the Holiday Lodge's dancing and entertainment proceedings.

Scott, whose home is in Auburn, Calif., is well known in the Sacramento area, having appeared in the Music Circus and in concerts at Sacramento.

Rosa Linda, a recording artist, has been featured in virtually all entertainment mediums and has accompanied Metropolitan Opera stars.

Entertainment and dancing continues from 8:30 p.m. to 5:30 a.m. at the Holiday Lodge, three miles west of Reno on Highway 40.

HIS AND HERS PROGRAMS

NEW YORK — Different programs are handed out at the Broadway farce "Pajama Tops" to male spectators and their distaff companions.

The playbill marked "His" has cheesecake photos only of June Wilkinson, the show's star. The one labelled "Hers" has a demurely gowned Miss Wilkinson on the cover, and on inside pages includes pictures of other members of the cast, modestly attired.

Nordic Nocturne
Mills High School Graduation Night
June 13, 1963
Thunderbird Hotel - Crystal Ballroom

Buffet Supper 11:00-12:00 p.m.   Continental Breakfast 5:00-6:00 a.m.

Slices of Choice Rounds of Beef
au Sauce Piquante
Molded Salads — Tossed Green Salads
Assorted Relishes — Hot Rolls
Shortcake
Coffee, Tea, or Milk

Chilled Juice
Breakfast Rolls
Hot Chocolate or Coffee

Continuous Program

Dancing: 10:30 - 5:00 A.M.
Sal Carson and his Orchestra

* * * * * *

Bingo — Prizes
Bingo Lounge: 1:00 - 4:00 A.M.

* * * * * *

Top Entertainment Acts:

Donna Theodore - "Gay Nineties" Vocalist
Señor Armondo - Master of Magic
Roy & Jess - Folksingers and Comic Duo
Freddy Paris - Top Vocalist recently appearing
at "The Purple Onion" and "Frenchies"

Dance Contests - Prizes   Group Participation Events
Individual Favors   Valuable Door Prizes

Holiday Lodge. Nevada State Journal and Reno Evening Gazette. August 3, 1963.

(Right) Mills High School Graduation Night at the Thunderbird Hotel. June 13, 1963.

(Bottom left)Sal at the San Mateo Hillsdale Inn. April 3, 1964. San Francisco News-Call Bulletin

SAL CARSON and his orchestra are entertaining in the King Henry Room at the Hillsdale Inn in San Mateo.

On the Peninsula

SAL CARSON, one of the most sought-after personalities in show business, opened last Wednesday with his orchestra at the plush Hillside Inn in San Mateo. Sal, who's acted as musical director for Mel Torme, June Christy, Four Freshmen and Hi-Los, has a new record out entitled "Mama's Gone Goodbye" that's been getting plenty of play from the disc jockeys lately. . . Seen dining at

On the Peninsula, April 1964

Holiday Lodge match cover

"GOOD DANCING NEEDS GOOD MUSIC"
SAL CARSON
ORCHESTRAS AND COMBOS
Direct from the Holiday Lodge in Reno

1964

SAL CARSON
TRUMPET
AND VOCALS

SAL CARSON . . . Fresh From These Extended
Engagements:
Sir Francis Drake Hotel .... San Francisco
Fack's .... San Francisco
New Frontier Hotel .... Las Vegas
Hoberg's Resort .... Lake County
Stateline .... Lake Tahoe
El Dorado Hotel .... Sacramento
In addition he has accompanied such stars
as JUNE CHRISTY, FOUR FRESHMAN, HI-
LO'S, MEL TORME...while his combos and
orchestras are continually being booked by
colleges, high schools, conventions, social
clubs; in fact, for any occasion that calls
for danceable music.
EXPERIENCE—Suggestions to help make
your next affair a memorable event.
DANCEABLE MUSIC—Any style of music
for any style of party.
FAIR PRICES—By furnishing a group to fit
your budget from Trios to Full Orchestra.
FOR IMMEDIATE ACTION,
WRITE OR PHONE NOW
SAL CARSON
ORCHESTRAS - COMBOS
BAyview 1-6194 or SKyline 2-6942
(Out-of-Town, Call Collect)
715 35TH AVENUE, SAN FRANCISCO 21, CALIF.

A Sal promo, 1964

Newspaper ad. ca 1964

THE **SAL CARSON SHOW**

featuring
DONNA THEODORE
CAROL MOORE &
ROSA LINDA

HOLIDAY LODGE

3 MILES WEST OF RENO
ON HIGHWAY 40

For Reservations:
Accommodations or Dining...
Phone 329-8401
Lawton's Springs
3 Miles West of Reno, Nevada on Highway 40
On the River

BUD RUPPERT'S
HOLIDAY LODGE

Holiday Lodge flyer. ca 1964

Holiday Lodge Opens

Bud Ruppert's Holiday Lodge, a new landmark at the site of an old one on Highway 40 West, is opening formally in a grand manner this weekend.

Both Friday and Saturday of this weekend are grand opening days with festivities highlighted by the Sal Carson show. Featured in the show are bandleader-vocalist Carson himself, songstresses Donna Theodore and Carol Moore who have much to offer in eye and ear appeal, and musician Bill Perkins, regarded as one of the most talented tenor and baritone sax players on the Pacific Coast.

The Holiday Lodge, "Nevada's most recreational resort," is three miles west of Reno at the site of historic Lawton Hot Springs on the banks of the Truckee River.

The brand new luxury motor lodge with 100 units is one of a string of Holiday Lodges owned by Ruppert in the West. The Reno area lodge is unique in the group in that it provides a gaming casino.

Approval of the gaming operation at the Holiday Lodge was given this week by the state Gaming Control Board and the Gaming Commission.

General Manager Stanley Simmons has announced that other attractions include completely restored mineral baths and a nine-hole golf course. The new golf facility which runs along the river just west of the lodge was designed by Robert Baldach of Fresno, a highly regarded expert in the field.

The new luxurious motor lodge was built by Don DeRoza Inc. The vice president of the firm, C. E. Crandall, is a principal in the lodge with Ruppert and Simmons.

Other attractions to support the title "Nevada's most recreational resort," include a restaurant with banquet facilities to handle 400, a nine-hole putting green, cocktail lounge, swimming, horseback riding, packtrips, shuffleboard and dancing.

Simmons has pointed out that the lodge is designed to appeal to tourists and local residents alike. He predicts a high degree of popularity among the people of Reno and Sparks because of dancing to the music of Sal Carson's orchestra and all the lodge's other attractions.

Most of Nevada's resorts, he noted, put the emphasis on tourist attractions. Simmons commented:

"One big item which is missing throughout Nevada is dancing, simply because it doesn't fit in with the volume business philosophy of casinos. It's enjoyable but it doesn't produce much in the way of revenue.

"But we feel dancing is an important part of a gracious resort."

Sal Carson is one of the best known dance band names on the Coast. He has been booked for extended engagements in San Francisco, Las Vegas, Lake Tahoe and Sacramento.

Songstress Donna Theodore is a beautiful young brunette who belts a song with the best of the belters. She has appeared in various clubs including those on the Las Vegas Strip. Donna is being groomed for a Hollywood career.

Carol Moore, newest attraction in the Sal Carson Show, is a voluptuous blonde with a reputation as a great song stylist and dance band vocalist. She has been featured with a number of top-rated orchestras.

A 45-rpm recording by Sal Carson's orchestra has just been released. It couples "Mama's Gone Goodbye" and "She's My Baby,"

SAL CARSON

CAROL MOORE

DONNA THEODORE

HOLIDAY LODGE grand opening entertainers include bandleader-vocalist Sal Carson and songstresses Donna Theodore, a brunette, and blonde Carol Moore. The three, pictured above, are joined by saxophone star Bill Perkins as featured performers in the lodge's Sal Carson Show. A "single" attraction at the lodge is pianist Rosa Linda, a recording artist.

Holiday Lodge Opens. ca 1964

The main lodge takes full advantage of the splendid view looking out across the river to the high Sierra. Cocktail lounge, casino and dining room all open onto the exquisite scenery. A beautiful stone fireplace is the focal point in the expansive interior. The dining room will seat groups up to 400. And, the Holiday Lodge will institute a dance policy starting with Sal Carson, the popular band leader from Northern California this summer Entertainment is also planned.

Insert for the flyer

(Below)
Ad for Skyline Club in Billings, Montana. Mid 1960's

Letter from John Armstrong the president of Armstrong College. May 27, 1963

Casual Contract Blank

AMERICAN FEDERATION OF MUSICIANS
of the United States and Canada
Local Number 6

Federal Employer's No._____

State No._____

Insurance Carrier's
Policy No._____

THIS CONTRACT for the personal services of musicians, made this_____ day of_____, 19_____

between the undersigned employer (hereinafter called the "employer") and_____ musicians (hereinafter called
"employees").
(Including the Leader)

WITNESSETH, That the employer hires the employees as musicians severally on the terms and conditions below, and as further specified on reverse side. The leader represents that the employees already designated have agreed to be bound by said terms and conditions specified on reverse side. Each employee yet to be chosen shall be so bound by said terms and conditions upon agreeing to accept his employment. Each employee may enforce this agreement. The employees severally agree to render collectively to the employer services as musicians in the orchestra.

_____ as follows:

Name and Address of Place of Engagement_____

Date(s) of Employment_____ Hours of Employment_____

Type of Engagement (specify whether dance, stage show, banquet, etc.)_____

WAGES AGREED UPON $_____ including $_____ 5% Employer Pension payable to A.F.M. & E.P.W. Fund.

This wage includes expenses agreed to be reimbursed by the employer in accordance with the attached schedule, or a schedule to be furnished the employer on or before the date of engagement.

To be paid_____
(Specify when payments are to be made)

Employer's Name	Leader's Name	Local No.
Signature of Employer	Signature of Leader	
Street Address	Street Address	
City State	City State	
Phone	Booking Agent	Address and telephone number

NAME OF EMPLOYEES	Local Number	S. S. Number	Wages	Pension

FOR OFFICE USE ONLY

Contractor's No.	Contractor's Name	Date of Job	Place of Engagement	No. of Days	Start Time	Contract No.	County	Day of Week	No. of Men	No. of Hours	Job Type	Type Emp	Traveler	Agent	Work	Dues	Pension

Sal had to complete the form for each casual

A 1964 casual. (l to r) Shelly Denny, Bill Nawrocki, and Sal.

'Sounds of Big Bands' For Westlake's Affair *1967*

"Sounds of the Big Bands," as played by Sal Carson and his 18-piece Astro recording orchestra, will fill the air Saturday night at beautiful Elks Lodge, South San Francisco, when Westlake Shopping Center Merchants Association stages its annual Spring Informal Dinner Dance.

Original arrangements, reminiscent of the likes of Harry James, Tommy Dorsey, Benny Goodman and Glenn Miller, with many of the originating sidemen who played with those greats, are on tap for the more than 200 merchants, their wives and guests.

The Carson band features Miss Mackie Brooks on vocals, Billy Nawrocki on drums and Bill Perkins on tenor saxophone. Miss Brooks headlined

at many of the Lake Tahoe area supper clubs before joining with the Carson crew, while Nawrocki has been called "the closest thing to the great Buddy Rich" (featured drummer with Harry James). Perkins is a former Benny Goodman sideman who made the now famous "Mission to Moscow" with the King of Swing for the State Department

In all, it will be a night to remember for the Association and its guests. The elegant, new Lodge ballroom is being transformed into a virtual picture garden for the occasion. Special staging, atmospheric props, flowers and Hollywood lighting effects will transform the ballroom into a "breath of Spring".

Westlake Shopping Center Merchants Association annual Spring dinner dance. Elks Lodge in South San Francisco. ca 1967

Westlake
SHOPPING CENTER
Suite 289 Westlake Bldg. • 375 South Mayfair Ave., Daly City, California

January 5, 1967

To Whom It May Concern:

This is to introduce and to recommend Sal Carson, who for the past five years has been the bandleader and supplier of musicians for The Westlake Shopping Center and The Westlake Merchants Association.

He is an excellent musician, a hard worker and dedicated above reproach. He is well acquainted with and highly thought of by the Metropolitan Bay Area Press and Radio. I have personally observed his work in numerous hotels and supper clubs, as well as enjoying his music at Hoberg's Resort, Lake County. He has a special facility for developing good public relations with all.

I know from being his employer over a ten year span, as well as from close personal friendship, that he is a fine man.

I cannot think of anyone better suited from any point of view for a position of trust and reliability in the field of music and/or entertainment.

Sincerely yours,

Gene L. Perry
Advertising - Promotion Director

An excellent letter of recommendation by Gene L. Perry. January 5, 1967

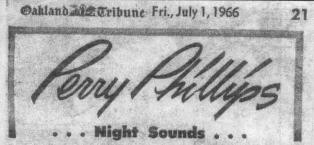

Jack Rosenbaum

★ ★ ★

SELECTED SHORTS... Sandy Black, vocalist on bandleader Sal Carson's new album, "Honey Dear," is an understandably confused girl when asked where she can be reached. "Well," she explains, "I live in Dublin across the bay; my mailing address is Hayward; if you want to phone me, call Pleasanton information, and I pick up packages mailed to me in Castro Valley."

A sign at Powell and California reads, "No Left Turn, Cable Cars Excepted." (A neat trick. There's no left turn track) ... The Doggie Diner's Al Ross suggests where to send Cassius Clay when he's drafted. To Fort Bragg, N.C., natch.

Nostalgia: When's the last time you saw a youngster jumping rope, playing jacks, hop scotching, hula-hooping, shooting marbles? What DO the kids do for excitement these days?

Repartee: Marty Leaver, the United Air exec, introducing Major-Gen'l Andrew Lolli at a banquet, "It's quite an honor for a one-time humble corporal to present a general." Responded the General," it's an honor to have a former corporal introduce a former private first class."

Jack Rosenbaum column February 20, 1966 in the <u>San Francisco Examiner & Chronicle</u>

... Night Sounds ...

If big bands are passe, you couldn't prove it by Tony Martin, who operates the Ali Baba Ballroom here in Oakland.

Sid Hoff has been there for years and is replaced only for a two-month vacation during the summer. Sid is set for his annual rest later this month, and Tony is going all-out in the band replacement department by bringing in a new band each week while he's gone. Could just about label it the "Battle of the Bands."

The summer lineup includes the orchestras of Jim Diamond, Maury Wolohan, Benny Meltzer, Jimmy Blass, Paul Law, Ray Hackett, Jack Fisher and Sal Carson.

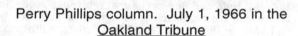

I was particularly happy to find the name of Sal Carson on Tony's list. Sal's an Oaklander and has been building a name for himself the past two years. Adds up to a lot of good dance music coming the Ali Baba's way this summer.

★ ★ ★

Perry Phillips column. July 1, 1966 in the <u>Oakland Tribune</u>

Ali Baba ad in the <u>Express</u>, May 15, 1981. Just to demonstrate how long Sid Hoff was there.

- **35 YEARS AGO**, on May 17, 1946, we announced our grand opening
- **SATURDAY NIGHT**, MAY 16, 1981, we celebrate our 35th year as America's premier ballroom

Join us for our 35th Anniversary Party!

- Free buffet/cash bar
- Island Holiday for 2
- Jitterbug contest
- Costume contest—'40s style
- Ballroom dancing to Sid Hoff's 10-piece band—singles welcome
- Plus other prizes and surprises

Remember: "An evening of dancing is an inexpensive extravagance."

Ali Baba • 111 Grand Ave., Oakland • 451-7040

Gentlemen: coat & tie   Ladies: dressy attire

Sid Hoff was born August 25, 1913 in Chicago. He died September 23, 2002 in Alameda, CA. Was living in Oakland, CA. Photo courtesy of Richard Feinberg.

Sid Hoff and his Orchestra at the Ali Baba. Photo courtesy of Richard Feinberg

Perry Phillips

... Night Sounds ...

Tony Martin's big lineup of bands during the summer, at the Ali Baba, is nearing the end with mainstay Sid Hoff and his orchestra returning soon. Sal Carson and his orchestra open tomorrow night as the final band in this series, which has proven quite popular at the Ali Baba. Sal is a local lad, in case you didn't know. He's been very active in the band business for years and recently recorded a big band album that received much play on local stations.

Vacationers who make Hoberg's in Lake County their annual rest spot know Sal Carson well. He's been a regular there for years. Obviously Sal and his boys make good music or they wouldn't be invited back to Hoberg's year after year. In any event, Sal has many friends in the Eastbay who will certainly be dropping by the Ali Baba to say hello and to dance to his big band sounds. As for that upcoming big band record dance at the Ali Baba, it is well past the planning stages. To

SAL CARSON

top off that evening, one of the big band era's top singers will be on hand to help make it a memorable event. I'm going to hold off giving you her name for now as a way of maintaining interest and injecting a little suspense into the event.

Ad for Sal at the Ali Baba

Perry Phillips Column in the
Oakland Tribune,
September 13, 1966

Citation from the National Ballroom Operators
Association. September 19, 1966

Sal, 1967

Lori English with Sal's band. Names of band members not known except for
"Howie" Segerson (on Sal's left) ca 1967

USO Fund Aided by Hope Show

A group of stars, headlined by comedian Bob Hope, raised more than $12,000 to construct a USO clubhouse at the Da Nang Marine Corps base in Vietnam, it was announced yesterday.

KSFO disc jockey Jack Carney, who headed the benefit at Masonic Auditorium Friday night, said that there was a standing room only crowd, with more than 3000 tickets sold.

In addition to Hope, the performers included Ed Ames of the former Ames Brothers singers; singers Tommy Leonetti and Donna Fuller; Judy Mac, singer and San Francisco's "swim" girl; Turk Murphy and his band and Sal Carson and his orchestra.

During the performance Hope was presented with a "Thanks for the Memory" petition signed by 1000 wounded veterans at Letterman General Hospital.

The petition said, "You've never forgotten us, we'll never forget you," and each veteran noted the time and place — Korea, World War II

— he had seen Hope perform.

Hope also talked by satellite to Marine General Lewis Walt in Da Nang who praised San Francisco as the first city in the United States to build and equip a USO lounge in Vietnam.

Clipping about the USO fund show. <u>San Francisco Examiner & Chronicle</u>, May 21, 1967

```
               USO BENEFIT PERFORMANCE

MASONIC AUDITORIUM        FRIDAY        MAY 19, 1967        8:30 P.M.

BOB HOPE                                 PHYLLIS DILLER
ED AMES                                  TOMMY LEONETTI
DONNA FULLER                             JUDY MAC
MARK ZELLER                              THE TRIO ORPHEO
PATTI MOORE &                            MISS CALIFORNIA
BEN LESSY                                MISS SAN FRANCISCO

TURK MURPHY'S DIXIELAND JAZZ BAND

SAL CARSON'S ORCHESTRA
UNITED STATES MARINE CORPS BAND
SIXTH UNITED STATES ARMY BAND

MASTER OF CEREMONIES------------------------ KSFO'S JACK CARNEY

SPECIAL GUEST:  GENERAL WALLACE M. GREENE, JR.
                COMMANDANT, U.S. MARINE CORPS

FASHION SHOW PRESENTED BY DELTA AIRLINES
MISS CALIFORNIA'S GOWN BY 20TH CENTURY FOX
GOWNS AND FASHION WARDROBE BY JOSEPH MAGNIN

LIMOUSINE SERVICE COURTESY NATIONAL EXECUTIVE SERVICES (NES)

PHOTOGRAPHY BY GERALD FRENCH

GRAND PRIZE: VACATION FOR TWO, VIA DELTA AIR LINES, TO THE
             BEAUTIFUL ISLAND OF JAMAICA


The USO BENEFIT PERFORMANCE has been produced and directed by:

              JACK CARNEY & DICK SMITH
```

USO Benefit program, May 19, 1967

Mel Torme. Born: September 13, 1925, Chicago..Died June 5, 1999, Los Angeles

Bob Hope, a very funny guy who did so much to entertain our service men and women not to mention the whole country

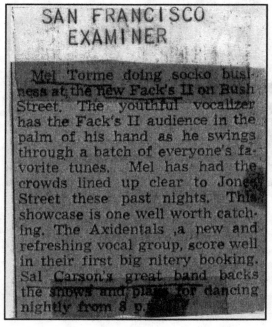

Fack's II with Mel Torme. San Francisco Examiner, 1967

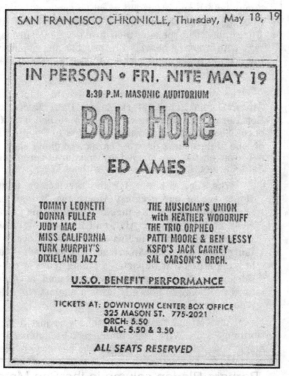

Ad in the San Francisco Chronicle, May 18, 1967

THE MARQUEE
By Barbara Bladen

Praises Sung of Soldiers and God

The USO Benefit at the Masonic Auditorium Friday night reminded me of the thrilling shows staged during the war years for Bond Drives. There'd be more movie stars on the bill than you could see live at the Golden Gate theater in a year. And they were so enthusiastic, so full of patriotism and optimism we were left giddy with excitement.

While the feeling wasn't quite the same, in spite of the rousing United States Marine Corps Band, 22-piece Sal Carson's orchestra and ten top acts, the impact of the benefit left the 2,700 people who attended with a feeling of pride in out boys in Vietnam.

Bob Hope made it more than just a parade of show business personalities. A phone call from Da Nang was transmitted by Satellite and we heard the voice of the general in charge of 75,000 marines there express their gratitude to those who were contributing time and money to build the Golden Gate USO Lounge in Da Nang.

We've never seen Hope so serious. He was plenty funny before and after, but when he spoke of "looking into the faces of one hundred thousand guys last Christmas" and spoke of their bravery and courage, it was with a heavy heart. "I'm praying and hoping we get a great break in this war, we need it," the comedian said.

The crowds were most receptive to singers Ed Ames, Donna Fuller, Mark Zeller, Patti Moore and Ben Lessy, Tommy Leonetti, Judy Mac and Trio Orpheo. No one explained what happened to Phyllis Diller, one of the show's drawing cards who didn't show up nor was an excuse offered by master-of-ceremonies Jack Carney. It was a fine show without her.

Who speaks better for the servicemen than Hope, one of our greatest Americans, a man to admire and respect. He mentioned performing last week at Montgomery, Ala., and the next night at Indiana University. "In this country 99 per cent of the people are real American," he offered. And hearing him say it imparted a strong sense of confidence in this era when suspicions and accusations are being so liberally leveled against our college students.

"I understand the Haight-Ashbury is just a large rummage sale. With live rummage," he quipped. "A hippie is a girl with a nice figure who has gone to pot,"

Barbara Bladen column in the San Mateo Times, May 22, 1967

"Christmas Magic", December 14, 1967. Hotel Mark Hopkins.

Hotel Mark Hopkins.

Astro Recording Co., established in 1968

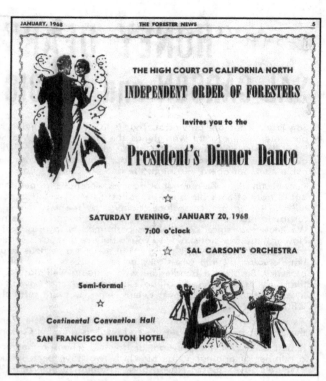

Dinner Dance January 20, 1968.
Independent Order of Foresters.

STEREO **1001** MONO

SIDE ONE

HONEY DEAR
(2:15) (Hunt-Melrose) Miller Music Corp.

HELLO, DOLLY
(1:37) (Herman) Edwin H. Morris Co., Inc.

THIS IS ALL I ASK
(2:37) (Jenkins) Massey Music Co., Inc.

WHERE WAS LOVE (Bossa Nova)
(2:04) (R. G. Brown) Carleen B.M.I.

MAMA'S GONE GOODBYE
(2:34) (Bocage-Peron) Pickwick Music Corp. &
Jerry Vogel Music Co.

THE NEARNESS OF YOU
(3:45) (Carmichael-Washington) Famous Music Corp.

SIDE TWO

SO BEATS MY HEART FOR YOU
(2:30) (Ballard-Henderson-Waring) De Sylva, Brown & Henderson, Inc.

THROUGH ALL THE YEARS
(2:21) (R. G. Brown) Carleen B.M.I.

SHE'S MY BABY
(2:10) (Cohn-Cohen-Ascher-Carson) Cireco Music B.M.I.

MY LOVE FORGIVE ME
(2:25) (Pallacicini-Mescoli-Lee) Gil Music Corp.

MOBILE (Alabama)
(2:25) (Gordon) Tree Pub. Co., Inc.

Tune selections for Sal's LP., 1968

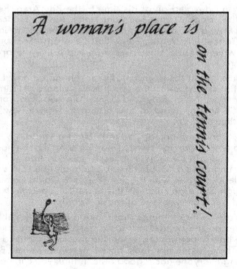

Honey Dear" LP. Personnel – Sal Carson,
leader, trumpet, vocals. Trumpets: Billy
Catalano, Jr., Fred Radke, Chuck Marcoe,
Dale Thompson, Larry Viau.. Saxes: Bill
Perkins, Hal Wylie, Alan Hoeschen, Bob
Davidson, Terry Summa (flute), Bill Byrne,
Howie Segurson.. Rhythm: Bill Nawrocki,
drums; Herb Andrade, piano; Andre Garand,
bass; Bill McCubbin, guitar. Trombones: Jack
Sava, Gordon Messick, Dick Leland, Ron
Kaponat. Arranger: Bob Sisco. (Recorded in
two sessions) **ASTRO RECORDS**

–119–

"HONEY DEAR"
SAL CARSON and his BIG BAND

San Franciscans are provincial. That is to say people living here in the bay area are quite content with things the way they are. We San Franciscans have definite likes and dislikes about almost everything. We definitely like our weather, our wierd architecture, our fabulous restaurants, our antiquated cable cars, our opera, our night life and Sal Carson's Band.

To try estimating the number of dancers who have tripped the light fantastic out in front of Sal's big band in the last fifteen years is impossible but I can tell you that at Hobergs alone (Hobergs by the way is one of the greatest resorts in the world and fortunately is just a hundred miles northeast of us). We know that since 1947 Sal has performed for over a million vacationers. Now if these few statistics lead you to believe that Sal is extremely successful in the band business, you're right. But there is a perilous trap that too many bandleaders fall into when they achieve success. I am talking about complacency. So often a bandleader who is doing well stops trying to develop the sound of his band. We all have heard bands that haven't changed a note in most of their book in over twenty years, but that certainly isn't the case with Sal.

As you listen to this album you'll find a taste of Basie, Zentner, Ellington, the Dorseys and James, but the end result is pure Sal Carson.

Robert G. Brown, the principal of Havens, School in Piedmont, has written a number of original songs of which two have been included in this LP: "Where's Love" (Bossa Nova), and "Through All the Years."

Arranger Bob Sisco, formerly with Earl Grant, has done an excellent job in patterning arrangements around Sal.

Also, this album introduces Gene Scott singing "My Love Forgive Me," who was discovered by Sal while appearing at Reno's Holiday Lodge.

Sal hasn't devoted all of his time to the Bay Area. Between engagements at the Mark Hopkins, the Fairmont Hotel, the Sir Francis Drake, Focks, the Off Broadway, and every other good room in Northern California, he has worked Lake Tahoe, Las Vegas, Reno, Salt Lake City, Spokane, Portland, and in the days when the big bands were on radio live, he appeared on every major network.

Listening to, on the average of over a hundred new LPs every week as I do, I find that all too often the emphasis is placed on gimmicks and shock value rather than the melody and danceable beat. You only need listen to thirty seconds on any band in this album to realize how great the Carson band is to dance to.

"Sal", I once remarked, "a Frank Sinatra you ain't." But still Sal has a way with a lyric. Listen to "Honey Dear," a song that he has been singing for many years, and after you hear it see if you can think of anyone else you would rather hear sing it. (Bobby Breen is unavailable.) Sal's dad, Giuseppi Carcione, sang leading roles with the San Francisco Opera Company in the twenties and although Sal didn't inherit the beautiful operatic tenor voice of his father, he did get a sincere love of music from him.

There are so many things that make a band enjoyable and it isn't all sound. A band on the bandstand has a personality and I know you have seen big name bands performing when the musicians looked as if they couldn't care less. They sometimes look bored or even worse. But when Sal's band is working everyone has a good time. I think you can hear that in this recording. These are swinging musicians who are enjoying every minute and if you close your eyes you can see Sal running around in front of the band waving his trumpet like a mad man.

If you have a few minutes take a listen to this album. I know you will enjoy it for listening or for dancing. Better still, buy it. (Sal has a hundred thousand of them in his garage.)

JACK CARNEY
KSFO — San Francisco

LP liner notes by Jack Carney, a radio and TV personality. Sal was on Carney's TV show once a week for six months.

The Good Time Washboard 3 was also part of the entertainment at The Firehouse Frolic (opposite Page). The washboard player is good friend, Wayne Pope. The other two members are Bruce Bratton and Peter Arnott (Seated). Ca 1960's.

"A Night in Paris" at the Commercial Hotel in Reno. December 1968

Firehouse Frolic, a benefit for the Lincoln Child Center. March 16, 1968 at Firehouse East, Oakland, CA.

SHOW OF STARS

★ ONE NIGHT ONLY ★

★ ONE NIGHT ONLY ★

Guest Star

CAROL CHANNING

Bonanza's

★ DAN 'HOSS' BLOCKER ★ PAT BOONE

★ TONI LEE SCOTT & THE SAL CARSON BAND

Jack Carney, Master of Ceremonies

BENEFIT FOR THE 7TH STEP FOUNDATION

A non-profit Organization dedicated to the rehabilitation of ex-convicts and juvenile delinquents

COW PALACE ★ SAT., MARCH 23

8:30 P.M.

Tickets 584-2480 and 431-0722 — Cow Palace and Downtown Center Box Offices

Donation: $5.00, $4.00, $3.00, $2.00

161

"Show of Stars" at the Cow Palace, March 23, 1968.
Carol Channing was there.

7TH STEP FOUNDATION

★ SHOW OF STARS ★

COW PALACE ☆ MARCH 23 ☆ 8:30 P.M.

PROGRAM

Jack Carney, Master of Ceremonies

Starring

FRANKIE AVALON
DAN 'HOSS' BLOCKER ★ PAT BOONE
— SAL CARSON'S ORCHESTRA —
CAROL CHANNING ★ PAUL FORD
JACKIE GLEASON
MAHALIA JACKSON'S LADIES OF SONG
OTTO PREMINGER
ROBERT ROGER and the RAMA MUSIC CO.
CAESAR ROMERO ★ BILL SANDS, (founder)
TONI LEE SCOTT

Sponsors

LEE BARY, Chairman
National Board of Governors

EDWARD GAUER, President
Bow/Arkin

GEORGE W. GERBER, President
Imperial Oil and Grease Co., Inc.

CHARLES QGUILD, Publisher
San Francisco Examiner

LOUIS LURIE, Esquire

This benefit is presented with the approval of Theater Authority, Inc.

★ ★ ★ ★ ★ ★ ★ ★ ★

DON'T FORGET

7TH STEP FOUNDATION'S THIRD ANNIVERSARY DINNER

"Show of Stars" program.

In San Francisco
it's the

COW PALACE

Greatest Show Place in the West

SHOW OF STARS

CAROL CHANNIN

TONIGHT ONLY 8:30 P.M

and the PAT BOONE SHOW with
DAN "HOSS" BLOCKER and
MAHALIA HACKSON'S
LADIES OF SONG —
→ SAL CARSON'S BIG BAND

Tickets: $5, $4, $3, $2 — Downtown Center
Box Office, 825 Mason St. — Cow Palace —
Sherman Clay Oakland — San Jose Box Office

COW PALACE ● 584-248

Newspaper ad for "Show of Stars", March 23, 1968

The Cow Palace flyer

−122−

Sylvia Gaylord

Some Gaylord clippings

"Music—Society Style," as played by Sal Carson and his Hotel orchestra, will fill the air Saturday night at Millbrae's Thunderbolt Hotel when The Westlake Shopping Center Merchants Assn., holds its Fourth Annual Spring-Summer Dinner Dance.

Nostalgic arrangements, remininscent of Russ Morgan, Freddie Martin, Dick Jurgens, Guy Lombardo and the big band greats, will greet more than 200 merchants, their wives and distinguished guests.

The Carson band features lovely Sylvia Gaylord on vocals. Miss Gaylord has headlined at many of the top Las Vegas and Reno supper clubs, namely The Desert Inn, Flamingo Hotel, Harrah's South Shore Room and the Holiday Hotel.

Also featured in the Carson aggregation are Drummer Billy Nawrocki (noted for his Buddy Rich style), Pianist Herb Andrade, who sat in many years with an early Woody Herman Herd, and Trombonist Sammy Blank, who has been noted as "a show in himself."

Honored guests will include Mayor Bernard (Bud) Lycett, Councilmen Micheal DeBernardi, Frank Pacelli, Anthony Giammona, Edward Dennis, City Manager Edward Frank, City Attorney Albert Polonsky.

Sylvia Gaylord
To Sing

Sal Carson
To Play

Clipping of gig at the Thunderbolt Hotel. Late 1960's

A trio gig. Sal with Herb Andrade at the piano and the bass player is the famous Mr. Unknown.

Victor Green, late 60's. "A hot drummer who worked mostly with the Whittington Sisters. Worked a lot of casuals with us. In the I-80 Band". Sal's wife, Kathleen came up with the band's name

FRANK LAPIERRE

(Post Columnist)

'Poor Soul' Returns

verbal scuffle with several Japanese Zengakuren students at the school.

As usual, RFK won the debate hands down and received an ovation from the hundreds of kids attending, plus the millions of people who watched the talk on television.

☆   ☆   ☆

WESTLAKE SHOPPING CENTER'S JIM TREVOR has sent out a letter (dated 11 June) to all Westlake merchants asking them to look into the possibility of taking on some summer help.

Requests for help should be directed to the Rev. Howard Bryant (Daly City Information and Referral Center, 6634 Mission Street), Michael Orlich (Thornton High School), or James Grealish, (Westlake Bowl), all in Daly City.

Trevor noted in his letter that "statistically, Daly City has been perhaps apathetic regarding this national problem . . ." and expressed the hope that community leaders would undertake

☆   ☆   ☆

THOSE SWINGING WESTLAKE MERCHANTS had their night out again Saturday and danced till dawn to the unforgettable tunes of Sal Carson and his Big Band. There just ain't too many of those sounds around no more. It was a double occasion: The Merchants got together and danced while restaurateur Bruno Scatena sadly noted it was his 49th birthday (he noted it with a straight face).

And photog Doug Mack gets First Prize for his dancing interpretation of Carson's Sugar Blues number. Runnerup spots to al and Shriley Polonsky and city manager Ed Frank.

Mrs. Ed King discounted rumors that she might run for the Daly City council, much to the relief of her table companions which included Mayor Bernard (Bud) Lycett. Actually, observers noted it was Ed (VP of Doelger Enterprises) that first brought up the subject.

1960's – 1970's promo flyer

Frank La Pierre column in The Post, June 26, 1968

Helen Munroe also worked with Sal in the late 60's. "She was the wife of one of our piano players. Very good singer".

Charlyne Lewis, late 60's. Vocalist with the band.

Still another one in the 60's, Linda Rockey.
Photo by Mel Levine.

Sal Carson flyer, 1969

Saturday January 4, 1969

Evening

Circus and columnist Earl Wilson, who
presents the awards. Buddy Schwab,
dancers; Mitchell Ayres conducts the orchestra. (60 min.)

Highlights

"Once-a-Year Day," "The Straight
 Life," "Little Green Apples" ....Bing
"Come to the Ball," "My Dreams Are
 Getting Better All the Time," "Great
 Balls of Fire" ....Tiny Tim
"Ring-Around-a-Rosy Rag" ....Judy
"Mornin' Glory" ....Bobbie
"Okolona River-Bottom Band"
 ....Bing, Bobbie

32 [COLOR] BOXING—Las Vegas
36 BAY AREA SPORTS
38 [COLOR] NEWS—Gary Ashman
10:00 **5** **10** **12** MANNIX—Crime Drama
[COLOR] A friend's call for help sends
Mannix to a remote forestry station. A
sinister picture develops as the detective
is shot at, menaced by a fanatical sheriff and dumbfounded by two women who
claim to be the friend's wife. Mannix:
Mike Connors. (60 min.)

Guest Cast

Laura Giles ....Madlyn Rhue
Sheriff Hale ....John Milford
Bill Chase ....Fred Beir
Carol Chase ....Beverlee McKinsey
Dr. Harris ....Edward Franz
Tom ....Art Metrano
Kessler ....Hal K. Dawson

9 BLACK JOURNAL
[SPECIAL] [COLOR] A report on major
news events of 1968 as they have affected
Black America. Participants include poet-
playwright Le Roi Jones; author Claude
Brown ("Manchild in the Promised
Land"). Dan Watts, editor of Liberator;
Andrew Young of the Southern Christian
Leadership Conference; Mrs. Kathleen
Cleaver, wife of Black Panther Eldridge
Cleaver; Julian Mayfield, co-author and

38 [COLOR] GROUND ZERO
40 [COLOR] GOLF FILM
10:05 **40** LES CRANE—Discussion
[COLOR] Topic: Buddhism and Christ-
ianity. Guest: Dennis Weaver. (60 min.)
10:30 **2** JACK CARNEY—Variety
[DEBUT] [COLOR] Radio disc-jockey
Jack Carney is the host for this ninety
minute variety show featuring the Sal
Carson orchestra, singers Lisa Marne
and Steve Situm. Tonight's guests include singers Ed Ames, Joannie Sommers
and the Cowills; and comics Ronnie Schell
and Jerry Van Dyke. (90 min.)
7 [COLOR] OH, MY WORD!—Game
7 MOVIE—Musical
[COLOR] "Can-Can" (1960), a lavish
adaptation of the Cole Porter-Abe Bur-
rows stage hit. In Paris during the
1890's, a lawyer is both lover and valiant
defender of a cafe owner, who runs afoul
of the law for presenting the scandalous
can-can. Frank Sinatra, Shirley Mac-
Laine, Maurice Chevalier, Louis Jourdan,
Juliet Prowse. (Rerun; two hours, 30 min.)
11 HERE COME THE STARS
[COLOR] Guests are Martha Raye and
her daughter, singer Melody Condos; Billy
Daniels; comics Marty Allen, Dave Barry
and Dick Patterson; and singer Morgana
King. George Jessel is the host. (60 min.)
13 MOVIE—Adventure
[COLOR] "Ride the Wild Surf." (1964)
Surfing footage highlights this sand-and-
surf saga. Three surfers arrive at Hawaii's Oahu Island for an international
competition, only to find themselves
"wiped out" by three pretty girls. Tab
Hunter, Fabian, Shelly Fabares, Barbara
Eden, James Mitchum, Peter Brown, Anthony Hayes, Susan Hart, Catherine Mc-
Leod, Murray Rose, David Cadiente. (Two
hours)

Ed Ames. Born July 9, 1927 in
Malden, MA. He lives on a horse
ranch in Utah.Photo on cover of LP

First appearance on the Jack
Carney show. January 4, 1969

Letter from John McGuire, January 1969

THE CORMAC PUBLISHING CO.

408 ANDOVER STREET
SAN FRANCISCO, CALIFORNIA 94110 • **PHONE (415) 647-2037**

January 3, 1969

Mr. Sal Carson
127 Hardie Drive
Moraga, California 94556

Dear Sal:

I thought that you and the orchestra were superb
last night.

The arrangements were tight and the music crisp,
all in all you had a good sound. I fail to see where
Doc Seversen is any better.

Any success Jack Carney and the show should enjoy
must certainly take into consideration your splendid
musical contribution.

In case you forgot me, I am the writer you met last
Monday at our program conference in Jerry Diamond's
office.

Cordially yours,

John

John McGuire

Note about the January 11, 1969 show.

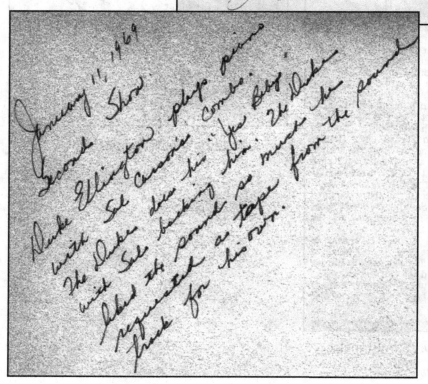

Duke Ellington was born April 29,
1899, Washington DC. He died
May 24, 1974 in New York City.

Jack Carney was born August 23, 1932. He died November 27, 1984 in St Louis of a heart attack while taking a scuba diving lesson in a swimming pool. Publicity photo for a fund raiser. Courtesy of San Francisco Public Library, History Section

Wed.-Thurs., Jan. 15-16, 1969 ★ San Francisco Progress 23

Jack Carney Second Sat. Night Channel 2 TV Show Top Entertainment . . . It Was Fast Moving, Entertaining, and Well Produced . . . 10:30 P.M. till Midnite.

In Jack Carney's second television show over Channel 2 on Saturday last, he succeeded in eliminating all the bugs that were on the first episode . . . Here the real Carney showed thru, a Carney whose humanness and warmth and an uncanny ability for fast thinking and erudition became part and parcel of an hour and one-half that embodied everything that a program of its type should—and that's "Entertainment" . . . his guests were chosen with more care . . . Jack kept the program moving with diversified people such as Private Eye Hal Lipset . . . Oakland Raider Linebacker Ben Davidson . . . Barrister Ron Winchell . . . Tommy Butler and the Magnificent Four . . . from the Hungry i Hedges and Donavan and the piece de resistance and that was the incomparable Duke Ellington, who is a pleasure to listen to, both as a conversationalist and songwriter and pianist . . . Even his regular singer Sinnet did an outstanding job in singing "On A Clear Day" . . . He seemed to have lost his stiffness because frankly we liked him not at all on the first program . . . Sal Carson as Musical Director had his ork muted and swinging in tempo and did the kind of job we know Sal is capable of doing . . .

As for our old and valued friend Jack Carney, he's easy to listen to, doesn't hog the floor, kept his guests at ease and all in all did an outstanding job . . . Watching TV is not our forte but for a change the last two Saturdays we watched the Carney show . . . the first mmmmm, the second socko . . . Tune in Channel 2 every Saturday at 10:30 p.m. to midnite for the Jack Carney Show and watch 1½ hours of delightful television.

Review of the Jack Carney Show. San Francisco Progress. January 15, 1969

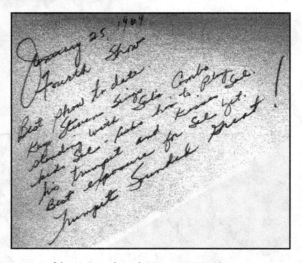

Note on the January 25 show

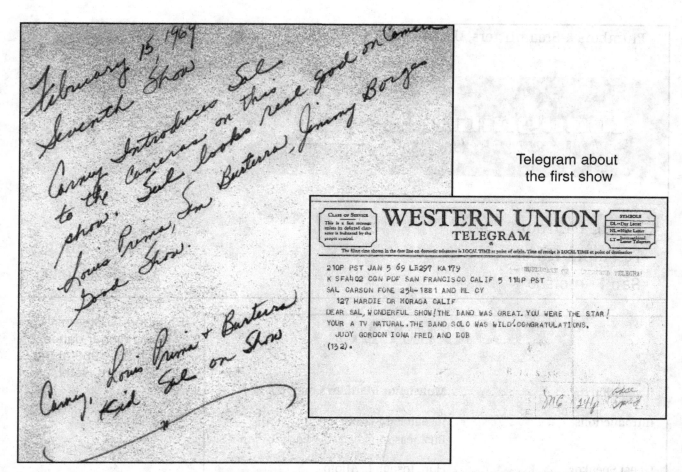

February 15, 1969
Seventh Show

Carney Introduces Sal
to the cameras on this
show. Sal looks real good on Camera.

Louis Prima, Sm Butera, Jimmy Borga
Good Show.

Carney; Louis Prima + Butera
Kid Sal on Show

Note about the February 15, 1969 show

Telegram about
the first show

Telegram about
the first show

WESTERN UNION
TELEGRAM

210P PST JAN 5 69 LB297 KA179
K SFA402 CGN PDF SAN FRANCISCO CALIF 5 114P PST
SAL CARSON FONE 254-1881 AND ML CY
127 HARDIE DR MORAGA CALIF
DEAR SAL, WONDERFUL SHOW! THE BAND WAS GREAT. YOU WERE THE STAR!
YOUR A TV NATURAL. THE BAND SOLO WAS WILD! CONGRATULATIONS.
JUDY GORDON IONA FRED AND BOB
(132).

Louis "Louie" Prima was
born December 7, 1911 in
New Orleans where he died
August 24, 1978. He was a
very good horn player. Just
listen to his recordings prior
To Las Vegas.

Plumbers & Steamfitters, UA Local 38

Recognitions '69
AWARDS TO VETERANS / SALUTE TO YOUTH

Grand Ballroom
Fairmont Hotel
San Francisco

Saturday Evening
March 29, 1969

PROGRAM

Invocation . . . . Monsignor Matthew Connolly

Introductions . . . . Joseph P. Mazzola
Business Manager, UA Local Union #38

Guest Speaker . . . . Hon. Joseph L. Alioto
Mayor of San Francisco

Remarks by Honored Guest . . . . Peter T. Shoemann
General President

Entertainment . . . . Jack Carney
Master of Ceremonies

Dancing . . . . Music by Sal Carson Orchestra

Plumbers & Steamfitters
Union dinner dance.
March 29, 1969 at the
Fairmont Hotel.

Program for the dinner
dance. Plumbers &
Steamfitters Union

Fairmont Hotel, San Francisco, California

Early postcard,
Fairmont Hotel

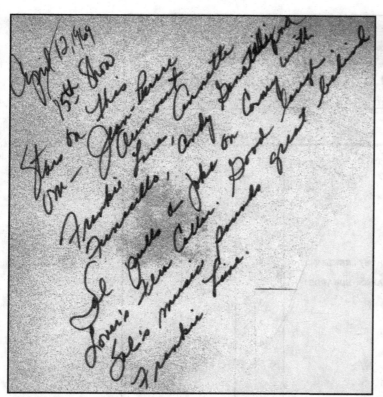

Note about the April 12, 1969, Jack Carney show

Frankie Laine was born March 30, 1913 in Chicago. He died February 6, 2007 in San Diego, CA, Along the way he had many records. "Jezebel", "That's My Desire","That Lucky Old Sun", to name a few.

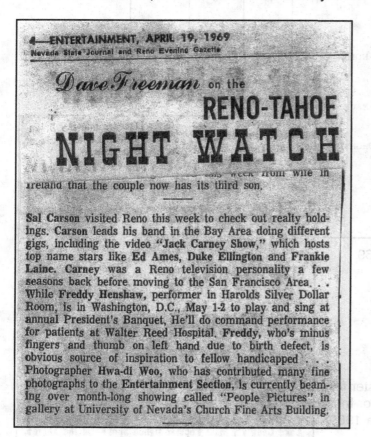

4—ENTERTAINMENT, APRIL 19, 1969
Nevada State Journal and Reno Evening Gazette

Dave Freeman on the

RENO-TAHOE
NIGHT WATCH

...week from wife in Ireland that the couple now has its third son.

Sal Carson visited Reno this week to check out realty holdings. Carson leads his band in the Bay Area doing different gigs, including the video "Jack Carney Show," which hosts top name stars like **Ed Ames, Duke Ellington** and **Frankie Laine.** Carney was a Reno television personality a few seasons back before moving to the San Francisco Area . . . While **Freddy Henshaw,** performer in Harolds Silver Dollar Room, is in Washington, D.C., May 1-2 to play and sing at annual President's Banquet, He'll do command performance for patients at Walter Reed Hospital. Freddy, who's minus fingers and thumb on left hand due to birth defect, is obvious source of inspiration to fellow handicapped . . . Photographer **Hwa-di Woo,** who has contributed many fine photographs to the **Entertainment Section,** is currently beaming over month-long showing called "People Pictures" in gallery at University of Nevada's Church Fine Arts Building.

Dave Freeman column in the Nevada State Journal and Reno Evening Gazette, April 19, 1969

TV Guide, May 3, 1969

The Jack Carney Show

KTVU CHANNEL 2   SAN FRANCISCO·OAKLAND

TAPING DATE 1 MAY 1969   PLAY DATE 3 MAY 1969

GUEST OR ACT	LENGTH	ELAPSED TIME	AREA
THEME, JON-JON CARNEY & RICKY HERRICK WITH CARDS	3	3	
SAL CARSON'S BAND - DIXIE NUMBER	3	6	
FIRST SPOT BREAK	2		
INTRO ANTHONY NEWLEY AT HOME BASE	7	13	
SECOND SPOT BREAK	2		
INTRO NORMA FOSTER AT HOME BASE WITH ANTHONY NEWLEY	4	17	
(POSSIBLE DANCE BETWEEN NORMA FOSTER & AARON EDWARDS)			
HOME BASE: NORMA FOSTER, ANTHONY NEWLEY	3	20	
THIRD SPOT BREAK	2		
ANTHONY NEWLEY - SONG I	4	24	
INTRO JOHN GREGORY DUNNE	5	29	
FOURTH SPOT BREAK	2		
INTO AUDIENCE WITH JOHN DUNNE, NORMA FOSTER, ANTHONY NEWLEY	7	36	
FIFTH SPOT BREAK	2		
INTRO JOHN HARTFORD - SINGS 2 SONGS	7	43	
JOHN HARTFORD AT HOME BASE WITH JOHN DUNNE, NORMA FOSTER, ANTHONY NEWLEY	4	47	
SIXTH SPOT BREAK (DUNNE OUT?)	2		
FASHION SHOW - TEENS MODELING FASHIONS FROM MACY'S	8	55	
SEVENTH SPOT BREAK			
HOME BASE: JOHN HARTFORD, NORMA FOSTER, ANTHONY NEWL			
EIGHTH SPOT BREAK			
GOOD NIGHT; THE SUMMER WINDS - SONG I			

Layout for Jack Carney Show. May 3, 1969

Poster for
Konocti Harbor Inn,
ca 1969

♪ San Francisco's Favorite

SAL CARSON AND HIS BAND

DANCE AT KONOCTI HARBOR INN

EVERY FRIDAY & SATURDAY NITE

COME TO THE LUPIYOMA ROOM

Lake County's Most Popular Dance Spot - On the Shores
of Clear Lake. Dancing from 9:30 till 1:00.

TURN OFF KELSEYVILLE ROAD ONTO SODA BAY ROAD. DRIVE 5 MILES TO KONOCTI HARBOR INN

SAL CARSON and his band are always a great success wherever they play. Sal's own superb trumpet style and sound have been enjoyed by dancers and music lovers at such top places as the Mark Hopkins and Fairmont hotels in San Francisco, Holiday Lodge, Reno and Riviera Hotel, Las Vegas. This season Sal and his band can be heard at Clear Lake's own Konocti Harbor Inn Friday and Saturday nights.

Konocti Harbor Inn clipping, ca 1969

Konocti Harbor Inn ad, ca 1969

Dwight Newton column. San Francisco Examiner, August 2, 1969

Club North Shore, ca September 1969

Ad, North Shore Club flyer. October 1969

North Shore Club flyer.
October, 1969

Clipping North Shore Club flyer. October 1969

Around Las Vegas, Reno & Lake Tahoe

(by SYD GOLDIE)

SAL CARSON AND ORK OPEN OCT. 2nd AT JIM HUME'S NORTH SHORE CLUB HOTEL

Sal Carson, San Francisco's own music man and Reno ranch owner, his trumpet and band, will open at Jim Hume's North Shore Club Hotel, Crystal Bay, Lake Tahoe, Nevada, for 3½ weeks engagement. Opening night is Oct. 2nd thru Oct. 26th. Sal has been running back and forth between Reno and San Francisco twice a month for the past six years. Why? To keep on top of fast changing developments around his ranch. Sal's 50 acre ranch is on the beautiful Truckee River right on Interstate 80 and it adjoins the Holiday Lodge property which is now undergoing a $4.2 million expansion program (seven story hotel and showroom being added). By accepting the engagement at the North Shore Club Sal will save a lot of traveling in October. He is going to spend his Wednesdays (the band's night off) at the ranch. Sal is looking forward to seeing his Bay Area friends at North Shore Club Hotel. For some real great dinners and great music, get yourself on up there.

Group of clippings about North Shore.

Carson Headlines North Shore Club

Sal Carson and his band will appear at Jim Hume's North Shore Club Hotel at Crystal Bay, Lake Tahoe, through Oct. 26.

Sal Carson was the musical director, in San Francisco, for The Bob Hope Show, The Roger Miller Show and The Carol Channing Show. Sal's Band has also played for singers Ed Ames, Pat Boone, Frankie Avalon, Rusty Draper and many other great vocalists.

Sal Carson's Orchestra was chosen to play for San Francisco's Mayor Joseph L. Alioto's Inaugural Dinner reception in the Grand Ball Room at The Fairmont Hotel and the late Robert F. Kennedy's $100.00 a plate dinner at the Palace Hotel.

For the past four years, Carson has appeared primarily in the San Francisco area, however he is no stranger to the Nevada scene. He owns a 50-acre ranch west of Reno on Interstate 80.

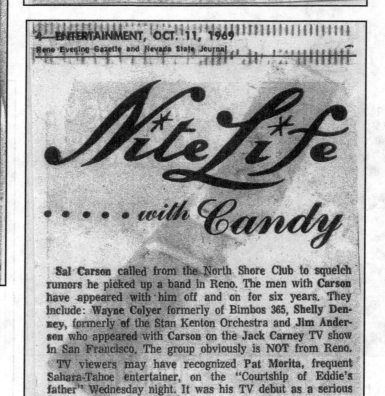

4 — ENTERTAINMENT, OCT. 11, 1969
Reno Evening Gazette and Nevada State Journal

Nite Life
..... with Candy

Sal Carson called from the North Shore Club to squelch rumors he picked up a band in Reno. The men with Carson have appeared with him off and on for six years. They include: Wayne Colyer formerly of Bimbos 365, Shelly Denney, formerly of the Stan Kenton Orchestra and Jim Anderson who appeared with Carson on the Jack Carney TV show in San Francisco. The group obviously is NOT from Reno.

TV viewers may have recognized Pat Morita, frequent Sahara-Tahoe entertainer, on the "Courtship of Eddie's father" Wednesday night. It was his TV debut as a serious actor.

Sal Carson

The talented entertainer is making his own sounds nightly at the North Shore Club, Lake Tahoe. Carson is almost a native Nevadan ... he owns a large ranch just outside of Reno.

4—ENTERTAINMENT, OCT. 18, 1969
Reno Evening Gazette and Nevada State Journal

NiteLife
.....with Candy

Sal Carson was frantic last week when he lost his trumpet. It seems members of the John St. John Trio hid the trumpet in the North Shore Club until 20 minutes before Carson went on. "What could I do?" he asked with a sly

Group of clippings about North Shore.

Sal Carson

The talented entertainer is making his own sounds nightly at the North Shore Club, Lake Tahoe. Carson is almost a native Nevadan ... he owns a large ranch just outside of Reno.

* * *
SAL CARSON AND ORK CLOSE SUCCESSFUL SEASON AT CRYSTAL BAY CLUB, LAKE TAHOE

Sal Carson and his Band closed last Sunday Night after a very successful engagement at the North Shore Club Hotel at Crystal Bay, Lake Tahoe. Closing night (which ran thru the wee hours of the morning) was something to witness. Sal's Band was joined (for fun) by musicians Ted Stevens (Connie Stevens' dad), Charlie Blackwell (formally with Count Basie), two members of his band, who are appearing at Harvey's at Stateline, Lake Tahoe and trombon player from The Mapes Hotel in Reno. The Jam Session from then on was wild.

Sal has lined up some of these musicians for his one nighters around San Francisco during the next two months.
* * *

Feminine Touch

Everybody's got a theory on the Zodiac killer. One detective's little helper brought a "Wanted" poster into the Hall of Justice on which he had daubed lipstick. "See," he exclaimed, "this proves Zodiac is a woman!" . . .

Blacks are expressing pride in the latest school dep't breakthrough — the probable appointment of a black supt. of schools in Oakland. But did you know the first chairman of the San Francisco school board, back in 1848, was a Negro? Civic leader William Leidesdorff was, additionally, a hotel owner and operator of the first steamship on S.F. Bay.

★ ★ ★

LIFE IS LIKE THIS: Bandleader Sal Carson reports from Tahoe's North Shore Club that the early snow caused four golf-playing conventions to cancel. So, right after the cancellations the sun came out . . . The old Amazon Theater in the outer Mission reopens today as the Apollo with major American movies and Spanish subtitles. First attraction: "True Grit."

Auto salesman Lou Menconi made two deliveries in one trip yesterday. He took a brand-new Mercury to the Douglas O'Connor home in San Rafael just as Mrs. O'Connor had labor pains. Menconi headed right back to S.F. and just as they arrived at French Hospital so did little Heather Marie. Everybody's fine.

Street Scene, Pine and Taylor: A motorist with out of state license stopped beside a cab and asked, "Where's the Mark Hopkins Hotel?" The cabbie didn't know. A passerby, Mary Pearson, pointed to the Mark — two blocks away.

★ ★ ★

More North Shore items

Halloween was celebrated in royal style a day early Thursday at John Ascuaga's Nugget. The world champion apple bobbing contest was held in the pit area (80 cases of apples were used); a free cocktail party was held and all customers and employes in costume were admitted free to the cocktail show at 11:30 p.m. Bertha and Tina made appearances throughout the casino during the festivities . . . followed close behind by two housekeepers. All in all the evening was WILD.

Perhaps you noticed Sammy Davis Jr. didn't show up for his Harrah's Reno stint. Flip Wilson filled in for three nights and then Frankie Laine took over. Wilson did a fantastic job filling in on such quick notice . . . he's a super talented guy. Sammy Davis does have his problems though . . . when he closed at Harrah's Tahoe he invited 50 close friends to a party and ended up with more than 800 free loaders.

Sal Carson, back in San Francisco after a successful stint at North Shore Club, phoned to say he'll probably be back at Tahoe next spring. Rumor has it his group may entertain in Reno sooner than that.

"Then Came Bronson," starring Michael Parks, will be filming all day Saturday and Monday at Lake Street and Commercial Row. The television series just finished filming in Wyoming and Colorado. When the series begins filming at Lake Tahoe (tentative) the staff may take more than 60 rooms in the Sahara-Tahoe.

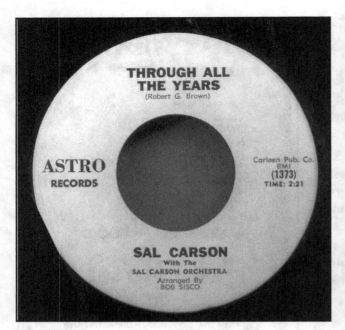

THROUGH ALL
THE YEARS
(Robert G. Brown)

ASTRO
RECORDS

Carleen Pub. Co.
BMI
(1373)
TIME: 2:21

SAL CARSON
With The
SAL CARSON ORCHESTRA
Arranged By
BOB SISCO

FAR ACROSS
THE DEEP OCEAN
(Robert G. Brown)

ASTRO
RECORDS

Carleen Pub. Co.
BMI
(1372)
TIME: 2:35

SAL CARSON
With
THE GLENNS
And The
SAL CARSON ORCHESTRA
Arranged By
BOB SISCO

Recordings

Sal

Harvey's sign.
ca 1960's

Chapter 7
The 70's

The 1970's turned out to be even more busy than the 1960's. Many of his gigs were of longer duration and at some of the best hotels in San Francisco and elsewhere. Sal received recognition for all he did to help the Special Olympics, he became a prominent band leader in the Reno-Tahoe area and had many outside the Bay Area engagements.

In the 70's Ralph Edwards, famous for his "Truth or Consequences" show, achieved very high ratings for his "This Is Your Life" TV show. Sal was invited to be on the show honoring Barbara Eden and rightfully so as he gave Eden her first chance in the entertainment field. Prior to that she was a secretary.

Sal had gigs at the San Francisco Press Club, all the major hotels, clubs and the Konocti Harbor Inn which was an important engagement and led to others.

The Home Savings and Loan Association became a major part of Sal's career resulting in a number of gigs. In addition he was spending more time performing at the top Reno-Tahoe hotels.

Another giant step went from 1974 to 1979 when Sal led the forty-one piece orchestra for the 49'ers Football team. Not just the football games, but many private parties. This is the subject of Chapter 8.

Next is about Bill Armanino the owner of Armanino Products and a prominent person in the Italian section of San Francisco, especially North Beach. Armanino hired Sal to put together a 32-33 piece band to back Vic Damone on an LP. Armanino wanted to record one song in particular, a pretty ballad, "Christmas In San Francisco". Other than that he let Sal run with the project. That's a good example of a band leader's dream. What follows is a transcript of a portion of our interview.

Sal: We had a 32-33 piece band, a beautiful big band. I got the best musicians available, some out of Las Vegas. Some doubled on oboe or other instruments. Truly top musicians. So that time he had me helping Vic Damone and his accompanist, I forget his name, called me because he needed this and that. So I went to a store in San Francisco so we could rent different things in time before the session. The session was in 1979 and we recorded about 16-18 songs. So we had all the equipment up from LA and San Francisco. It was a big production.

Jim: That had to be an expensive production.

Sal: Very, very expensive production. We set up and had a rehearsal the day before the session. Did the whole album as a back-up. The record session was done live. Big dinner party honoring Diane Feinstein. I believe she was running for mayor. All her group was there. The place was jam packed. Before the session our band played for about one hour. Dinner music, entertainment, a good hour, maybe an hour and a half. Took about a fifteen minute break and then did the recording session. Before the session there were speeches which they recorded and gave me a copy. It was a very big evening. Combination of the session, Feinstein running for mayor, national coverage.

Jim: Why was Armanino backing this thing?

Sal: Good question.

Jim: That's not his normal business.

Sal: I think at the time he wanted to be given an appointment. That was one of his motives.

Jim: He spent a lot of money.

Sal: He spent a fortune. Just the band was expensive.

Jim: I would think so. That was a lot of pieces. Just that alone. Bringing all that stuff from LA.

Sal: The rehearsal before was more than a thin dime. The night of the performance was about ten thousand just for the band. It was a very successful evening

Jim: By the way, what was his first name?

Sal: Bill

Jim: Bill Armanino.

Sal. There was a comedian who came up from Hollywood to MC the whole event and to make some of the announcements on the record session. Nice part about the record session was the mention of Sal Carson twice. Gave us some good compliments right in the session. Naturally it made me feel pretty damn good.

Jim: Of course it did.

Sal: Anyway, after the record session I was invited to Benito's a nice restaurant. It was a pretty good party.

Jim: And that wasn't cheap either. This guy knows how to spend money.

Sal: It was a lot of money. Of course he also had to pay Vic Damone and his personal accompanist. About one week before the session he had a keyboard player, drummer and bass player. That was it. I got the rest of the band for the Fairmont. One week of being very busy. I was very happy that night. Everyone was happy. There were parties before the session at a fancy restaurant. Before and after that Bill Armanino had his own TV show.

Jim: You mean as a sponsor.

Sal: Yes. In the afternoon for once a week. Had the big band and different entertainers, always a big name.

I asked Sal about the vocalist Sylvia Gaylord. Here's what he told me: "She was a very professional singer who worked with 'Fatha' Hines, Ernie Heckscher, John Cardoni, a good friend of mine and others. Singers in those days did not just sing in one band because there were many one-nighters for conventions, private parties and what have you. Sylvia was really, at that time, a top draw in town. Very pretty and great. She knew how to handle an audience and how to put over a song with style. People liked her very much".

So the 70's were great. He backed such stars as Vic Damone in the unforgettable recording session, Connie Haines, Danny Kaye, Helen O'Connell, George Raft, Della Reese, Kay Starr, The Whittington Sisters and others. Some members will never forget performing at the San Francisco Zoo in front of the lion's cage. One lion had to heed the call of nature which required a change of clothes for some of the band members who were close to the lion cage.

Lynn Bali and Les Brown. Lynn sang a few tunes one night with the Les Brown Band in San Francisco. She worked with Sal in the 1970's and early 80's. Very popular singer.

Utah postcard

Harvey's in the early 70's

Hotel Utah postcard. Sal had some long gigs there.

THERE WAS A surprise entertainer in the Fairmont Grand Ballroom during the Sailors Union of the Pacific banquet. Maestro Sal Carson gave the downbeat for "Danny Boy" and even to his astonishment Father Heaney, the Port chaplain and head of the Apostleship of the Sea, stepped on stage and in a rich tenor accompanied the band. A resounding ovation.

Clipping about Sal and Father Heaney, ca 1970's

–142–

Lori English did some vocal work with Sal, ca 1970's. Another good looking singer with style.

The Sal Carson Band will be appearing in the Tiki Lounge at the Top of the Wheel, Harvey's Resort Hotel, South Lake Tahoe, Tuesday through Aug. 2, alternating with Ron Rose and Lady D.

Sal Carson is one of the top trumpeters in show business today.

He was the musical director in San Francisco for the Bob Hope Show, the Roger Miller Show and the Carol Channing Show.

Sal and his band specialize in the popular Top 40 tunes of today and along with the great standard songs of the '40s, '50s, and '60s. They have the ability to round out their performance with everything from the Hora to the Hawaiian Wedding Song.

"My whole idea is to hit the people with nostalgia," says Sal, a man who has brought the sounds of Count Basie, Glenn Miller and the Dixieland greats.

This year will be the third season the Carson's 45-piece band plays for the San Francisco 49er's during their home games in Candlestick Park.

Starring among those members of the band to appear at Harvey's is Sylvia Gaylord, a beautiful and talented vocalist.

Harvey's Top of the Wheel, ca 1970's

(Top left) Special Olympics Award to Sal. Presented by Alan Gehring at the Hyatt Hotel. ca 1970's

(Bottom left) Top of the Wheel clipping, ca 1970's

Sal Carson Band to play

The Sal Carson Band will be appearing in the Tiki Lounge at the Top of the Wheel, Harvey's Resort Hotel, South Lake Tahoe, Tuesday through Aug. 2, alternating with Ron Rose and Lady D.

In the Theatre Lounge are the Leland Four (through Sunday); Sun Spots (through Aug. 1); Tunes Plus One (through Aug. 1); Ernie Menehune (through Tuesday) and the Esquires (through Monday).

Opening in the Lounge Tuesday is Rita and the Rebels through Aug. 9. Big Tiny Little opens Monday and stars through Aug. 15.

Conchita is in the Entertainment Center at Harvey's Inn through Aug. 2.

Sal Carson is one of the top trumpeters in show business today.

He was the musical director in San Francisco for the Bob Hope Show, the Roger Miller Show and the Carol Channing Show.

Sal's band has also played for singers Ed Ames, Pat Boone, Frankie Avalon, Rusty Draper and many other great vocalists.

Sal and his band specialize in the popular Top 40 tunes of today and along with the great standard songs of the '40s, '50s, and '60s. They have the ability to round out their performance with everything from the Hora to the Hawaiian Wedding Song.

"My whole idea is to hit the people with nostalgia," says Sal, a man who has brought the sounds of Count Basie, Glenn Miller and the Dixieland greats.

This year will be the third season the Carson's 45-piece band plays for the San Francisco 49er's during their home games in Candlestick.

Top of the Wheel article, ca 1970's. Photo of Sylvia Gaylord

Harvey's ad. August 12, 1970

Tiki Lounge performer

Sal Carson Band entertains at Harvey's

Sal Carson and his Band are in the Tiki Lounge, Top of the Wheel, Harvey's Resort Hotel through July 3, alternating with the Ron Rose Sound.

Appearing in the Theatre Lounge are: Chris Wade (through Sunday); Sounds of Brass (through July 12); Jamie (through July 5); Tunes Plus One (through Sunday); and Frankie Fanelli (through Sunday).

Opening in the Theatre Lounge Monday is the Philthy McNasty Show (through July 10); Jack Lox and the Big Country Express (through July 3) and the Ernie Menehune Show (through July 17).

Sal Carson has signed a contract to make commercials with Andy Russell, singer extraordinaire.

Carson's 45-piece orchestra is the official San Francisco 49er band. The band plays the old tunes of Dorsey, Miller, Basie and Goodman and even a few Wayne King waltz-like tunes tossed in for the young-oldtimers.

The band is widely known for its versatility and ability to please any age bracket. Carson is not only a dedicated musician, but he's a musical contractor as well, heading, along with his big band, numerous combos of various sizes and mixed talents.

Carson has been an accompaniest to Bob Hope, Pat Boone, Ed Ames, Frankie Laine, Roger Miller, Kaye Stevens, Duke Ellington, Barbara Eden, Bobby Goldsboro, John Davidson and the Johnny Mann Singers.

Carson has a great talent for "feeling" the mood of th cers and requests at the Top of the Wheel are always wel His own superb trumpet style and sound have been enjo dancers and music lovers at the top hotels in the coun

POPULAR BAND LEADER Sal Carson, one of the top trumpeters in show business, is appearing with his band in the Tiki Lounge, Harvey's Resort Hotel through July 3. He alternates in the lounge with the Ron Rose Sound, which continues through Oct. 16.

Another Harvey's article, ca 1970's

SAL CARSON AND HIS ORCHESTRA - FEATURING
SYLVIA GAYLORD

HARVEY'S RESORT HOTEL, TOP OF THE WHEEL
STATELINE, LAKE TAHOE
OCTOBER 16, 1973 Thru OCTOBER 31, 1973

Harvey's
RESORT HOTEL
Lake Tahoe
South Shore, Stateline, Nevada
Phone (702) 588-2411

Sylvia
Gaylord

SAN FRANCISCO'S MUSIC MAN, SAL CARSON IS RETURNING TO HARVEY'S TOP OF THE WHEEL FOR YOUR DANCING PLEASURE. ENJOY THE GREAT TRUMPET SOUNDS OF SAL CARSON AND DANCE TO THE BIG BAND TUNES OF THE 40's, 50's, 60's and 70's.

SAL CARSON PROUDLY PRESENTS BEAUTIFUL AND TALENTED VOCALIST SYLVIA GAYLORD. SYLVIA RECENTLY HEADLINED IN THE VENETIAN ROOM OF THE FAIRMONT HOTEL. SYLVIA JONINED THE SAL CARSON ORCHESTRA FOUR YEARS AGO.

Sal, Gaylord promo

SF/CC
GREATER SAN FRANCISCO CHAMBER OF COMMERCE

EDWARD BRUSKE
general manager

January 23, 1970

Sal Carson
127 Hardie Drive
Moraga, California 94556

Sal:

Just a note of thanks to you and your orchestra for a job well done at the Chamber's Annual Dinner last Wednesday evening.

The extra time and effort that you gave us in not only producing a fine performance but also in working with the other entertainment, was outstanding. I know the Chamber of Commerce will certainly be calling on your services again in the future.

Enclosed you will find a check in the amount of $1,198.30, which covers the expenses for the evening of the 21st plus the piano rehearsal on Saturday, January 17th.

Thank you again.

Sincerely,

Ed Bruske

EB/lm

(Top left)
Sal in the 1970's

(Top right)
San Francisco Chamber of Commerce dinner. January 21, 1970

(Left)
Letter from Ed Bruske, the general manager of the Chamber of Commerce. January 23, 1970

Joan Blackman, singer and movie star. She first sang with Sal when she was only 16.

For "A Night to Remember," it is expected that Sal will show with Miss Blackman, who in 1972 was proclaimed one of the 10 Most Beautiful Women in the World. A former Hollywood star, turned vocalist, Miss Blackman has appeared in lead film roles opposite Elvis Presley (Blue Hawaii and Kid Galahad), Tony Curtis (The Great Imposter) and Jerry Lewis (Visitor to a Small Planet). She was also a regular on the TV series, Peyton Place.

We had occasion, thanks to John Nelson, VP and Gen. Mgr. of Oakland's Welsh & Bresee, Inc. Building Materials, to 'catch' the Carson Band playing for the company's well-patterned "Acapulco Getaway" fete Saturday night. Simply outstanding! The vocalist? None other than the extremely talented and enchanting Helen O'Connell, she of Jimmy Dorsey big band fame. Her awakening version of the great hit "Green Eyes" was a show-stopper to nigh the 800 folk in attendance. While on stage, Miss O'Connell did remark that she never had a band back her any better than Maestro Sal.

At one time, Sal had the opportunity to join Skinnay Ennis' contingent as lead trumpeter when that crooning leader was playing the Bob Hope radio show. But, Sal wanted to stay on his own; to remain in the Bay Area where he enjoys so much.

Article about Joan Blackman and Helen O'Connell, ca 1970's

The Lancers were backed by Sal at the Hilton Hotel, ca 1970's

Lee, Swan & Co.

COTTON
COTTON WASTE
COTTON LINTERS
COTTON GIN MOTES

IMPORT   EXPORT
350 TENTH STREET
SAN FRANCISCO 94103
CALIFORNIA

TELEPHONE
(415) 431-5544

CABLE ADDRESS
"LILEE"

June 3, 1970

Mr. Sal Carson
127 Hardie Dr.
Moraga, California 94556

Dear Sal:

Many thanks for your letter of June 1st. I will look forward to receiving the album "Honey Dear".

Sal, your music was outstanding, I saw people dancing that I know haven't danced in years. It was everything you said it would be and more!

Kindest regards,

LEE, SWAN & COMPANY

R. M. LEE

RML:sh

Letter to Sal

MERLE NORMAN
C O S M E T I C S

9130 BELLANCA AVENUE · · · LOS ANGELES, CALIFORNIA 90045
Area Code (213) 641-3000   Telex 653 437

June 8, 1970

Mr. Sal Carson
Sal Carson Orchestra
127 Hardie Drive
Moraga, California 94556

Dear Sal,

Thank you for your nice letter of May 27 ... it was a pleasure
doing business with you and the entertainment you provided us
was excellent.

The check for $2,725.00 which I left for you with Ted Deutsch
(as you requested) no doubt was obtained by you from him.

Enclosed is our check for $200 which should cover your "invoice
for additional items" plus extra expenses. I hope this is sat-
isfactory with you, Sal; and if not, please let me know.

Thanks again for all your help ....

Sincerely,

MERLE NORMAN COSMETICS

John E. Danley
Vice President, Franchising

JED:ltb
Enc.

Letter to Sal

RETAIL CONFECTIONERS Institute **INTERNATIONAL**

July 16, 1970
OUR 50th ANNIVERSARY

Mr. Sal Carson
Sal Carson Orchestra
127 Hardie Drive
Moraga, California 94556

Dear Sal:

"You pleased our convention registrants ! "

These five words tell the whole story. What more can I say?

Our Sunday evening House of Friendship Buffet Supper Dance, using the "Barbary Coast Theme", really "broke the ice"---started everyone off with a smile. The way you "sensed" the dancing crowd and gave them the music they wanted, is a tribute to your ability as a musician and as a showman.

Personally, I thought that our Tuesday evening 50th Anniversary Dinner-Dance, encased in that beautiful Garden Court, was the finest in our half century of operation. Again your music added just the convivial touch that made our registrants happy. As I looked out on the dance floor I'd swear that every member was a "twinkle-toes".

Thanks for helping make our Golden Anniversary a memorable one.

Most sincerely,

Tom Sullivan

Thomas J. Sullivan
Secretary-Legal Counsel

TJS:pt
Encl.

Letter to Sal

NATIONAL LIVE STOCK & MEAT BOARD

36 SOUTH WABASH AVENUE • CHICAGO, ILLINOIS 60603 • 312 / 346-6465

August 25, 1970

Mr. Sal Carson
Sal Carson Orchestra
127 Hardie Drive
Moraga, California 94556

Dear Mr. Carson:

Just a note of appreciation for the fine music your orchestra provided at the dance following our annual banquet. The songs played were most danceable. Everyone there thoroughly enjoyed the evening.

We look forward to having the opportunity of using your orchestra again in the not too distant future.

Sincerely yours,

Jacque Filiatreau
Assistant to the President

JF:bl

Letter to Sal

San Francisco
Stonestown, ca 1970's
(l to r) Frank Judnic, Nick
Jordon, Sal and Jack
Sava

Carol Doda was
backed by Sal at
Harrah's Tahoe.
Ca 1970's

Carol Doda at Tahoe

Singer Carol Doda says she "used to sound like Andy Devine."

That was before taking 10 exhausting years of voice lessons from Judy Davis, the Berkeley tutor who had helped such notables as Barbra Streisand and Merv Griffin.

Hard work paid off for the lovely San Francisco native, and the Andy Devine croaking was replaced by a "breathy and purring" voice that's been tabbed by reviewers as reminiscent of another blonde standout, Carol Channing.

Miss Doda will make her Nevada nightclub debut in the Stateline Cabaret of Harrah's Tahoe Wednesday, where she will be appearing nightly through April 20.

Broadway tunes, contemporary hits and delightful comedy bits comprise The Carol Doda Show.

"Show of Stars" at San
Quentin, ca 1970's

Annual Show of Stars
Returns to SQ

SAL CARSON'S HOUSE BAND

The show was kicked off by
Sal Carson's House Band. This
is a group of multi talented musicians who demonstrated their
expertise by doing their rendition of "A Train" and "Love
Will Keep Us Together."

"*Davre's*"

the restaurant division of ARA Services, Inc.
JOHN HANCOCK CENTER • SUITE 1519
875 NORTH MICHIGAN AVE. • CHICAGO, ILL. 60611 • (312) 787-3277

August 8, 1970

Mr. Sal Carson
Sal Carson Orchestra
127 Hardie Drive
Moraga, California 94556

Dear Sal:

I have processed your bill for payment. It may take
a couple of weeks, as it must go through our accounting
department in the Home Office in Philadelphia.

I was very pleased and very much enjoyed having you
play at the press party to open the Carnelian Room.
Everyone commented about how nice it was.

If we have any need in the future for an orchestra, we
will be sure and contact you.

Sincerely,

Timothy J. Canty
Director of Advertising
and Public Relations

TJC;cb

Letter from Timothy J. Canty, August 8, 1970

Airport Commissioner, Plumbers Union Leader Joe Mazzola phoned Sal Carson, San Francisco's Music Man, while on his ranch in Reno, Nevada, to report immediately with his band to Konocti Harbor Inn, Clearlake, to play for the gala Labor Day Weekend (Sept. 4th, 5th and 6th) planned at the fabulous resort.

Sal Carson has been dividing his time this summer between his huge land development in Reno and appearing at all of our top hotels here in San Francisco for convention parties; also his band played for the grand opening of The World Headquarters Bank of America Building, 52nd Floor Carnelian Room.

(Far left) Sunny Chow. Ca early 70's. A vocalist.

(Left) Konocti booking. San Francisco Progress, September 4, 1970

(Bottom lelft) Herb Caen article, San Francisco Chronicle, ca 1971

(Bottom right) The Whittington Sisters, San Francisco, ca 1971. (l to r) Paulete, Sal, Diane and Sonya

Park wonder who set a willow tree afire Sunday while barbecuing steaks (that's against regulations), we can tell 'em that this culprit, too, is an eminent Federal fellow ... Now it's the local musicians who are sore at Joe Alioto, because Sal Carson's band has been hired to play at the Mayor's big rally in Civic Aud. next Monday night when Sal isn't even a San Franciscan (he lives in Moraga). The fact that Carson's real name is Carcione may have had something to do with it ... No more Mr. Nice Guy: Candidate Harold Dobbs has decided to run a "tough" campaign, first indication being his blast yesterday at the Civic League of Improvement Clubs ("I don't want their endorsement — every four years they come out of the woodwork and try to play kingmaker") ... As though the waterfront strike weren't long and bad enough, the pollution caused by those 40-odd ships at anchor in the Bay is driving environment officials up the wall.

★   ★   ★

Capitol Square, 1408 - 5th Street, Sacramento, California 95814
Office of Secretary: P. O. Box 2631, Sacramento, California 95812
Phone 916 442-0411

California **ASSOCIATION of HIGHWAY PATROLMEN**

November 10, 1970

Sal Carson
P O Box 332
Moraga, California. 94556

Dear Sal:

Now that it's all over, the echos of the shouts have died
away, one fact still is mentioned occasionally, that is
"that was a damn good orchestra" we sure enjoyed the music.

What more can we say to a professional musician? Thanks Sal,
you provided the icing on the cake for us.

We are looking forward to seeing you soon and will certainly
enjoy attending one of your parties.

Sincerely,

R. L. Schiavone
Executive Manager

RLS/js

Reaction to Sal's performance
at a party. California
Association of Highway
Patrolmen. November 10, 1970

The Whittington Sisters
plus two. ca 1971.
(l to r) Paulete, Diane,
Barry Collier, Sonya and
Bonnie Collier.

A 45 recording by the Whittington Sisters. ca 1971 or 1972

AMERICAN PHARMACEUTICAL ASSOCIATION

The National Professional Society of Pharmacists

April 20, 1971

Mr. Sal Carson
P.O. Box 332
Moraga, CA 94556

Dear Sal:

Thank you for your very nice letter of April 15.

It was indeed a pleasure for us to utilize your services in providing entertainment for the 118th annual meeting of the American Pharmaceutical Association in San Francisco, March 28-April 2, 1971. Please feel free to use the American Pharmaceutical Association as a recommendation for your future solicitations.

We have not yet received a confirmation from Lucy Selenger, CBS News as to when the Mike Wallace show will be aired, but as soon as we do we will advise you accordingly.

With best personal regards, I remain

Sincerely yours,

George B. Griffenhagen
Associate Executive Director
for Communications

GBG:atd

Letter of appreciation

OAKLAND SCAVENGER COMPANY

2601 PERALTA STREET • OAKLAND, CALIFORNIA 94607

Telephone 465-2911

May 25, 1971

Mr. Sal Carson
127 Hardie Drive
Moraga, Calif. 94556

Dear Mr. Carson:

I wish to express my appreciation for the delightful evening that you gave us on May 22nd.

Mr. Carson, I could never thank you enough for your part in making this evening such an enjoyable one and a happy time for everyone.

I can't begin to tell you how many people approached me and expressed their compliments on the entertainment by you during the evening and they also showed appreciation over the little group singing along with one of your men at the bar at intermission time.

Your playing and singing was responsible for the spirit of festivity that prevailed and the songs that you played for our members really brought back some wonderful memories.

In closing, I wish to thank you again for agreeing to provide us with your entertainment on our very special evening.

Gratefully,

OAKLAND SCAVENGER COMPANY

Armando Rossi
Chairman

AR;bmc

Letter of appreciation

Pocketful of Notes

ME & MY BIG MOUF: Jim Browning, the U.S. Attorney here, read the riot act around the Fed'l Building yesterday after we blabbed about the photo of Mayor Alioto, captioned "Punch a Politician Today," in the hdqs. of the Organized Crime Strike Force. Breathing brimstone, ol' Jim strode around his empire and found two other displays that displeased him. One was a photo of Michael Metzger, the former Asst. U.S. Atty. involved in a dope case here, captioned "I know a narc when I see one." The other was a picture of Asst. Atty. Gen. Will Wilson, the Govt.'s chief criminal prosecutor, who allegedly borrowed $297,000 from the central figure in a stock scandal — this one posted over an ad reading "The Money Card — Your Friendly Banker Has It!" . . . All these goodies are now off the walls, and several of Browning's Bad Boys have been sentenced to stand in the corner.

★   ★   ★

CAENFETTI: If the Rangers over at Tilden Park wonder who set a willow tree afire Sunday while barbecuing steaks (that's against regulations), we can tell 'em that this culprit, too, is an eminent Federal fellow . . . Now it's the local musicians who are sore at Joe Alioto, because Sal Carson's band has been hired to play at the Mayor's big rally in Civic Aud. next Monday night when Sal isn't even a San Franciscan (he lives in Moraga). The fact that Carson's real name is Carcione may have had something to do with it . . . No more Mr. Nice Guy: Candidate Harold Dobbs has decided to run a "tough" campaign, first indication being his blast yesterday at the Civic League of Improvement Clubs ("I don't want their endorsement — every four years they come out of the woodwork and try to play kingmaker") . . . As though the waterfront strike weren't long and bad enough, the pollution caused by those 40-odd ships at anchor in the Bay is driving environment officials up the wall.

★   ★   ★

Herb Caen column. ca 1971. San Francisco Chronicle

★   ★   ★

MAYOR JOHN LINDSAY of New York appeared at the stage entrance, so movie-star handsome he makes Robert Redford look like Bennie Barrish. Bandleader Sal Carson (born Carcione) struck up "East Side, West Side" and the crowd went crackers. Lindsay strode onstage — he got here in time by canceling the Merv Griffin show — and delivered his patented, consumer-tested opening line: "My popularity rises in direct proportion to my distance from New York City." In his own speech, Mayor Alioto got off a great funny line, too — "My campaign will follow the high road of principles" — but nobody laughed.

★   ★   ★   1971

Another Herb Caen column. ca 1971

Sal Carson - Ponderosa Hotel

Sal Carson, his trumpet, and band will open in the lounge at the Ponderosa Hotel, Reno, on March 22. Sal's musical aggregation has played good conventional dance music with a wide variety of sounds and styles in such leading hotels as the Fairmont, the Mark-Hopkins, Top of the Wheel, Harvey's Resort Hotel, Lake Tahoe; the New Frontier Hotel in Las Vegas; Konocti Harbor Inn and Hoberg's Resort in Lake County. . . . El Smits, manager of the Villa Chartier, is offering free use of their many conference and meeting rooms to industrial and commercial firms from 2:30 p.m. to 5 p.m., Mondays through Fridays. Firms can reserve the famed facilities for seminars and afternoon meetings by contacting Gwen Penfold, the attractive catering manager . . . South City's New Southern was the recent site for two oratorical contests. They weren't just "rap" sessions with restaurant co-owner Reno Donati, they were organized contests sponsored by local civic groups, the Lion's Club and the Optimists. Participants were local junior high school students.

San Mateo Times, March 19, 1971

Sal Carson Konocti Harbor Inn

Keeping up with the musical capers of Sal Carson and his orchestra is no easy matter. These five musicians are so much in demand, they are booked months in advance. At this writing, Sal and his aggregation are scheduled to appear at Konocti Harbor Inn, located on Clear Lake (overlooking the marina below which is said to be the largest privately operated marina in the United States, Thursday, Friday and Saturday evenings through Labor Day. Incidentally, Konocti Harbor Inn is now offering a "Midweek Holiday" special (includes three days-two nights (Sunday through Thursday) which calls for immediate reservations. You'll find all kinds of recreation — sailing, horseback riding, golf, tennis, movies, fishing, plus gourmet dining, dancing, entertainment — and only two and one-half hours from the Bay Area. . . . The Charlie Blackwell Trio, direct from appearances at Lake Tahoe, display their musical artistry in the lounge at Villa Hotel nightly Tuesday through Saturday, from 9 p.m. The talented threesome has one of the smoothest dance sounds to hit the Peninsula. . . . Fresh pastry, including home made pies, cakes and various other goodies, can always be found at the New Southern restaurant in South San Francisco. You see, co-owners Reno and Julio Donati and Nick Sbarra also operate their own bakery, and one of their best clients is their restaurant.

Sal at Konocti Harbor Inn, ca 1971

OFFICE OF THE MAYOR
SAN FRANCISCO

JOSEPH L. ALIOTO

October 5, 1971

Mr. Sal Carson
Musicans Local No 6
230 Jones Street
San Francisco, California 94102

Dear Mr. Carson: *Sal*,

Again, I want to thank you for your hard work
and generous contribution of your talent in
arranging the musical program for the Alioto
Spectacular. The festivities were a tremendous
success and I am most grateful for your efforts.

With my very best wishes and appreciation for
your time, patience, and generosity.

Sincerely,

Joe Alioto

Joseph L. Alioto
Mayor

*Many thanks for all your
great help!*

Thank you letter from Joseph L. Alioto, the mayor of San Francisco. October 5, 1971

FIRST FEDERAL BUILDING

1717 NORTH HIGHLAND AVENUE • HOLLYWOOD, CALIFORNIA 90028

November 29, 1971

Dear Mr. Carson:

We are indeed happy to welcome you to Los Angeles to participate in "This Is Your Life", the exciting television production which this week honors someone in whose life and career you have played a part.

All of us at Ralph Edwards Productions are grateful that you have taken the time to be here to appear on the show, and wish that the few days you spend in Los Angeles will be memorable and joyful.

Cordially,

Richard M. Gottlieb
Executive Producer

RMG/smc

Welcome letter for "This Is Your Life". A Ralph Edwards Productions. November 29, 1971

Ralph Edwards Productions

FIRST FEDERAL BUILDING

1717 NORTH HIGHLAND AVENUE • HOLLYWOOD, CALIFORNIA 90028

November 29th

1971

Dear Guest:

Your visit to Los Angeles will be full of excitement and activity. To make your stay as simple as possible, here are some brief notes regarding your program:

VERY IMPORTANT: No doubt all our guests are aware that the very essence of THIS IS YOUR LIFE is the element of surprise for the subject. Therefore, may we ask you to discuss the show discreetly prior to the taping and not mention the true name of "You-Know-Who".

On Tuesday, November 30, 1971 we will meet you in the lobby of the Roosevelt Hotel at 10:00 a.m. for the drive to Cinema General Studios. A "Script-Read-Through" is planned, with our producer/director, to familiarize you with the lines written for you, to check veracity of facts, and to incorporate any necessary changes into the script.

Lunch will be served at the Studio about 12:00 noon.

Rehearsals are scheduled for the afternoon. The show will be taped at 6:30 p.m.

WARDROBE/MAKE-UP: Please bring with you, when we meet in the hotel lobby at 10:00 a.m., wardrobe you wish to wear during the taping. We will not return to the hotel again for the remainder of the day. Dressing rooms will be available for changing at the Studio.

AFTER THE SHOW: After the taping, a small after-show dinner party will be held to celebrate "You-Know-Who" in the Redwood Room (Mezzanine) of the Hollywood Roosevelt Hotel.

Three page advance information for "This Is Your Life". November 29, 1971

HOTEL SERVICES:

Meal Vouchers: Each of our guests is given vouchers
for meals taken at the Roosevelt Hotel. The vouchers
are dated, and your name or room number appear on each
one. Please hand the applicable voucher to your waitress in the Garden Room at the time you place your order.
Amounts over and above those shown on the meal vouchers
at the time your check is presented to you should be
settled by you at that time.

Vouchers may be applied toward food and beverages.
Alcoholic beverages are not included and may be settled
directly with the waitress.

Parking: If you are driving your own car to Los Angeles,
Ralph Edwards Productions will cover parking fees for two
nights in the Hollywood Roosevelt Hotel garage.

Tipping: Tipping of the hotel staff is not necessary
as a service charge is provided for the staff by Ralph
Edwards Productions.

Valet Service: You may avail yourself of the Valet
Service offered.

Phone Calls: Please feel free to make local telephone
calls free of charge. You may check with the hotel
switchboard operator for assistance on long-distance
calls. These are made at your own expense. Please
stop at the cashier's window before checking out to
adjust your personal bill for items other than those
covered by Ralph Edwards Productions.

INCURRED EXPENSES: If you incur expenses (transportation
parking, etc.) between your home and the airport at departure
and on arrival, please advise us so that we may reimburse you.

TRANSFER FROM/TO AIRPORT: Every endeavor is made to meet
our guests upon arrival at the airport. If you are not
personally met and take the airport limousine to the hotel,
please include this amount in your incurred expenses. We
will, of course, provide you with information regarding
limousine departures from the hotel for your return flights.

The Airport Limousine departs directly from the hotel's front
entrance.

FLIGHT RESERVATIONS: Pan American Airways and Trans World
Airlines have ticket counters in the lobby of the Hollywood
Roosevelt Hotel. Agents will assist you in every way to
make changes or onward reservations. If you prefer, I will
be glad to help you in any way possible.

EXTENSION: As the guests of Ralph Edwards Productions, your accomodations, meals, and non-alcoholic beverages are covered until the day following taping of the show. If you wish to extend your visit, we will be happy to assist you with reservations at the hotel. (Room rates at the Hollywood Roosevelt run between $22.00 to $24.00 per diem.)

BABY SITTERS SERVICE: If desired, the name of a Baby Sitters Service can be supplied to guests.

At the time of your visit we will not, as yet, know the date on which this show will be aired on your local TV station. As soon as a date has been set, we will advise you of the time, date and local channel.

We thank you sincerely for coming to California for this show, and for playing such an important part on "This Is Your Life."

Cordially,

Edda Shurman Witt
Guest Coordinator

ESW:kd

San Francisco Examiner

EDITORIALS OPINIONS COMICS
CLASSIFIED   OBITUARIES

OUR MAN ON THE TOWN

By Jack Rosenbaum

TV's "This Is Your Life" Feb. 16 will have a strong San Francisco flavor. It stars actress Barbara Eden, who, as Barbara Huffman, was a Miss San Francisco. (Gallantry forbids giving the exact year in the '50s). Barbara, then a secretary just out of Lincoln High, got her start in show business as a vocalist for two years with bandleader Sal Carson, who spent two secret days in Hollywood for the "Life" show.

"Our Man On The Town" by Jack Rosenbaum, ca 1971. San Francisco Examiner.

That's Ralph Edwards presenting a photo album to Barbara Eden at the climax of the "This Is Your Life" show. Standing far left is Sal and next to him is Ben Gazzara, a well-known actor. Sorry, I don't know the other names. November 1971

Two pages on Sal's portion, "This Is Your Life".

RALPH:

YOU BEGIN SINGING WITH BANDS
IN SAN FRANCISCO TO HELP
PAY FOR SINGING AND DANCING
LESSONS WHILE YOU'RE IN
HIGH SCHOOL.

SAL CARSON (VO):

IT ALL STARTED WHEN I SAW
BARBARA -- A LITTLE WISPY THING
WITH GLASSES -- SITTING
BEHIND A TYPEWRITER IN *the late*
HOWARD FREDERICK'S ~~BOOKING~~ *Theatrical*
~~OFFICE~~. *Agency*

RALPH:

ONE OF THE LOCAL BANDLEADERS
WITH WHOM YOU USED TO SING --
YOU HAVEN'T SEEN HIM IN MANY
YEARS -- FROM SAN FRANCISCO --
SAL CARSON.

RALPH:

WHAT HAPPENED TO GET BARBARA
FROM A DESK, TO IN FRONT OF
A BAND, SAL?

SAL CARSON:

I WAS IN HOWARD FREDERICK'S OFFICE
ONE DAY WHEN BARBARA WHISPERED TO
ME -- SHE WAS SUCH A SHY THING --
THAT SHE WAS A SINGER. I DON'T
THINK HER BOSS EVEN KNEW IT.
SO I SAID TO HER, "WHY DON'T
YOU COME OUT TO A JOB SOMETIME
AND I'LL LET YOU DO A COUPLE
OF NUMBERS". SHE DID, I LIKED
WHAT I HEARD, AND HIRED HER
FOR A NUMBER OF CASUALS. SHE
MAY HAVE BEEN A QUIET LITTLE
GIRL BEHIND THE TYPEWRITER, BUT
WHEN SHE GOT ON THE BANDSTAND,
SHE LET IT ALL OUT.

*Voice, personality
projection*

Another photo on stage of "This Is Your Life". (l to r) Ralph Edwards, Sal, Barbara Eden, Mr. Unknown and Ben Gazzara

HERB CAEN

MAYOR JOHN LINDSAY of New York appeared at the stage entrance, so movie-star handsome he makes Robert Redford look like Bennie Barrish. Bandleader Sal Carson (born Carcione) struck up "East Side, West Side" and the crowd went crackers. Lindsay strode onstage — he got here in time by canceling the Merv Griffin show —

TV's "This Is Your Life" Feb. 16 will have a strong San Francisco flavor. It stars actress Barbara Eden, who, as Barbara Huffman, was a Miss San Francisco. (Gallantry forbids giving the exact year in the '50s). Barbara, then a secretary just out of Lincoln High, got her start in show business as a vocalist for two years with bandleader Sal Carson, who spent two secret days in Hollywood for the "Life" show.

Herb Caen column. San Francisco Chronicle, ca 1972

Capwell's unveiling to benefit Symphony

1971

The Oakland Symphony Guild and Capwell's Oakland have announced plans for "An Evening On Broadway" on Sunday, Dec. 4 from 6:30 to 9 p.m. to benefit the Oakland Symphony and to premier Capwell's newly refurbished first and second floors.

Headlining the evening's events will be a special performance by song stylist Della Reese. The entertainment includes dancing to Sal Carson and his orchestra, a choreographed fashion show, gourmet hors d'oeuvres, wine and several door prizes with the grand prize being a special drawing for "An Invitation to Broadway," seven - day trip for two to Manhattan including theatre tickets and dinner at New York's famed Sardi's Restaurant.

Tickets at $12.50 each may be reserved with Charlotte Tudor, 220 Estates Dr., Piedmont, 547 - 4629. All proceeds collected through ticket sales will go directly to the Oakland Symphony.

"An Evening On Broadway". December 1971

Ralph Edwards Productions

FIRST FEDERAL BUILDING

1717 NORTH HIGHLAND AVENUE • HOLLYWOOD, CALIFORNIA 90028

December 6
1 9 7 1

Dear Sal:

Many years have passed since the days when Barbara
Eden first sang with your orchestra--but, oh, how
her memory clicked when she heard your voice from
off-stage!

Your presence gave Barbara very special pleasure
and illustrated that part of her career during
which she was in need of a helping hand. Thank
you for taking the time to be with us--and for
your help to our staff in preparing the show.

Sincere good wishes,

Ralph Edwards

Ralph Edwards

Mr. Sal Carson
127 Hardie Drive
Moraga, California

Letter from Ralph Edwards.
December 6, 1971

| LICENSE FEE $100.00 | STATE OF CALIFORNIA DEPARTMENT OF INDUSTRIAL RELATIONS DIVISION OF LABOR LAW ENFORCEMENT 455 GOLDEN GATE AVE., SAN FRANCISCO | LICENSE Nº A 272 |

ARTISTS' MANAGER LICENSE

San Francisco, California, April 1, 1972

MAIN OFFICE	BRANCH OFFICES
SAL CARSON, ARTISTS' MANAGER Salvatore J. Carcione, dba 228 Jones St. A-10 San Francisco, CA 91102	

having paid to the Labor Commissioner of the State of California the required license fee and
having deposited a Surety Bond in the penal sum of ONE THOUSAND DOLLARS is hereby
granted a license to conduct the business of an ARTISTS' MANAGER in the State of California
at the places designated above for the year ending March 31, 1973, in conformity with the
provisions of Chapter 4, Part 6, Division 2, of the Labor Code and the rules and regulations
issued thereunder by the Labor Commissioner.

**THIS LICENSE EXPIRES MARCH 31,
1973 AND MUST BE RENEWED ON
OR BEFORE THAT DATE.**

George W. Williams

State Labor Commissioner

*This license will protect no other than the person to whom it is issued nor any places other than those
designated in the license. The transfer or assignment of any interest in or the right to participate in the profits
of the licensee, without the prior written consent of the Labor Commissioner, is a misdemeanor.*

POST IN A CONSPICUOUS PLACE

ORIGINAL

Artists' Manager License,
April 1, 1972

At the San Francisco Press Club, ca 1972. (l to r) Sam Stern, former band leader (Sal worked with him), Dino Beneti and Sal. Photo by George Kruse.

Marya Lahoud did some gigs
with Sal in 1972

Thank you letter,
March 14, 1972

CAPELLA AUXILIARY
CEREBRAL PALSY CENTER FOR THE
BAY AREA, INC.

March 14, 1972

Mr. Sal Carson
127 Hardie Drive
Moraga, CA 94556

Dear Sal:

On behalf of Capella Auxiliary of the Cerebral
Palsy Center for the Bay Area, I wish to thank you once
again for the splendid job you did for our "Masque Ball".

Not only was your music perfect for our group,
but your cooperation during the evening really helped
to make the Ball a real success.

We are looking forward to an even greater
ball next year, and hope we can get together once again.

Sincerely,

Mary Valle

Mary Valle
President

P. S. Your check is enclosed.

San Francisco Examiner

Wed., May 3, 1972   ☆   S.F. Examiner

OUR MAN ON THE TOWN

By Jack Rosenbaum

★ ★ ★

SMALL WORLD: Bailbondsman Al Graf handled the release of a state employe for drunk driving and asked the routine question, "Where were you born?" The answer was Guthrie, Okla. An hour later came a call to bail out a federal employe, same charge, also born in Guthrie. Graf thought somebody was putting him on until the pair met next morning in court and recognized each other as high school classmates.

By coincidence, "Citizen Hoover" arrived yesterday, the day J. Edgar Hoover died. The book by Jay Robert Nash is highly critical, "the story of how Hoover, almost without interference, aggrandized his power and embellished his reputation." The sale, or non-sale, may determine whether the timing was right or wrong. . . . The rumors are popping again that Police Capt. (and attorney) Bill Conroy, who turned down an offer to become an aide to J. Edgar Hoover last year, will again be bidden to Washington for a ranking FBI post.

★ ★ ★

THE WORD around social circles is that Prince and Princess Rainier will grace our town this fall. . . . Bob Hudson forwards a "Business Opportunity" ad from the Mexico City News: "Acreage for sale adjoining nudist camp. Owner must sell due to failing eyesight."

Few musicians leave in the middle of a show to change clothes but it was a necessity for a couple of Sal Carson's bandsmen during the Oakland Police Athletic League circus at the Coliseum. The band was given an unfortunate location, directly in front of the lion's cage. Well, one frisky cat had no manners at all, and. . . .

Slogan of the Little People of America, an organization of midgets: "Don't Sell Us Short."

The lion did not enjoy swing music? May 3, 1972. Jack Rosenbaum column. "Our Man On The Town".

SERVICE EMPLOYEES INTERNATIONAL UNION, AFL-CIO, CLC

15th Convention Banquet

FAIRMONT HOTEL • SAN FRANCISCO, CALIF. • MAY 31, 1972

Fairmont Hotel Banquet. May 31, 1972

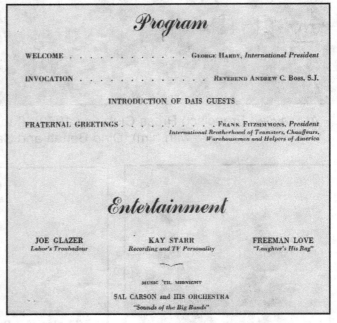

Program

WELCOME . . . . GEORGE HARDY, International President

INVOCATION . . . . REVEREND ANDREW C. BOSS, S.J.

INTRODUCTION OF DAIS GUESTS

FRATERNAL GREETINGS . . . . FRANK FITZSIMMONS, President
International Brotherhood of Teamsters, Chauffeurs,
Warehousemen and Helpers of America

Entertainment

JOE GLAZER	KAY STARR	FREEMAN LOVE
Labor's Troubadour	Recording and TV Personality	"Laughter's His Bag"

MUSIC 'TIL MIDNIGHT
SAL CARSON and HIS ORCHESTRA
"Sounds of the Big Bands"

Banquet program. May 31, 1972

Sal Carson

Sal Carson, the San Francisco Music Man, and his orchestra are headlining at Harvey's Top of the Wheel through Aug. 11. Carson recently did a "This Is Your Life" show with Barbara Eden. The orchestra comes to Stateline direct from the San Francisco Hilton Hotel, where during their two-week engagement they joined the Johnny Mann singers for five days. Carson is known for his versatility, playing old favorites but also keeping up with the Top 40 tunes. Sol's opening night, July 29, is said to be the biggest night the Top of the Wheel has had so far this year.

Stateline gig. July 29, 1972

MY HEART REMINDS ME

Also Known As "AND THAT REMINDS ME" Adapted From "AUTUMN CONCERTO"

Lyric by AL STILLMAN   Music by C. BARGONI

Kay Starr.
Born July 21, 1922.
Dougherty, OK. Photo
on sheet music. "The
Wheel Of Fortune" and
many other hits.

RON BATES   County Capsule

Daily City Record 11/10/72

Ron Bates col-
umn, Daily City
Record.
November 10,
1972

A REAL DALY CITY landmark fell this week and Daly City lost a real friend. Duffy's Tavern is just a bunch of rubble and the genial host, Red McGuire, is gone. Duffy's was a popular hangout for Daly City's finest and many a case was solved or opened there. McGuire was a large donor to the athletic programs of the city. He'll be missed.

WHO IS Percy Mercy?

THE VICTORY PARTIES at both Leo Ryan's and Lou Papan's were very nice. When Papan visited Ryan's at the New Southern Al Borelli's band played a Greek song and the crowd there was treated to a lesson in Greek dancing.

SPEAKING OF PARTIES we're looking forward to the annual bash put on by the Westlake Merchants Association. This year's will be on the 18th and the popular Sal Carson and his band will be there along with (sigh) Sylvia Gaylord. (Boy what a door prize she would make.) Gene Perry, who shares our love for the big band sound, says it'll be better 'n ever. Among those coming are the Jim Trevors, Ed Kings, Bud Lycetts, Tony Giammonas, McRobert Stewarts, Paul Hupfs, Roland Petrocchis, Keith Shrocks, Tony Zidiches and Al Polonsky.

JOHNNY SWANSON, the affable owner of the Westlake Bowl, joined an exclusive club this week. He was voted into USF's Hall of Fame along with seven others. Also in the Hall of Fame, elected several years ago, was another famous Daly Citian, former Mayor Bob St. Clair.

FAMOUS PEOPLE brings to mind another bit of little known knowledge we can share. Henry Doelger is related to Mae West. Yup, they're cousins.

THE SAN MATEO COUNTY Board of Supervisors backed the wrong horse, apparently, when they went against Proposition 20, the Coastside Initiative. The conservationists in the county are feeling their oats with the victory and have vowed to wave the vote under the noses of what they call "an unresponsive board."

Speaking of the Board of Supervisors, what ever happened to that strong letter from Daly City asking the county to complete construction of 2000 feet of storm drain?

Frank LaPierre

Embarrassed, Not Jubilant

INSTEAD OF JUBILATION over the presidential election (we predicted right here in this wonderful column that The President would sweep even South Dakota away from George M.), we feel embarrassed. Only now that the shock has worn off do we fully realize just how soundly the Democratic nominee was battered. All those pledges of support from bigtime Democrats. And the only one to deliver was Ted Kennedy. For our money those folks in Massachusetts were voting for Kennedy, NOT for McGovern. Time will tell.

BRENTWOOD LODGE is the place, and Big Game Night is the night, for the swinging Westlake Merchants shindig. The Hottest Horn around, Mr. Sal Carson, will be tooting his tunes while (gasp, wheez, choke, sputter) Sylvia Gaylord, the best thing that's happened to evening gowns since Cleopatra, will be warbling. The usual emcee will be Gene Perry. I mean, what can you say about Gene that hasn't already been said. What's that? Sorry, this is a family newspaper.

HERE 'TIS ...
Frank Freeman

Smoke Signal: Paid in Full.—

There'll be some mortgage burning May 6 at Calvary United Methodist Church, $150,000 worth. Loan was supposed to have been paid off in seven years (or was it eight?), anyhow extended to 15. Bishop R. Marvin Stuart will be down from S.F. to light the 4 p.m. fire. . . . • Mrs. Frances Enos, Maxine Casselberry, Jerold Casselberry & George Quay were Wayne Newton's guests at Harrah's in Reno last week. Come to think of it, his first fan club started in S.C. County in '61. . . . • See that Friends of Calif. Libraries attenders at a N. Calif. workshop here April 14 will have a noted spieler, the Speusippos of the S.F. waterfront . . . pardon, meant to say the Plato of the waterfront—Eric Hoffer. . . . • Wonder if you caught Sal Carson & his tootlers on "Hollywood Squares" the other night when the emcee said, " . . . & now a pause to sell a product" . . . & into the hot mike somebody blurted "Rita Hayworth!" Anyway, Sal & his sounds of Goodman, Ellington, Basie, James, Miller et al will be in S.J. & . . . . • Was told that A.R. (Bob) Morgan, pres. of County Bank, Santa Cruz, is mending at his 225-33 Mt. Hermon Rd. home, Spring Lakes Park, following surgery.

★ ★ ★

(Top left)
The Post. November 15, 1972. Frank La Pierre's column.

(Top right)
Frank Freeman column. San Jose Mercury. April 5, 1973

Dancers at the Italian Village in San Francisco, ca 1973

Another shot at the Italian Village dancers.

Dance party at the Jack Tar Hotel. March 10, 1973

DANCE PARTY

SAL CARSON
& his 16 Piece
ORCHESTRA
Saturday, MARCH 10, 1973
9:00 PM - 1:00 AM
JACK TAR
HOTEL INTERNATIONAL ROOM - VAN NESS & GEARY
SAN FRANCISCO
Sounds of the BIG BANDS

DANCE TO THE SOUNDS OF GLENN MILLER, DORSEY, BASIE,
JAMES AND SAL CARSON'S DANCEABLE MUSIC, FEATURING
THE GREAT TUNES OF THE 1940's, 50's & THE BEST OF
THE 60's & 70's. DOOR PRIZES AND DANCE CONTESTS.

APPEARING WITH THE ORCHESTRA, SCINTILATING SONG
STYLIST, SYLVIA GAYLORD AND TALENTED VOCALIST VIP
BARRY.

GOOD STREET PARKING AND REASONABLE PARKING IN HOTEL
GARAGE.

REASONABLE DRINK PRICES. NO COVER - NO MINIMUM

ADMISSION: $3.50 ADVANCE SALES, $4.00 AT DOOR
(Per Person)

FOR ADVANCE TICKETS, SEND CHECK OR MONEY ORDER
AND SELF ADDRESSED ENVELOPE TO: DANCE PARTY,
1409 LARKIN ST. SAN FRANCISCO 94109
OR PHONE FOR FURTHER INFORMATION 254-1881 or
221-6194

SAL CARSON ORCHESTRA
BIG BAND DANCE PARTY
HOTEL LEAMINGTON
AUGUST 4, 1973   9:00 P.M.-
$4.50   1:00 A.M.

SAL CARSON ORCHESTRA
BIG BAND DANCE PARTY
HOTEL LEAMINGTON
AUGUST 4, 1973   9:00 P.M.-
$4.50   1:00 A.M.

Two tickets for Hotel Leamington dance party. August 4, 1972

Schedule of Station KMPX air shots.

Poster for Circus Room. ca 1974

SAL CARSON AND THE BIG BANDS APRIL 7TH AT THE VILLAGE

Sounds of the Big Bands Dance Party, Saturday, April 7th, 9:00 p.m. to 1:00 a.m. at the Village (formerly the Italian Village) on Columbus St., featuring Sal Carson's 16 piece orchestra with beautiful vocalist Sylvia Gaylord and former newscaster Vocalist Art Brown doing a guest spot. There will be door prizes and a dance contest. The first Sounds of the Big Bands Dance party at the Jack Tar was a sell out by 10:15 p.m. The fine nostalgia dancing and listening to Carson's band playing the original arrangements of Artie Shaw's Begin the Beguine, Glenn Miller's In the Mood, Moonlight Serenade, Count Basie's April in Paris along with Sal Carson's new big band arrangements featuring the finest musicians in the country, most of them having played with Harry James, Woody Herman, Dorsey's, etc. No question about it. The Big Bands are back. Admission $4.00 advance at S.F. Ticket Center, all of the Macy stores or the Village. $4.50 at the door.

April 7, 1973. The Village. San Francisco Progress

NOW SHOWING
AT THE

CIRCUS ROOM

FRANK WELLS
The Singing Comedian
WITH
SAL CARSON
AND HIS MUSIC

Featuring Special Italian Dinners

HIGHWAY 50, STATELINE, NEVADA   PHONE EDGEWOOD 2241

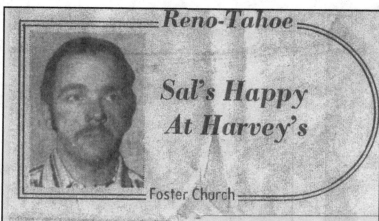

Reno-Tahoe

Sal's Happy At Harvey's

— Foster Church —

Sal Carson, the San Francisco Music Man, is orchestra-conducting these eves at Harvey's Top of the Wheel at Stateline. Sal, who is a popular figure around these parts, says he started out in life as Caricione, uses Carson as a show-biz name. He opened at Harvey's July 29 which, due to him or some other happy combination or circumstances, was the biggest night at Harvey's so far this season. Sal plays old standards but keeps up with the Top 40 tunes as well.

San Jose Mercury, Foster Church column, August 13, 1970

Marin Veterans Memorial Auditorium. November 2, 1973

Romaine photo of Mary Ann Meltzer. June 1974. Another vocalist for Sal

Lynn Bali and Sal at Harvey's Hotel, 1974

—173—

45 recording by Sal and Shirley Anne Bradley

(Right) Program for dinner dance at the Hyatt
Regency. December 5, 1974

(Below) Inside of program

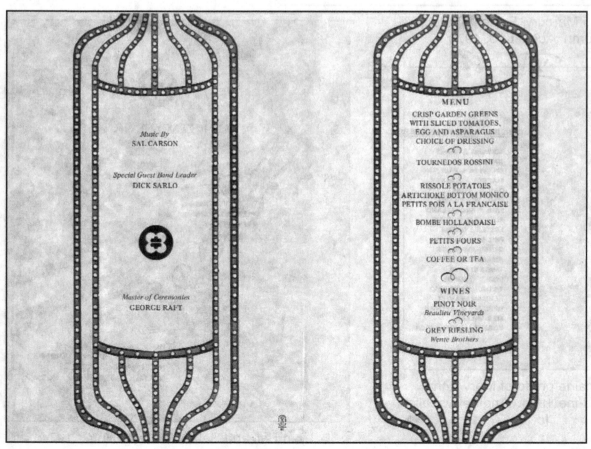

At the Hyatt Hotel, mid 70's. (l to r) In front: Bob Ferrera, Sal, Al Walcott, Lisa Polland, Mark Teel. In back: Jim Schlicht, Fred Radke.

George Raft. He was in many movies.

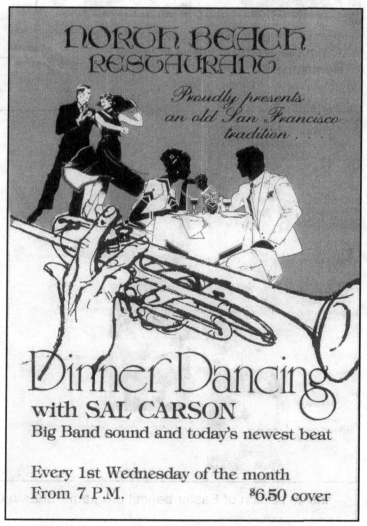

Five month gig at the North Beach Restaurant. Mid 70's

Helen O'Connell. She had some big hits with the Jimmy Dorsey Orchestra. Remember "Green Eyes", "Amapola", "Tangerine"?

Easter benefit. March 15, 1975

Troy Donahue, star of Godfather II

Sharon Carnes, featured singer of Merv Griffin and Lawrence Welk Show

Massimiliasso Baratta, international Italian movie and singing star

Sal Carson

Tony Romano

Inside portion of Easter benefit program: Sharon Carnes also worked at Yosemite with Sal

The Masthead
By GENE PERRY, EDITOR

Music, maestro, please . . . . . .

One of the nicest gestures of the year — and for a worthy cause, too — is upcoming Saturday, March 15 in San Francisco. It's "The Easter Bonnet Benefit Ball", sponsored by Varner-Warner Leasing Co.

The gig is being presented to aid the Easter Seal Society for Crippled Children and Adults of San Francisco, Inc. It is to be held at 548 Fifth St. (between Bryant and Brannan.)

Theme of the night will be "Easter Parade", nostalgia in the tradition of the motion picture of the same name.

Hollywood's Troy Donahue will be the evening's M.C. The dancing will spotlight our chum, Sal Carson and his brazen 16 piece big band, with Vocalist Tony Romano from Tommy Dorsey days. And therein lies the 'meat' for this column.

CARSON

If you didn't already know, Sal is the director of the large and new (46 piece) San Francisco 49er Band at Candlestick Park, which has struck a unique image and sound for Sunday adherents. A fine improvement from Kezar days past.

Sal bills himself as "San Francisco's Music Man", but this corner does not buy the moniker, for Sal and his trumpet have traipsed regions thru California, Nevada, Washington and Utah.

He not only heads the huge 49er contingent, which, by the way, includes a lady trombonist, a jumping and strong stage band which is skedded for the "Easter Parade", but also numerous combos of various sizes and distinctive talents. You see, he's a musical contractor, as well, and has hosts of artists and musicians, to fit many types of music and moods, in his files.

A loyal Democrat and staunch Unionist, Carson is probably best known for nigh his 20 years at Hoberg's Resort on Cobb Mountain, Lake County.

It was there he first met Gov. Edmond G. Brown, Jr., when the then young Brown was vacationing with his father. Sal was later to play the Governor's San Francisco Testimonial just days before Brown won election. His theme song, "Honey Dear", is still one of the elder Brown's favorites when Sal plays it 'shuffle rhythm' style, ala Jan Savitt.

In 1967 Plumbers Union Executive Joe Mazzola was looking for a 'name' group to enhance his already popular Konocti Harbor Inn at Clear Lake. He lured Sal away from Hoberg's. It was a happy four year engagement. We know, as your agent and his Bea never missed a summer stay at that delightful spa.

Unlike many of the prima donna leaders in the business, Pal Sal built his likeable reputation on being a nice guy to everyone, youngsters to senior citizens. We still laugh at the time when Carson, leaning over the Hoberg's Maple Room stage to hear a 10 year olds' request for "Bunny Hop", lost his balance and toppled into the late George Hoberg's punch bowl.

In a sense you might say Salvatore Giuseppe Carcione (his real name) is a 'star maker'. Such stunning talent as Barbara Eden ("I Dream Of Jeannie" — TV), Joan Blackman (Elvis Presley movies), Donna Theodore (with John Raitt on stage in "Oklahoma"), Gloria Craig (who left Sal to join the Ray Anthony band, prior to his 'Bookends', now appearing at Bruno Scatena's Joe's of Westlake-Fashionable Restaurant), and today's thrush, the beautiful Sylvia Gaylard, all began singing careers with Carson.

At one time, Sal had the opportunity to join Skinnay Ennis' band when that crooning maestro was playing the Bob Hope radio show. But Sal wanted to make it on his own and decided to remain in the area he enjoys so much. Skinnay, too, was a thoroughly likeable fellow, who in the early sixties met a violent death — while he was eating in a restaurant some food lodged in his throat and he choked to death.

No stranger to Union functions, Sal boasts of playing for Anthony Ramos' California State Council of Carpenters Ball at S.F.'s Sheraton Palace, Joe O'Sullivan's 90th Anniversary of Carpenters Union Local 22 at the San Francisco Hilton, and Joe Belardi's Culinary Workers, Bartenders and Hotel Employees bash, which headlined George Raft as M.C. and starred Shecky Greene and Keely Smith at S.F.'s Hyatt Regency.

Our own Dan Del Carlo had Sal provide music for his 1972 Testimonial (along with Violinist Sam Stern) at the Fairmont's Grand Ballroom.

If this sounds like an all-out endorsement for the Sal Carson crew, then that is just what it is intended to be. And, if you and yours can make it to the Easter Seal Society's "Easter Bonnet Benefit Ball", you'll be letting yourselves in for one of the swingingest sounds and nostalgic evenings to emerge since the good ol' days of Goodman, Dorsey, Miller, Lunceford, James and the rest of the greats. As added incentive, it's for a good cause.

And, now, maestro — the downbeat, if you please.

A second publicity photo of Helen O'Connell. She was born May 23, 1920 in Lima, OH. Died September 9, 1993 in San Diego, CA

The Masthead" by Gene Perry. An article about Sal. March 1975

Exterior photgraph of Bimbo's by Ed Lawless. May 18, 1980. I just cannot do a book without photos by Ed and Dottie Lawless' help.

SAL CARSON ORCHESTRA

COMBOS AND AGENCY

SAN FRANCISCO'S MUSIC MAN

127 HARDIE DRIVE, MORAGA, CALIFORNIA 94556

PHONE: 254-1881 OR 221-6194

March 20, 1975

Mr. Joseph S. Shribman
449 South Beverly Drive, Suite 201
Beverly Hills, Calif. 90212

This is to confirm the engagement of Helen O'Connell on June 4, 1975
at the San Francisco Hilton Hotel, Continental Ballroom, on Mason and
O'Farrell Streets.

Rehearsal scheduled for 4:30 P.M. Showtime approximately 8:00 P.M.
Net to Helen O'Connell through your agency $2,000.00 and a room at
the Hilton Hotel if possible or a first class hotel nearby. Am I
correct in assuming that Helen does a 40-45 minute show?

There will be an MC comedian on the show, Glen Heywood. We will have
a 14 piece orchestra.

Please sign on line below and return one copy to me. We will use this
letter as our contract. Also, please send me some of your pictures and
publicity with the signed copy. Looking forward to working with you
again.

Yours truly,

Sal Carson

Sal Carson

_____
Helen O'Connell

_____
Date

Band Leader, San Francisco 49'ers   Artists' Manager

Confirmation and contract. Continental Ballroom, Hilton Hotel.
March 20, 1975 for an engagement.

SAL CARSON
AGENCY
PHONE 254•1881

127 Hardie Drive, Moraga, California 94556

SAL CARSON . . . . S.F. 49'ers Bandleader --- Trumpet Virtuoso
ASTRO RECORDING STAR

SAL CARSON AGENCY: Reputable established agency.
OFFERING: Popular Rock, Soul, Top 40 Blues, Jazz,
Disco, & 50's Bands. Junior and Senior Dances and
Proms our specialty.
Weddings and Private Parties.

TOP PROFESSIONAL BANDS AVAILABLE

Top bands from throughout the country are available to us
through our associates in Los Angeles, New York and Las Vegas.

AVAILABLE FOR BOOKING:

NATURAL IMPULSES	ABEL	PABLO CURISE	MARYA (50's Band)
SWEET SUCCESS	MAGIC	VIP BARRY	CRUISIN (50's Band)
INTERSTATE 80	GRAND SLAM	TONY HALL	SAL CARSON BIG BAND
SELF EXPRESSION	FESTIVAL	CARICONE	JOHN HANDY
BAD WATER BRIDGE	JUBILLEE	GOLD LAME	TOWER OF POWER
SASS	EARTHQUAKE	CAL TJADER	STONEGROUND

The success of your next party or dance depends on
the success of your band. Call (415) 254-1881
or Write, Sal Carson, 127 Hardie Drive, Moraga, CA 94556

Sal Carson Agency flyer. Mid 70's

ICA FELLOWSHIP EVENING

An evening of dining, entertainment, dancing,
and fellowship in the Golden Gate Ballroom
7:00 p.m., May 15, 1975
Hyatt Regency, San Francisco

EVENING ENTERTAINMENT

Strolling Trio during Fellowship Hour

Duane Dancers

Sabah

Sylvia Gaylord

Mike Caldwell

Sal Carson's Society Orchestra

Down Memory Lane
New Orleans Conference

Previews of Washington, D.C. Conference

Drawing of Tour of Expo Prize
8 Day All Expense Paid Trip for Two to Hawaii

Dancing

ICA Fellowship
dinner dance.
May 15, 1975

The San Francisco scene on the menu by artist John Lewis is suitable for framing

Benefit for Casa Costanzo at Bimbo's 365 Club.
June 1, 1975

... The Social Circle ...

THAT WAS a smashingly elegant opening
the Oakland Symphony Guild gave Saturday
night to launch the fabled old Regilius
apartment building on its new, face-lifted
life. The party was shades of the 20's, when
The Regilius was built, and the 30's and
40's, when it was in its heyday. The scene
was perfect, from the vintage automobiles
parked in the curved, cobblestoned carriage
entrance, to the Oriental lanterns laced over
the back terrace, where Sal Carson's band

played for danc-
ing and singer
Connie Haines
entertained with
the likes of "I'll
Never Smile
Again," and
"You're Nobody
Til Somebody
Loves You." The
building's rear
verandah, whose
stairways criss-
cross down to the terrace (and almost to
Lake Merritt) in stately Mediterranean fashion, provided a perfect foil for party-goers
spilling out from the building's first floor
receiving rooms. The dinner, served from
round, white clothed tables on the verandah
(complete with white linen napkins), was a
gourmet's delight.

Robin Orr column. October 6, 1975

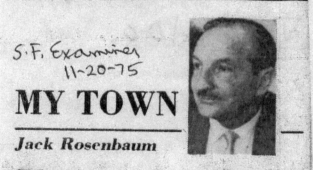

S.F. Examiner
11-20-75

MY TOWN

Jack Rosenbaum

Blowing his horn

Sour note: Bandleader Sal Carson, a paid-
up member of the Musicians Union, is hot at
the AFL-CIO. He played at the national
convention here Sept. 22 (the day President
Ford spoke) and is still waiting for his $350 fee.
National headquarters refers him to the local
office, and vice-versa.

My Town by Jack Rosenbaum, San Francisco
Examiner. November 20, 1975

Mayor Diane Feinstein (now a Senator) at the
Press Club of San Francisco. (l to r): Burt
Snyder, Keven Porter and Sal. 1976

ASTRO
431 BRYANT STREET
SAN FRANCISCO, CA 94107

SIDE I
1149 A

Brown-
Henderson
ASCAP
2:30

SO BEATS MY HEART FOR YOU
(Ballard-Henderson-Waring)
Sal Carson, His Trumpet & Orchestra

A 45 recording. 1974-1975.

San Quentin
"Show of Stars".
Program cover,
1976

San Quentin Show – the performers. Those jazz fans that like accuracy
will note the Phil Hofe in the Jimmy Diamond band should have been
spelled Phil Howe.

At the Fairmont Hotel. ca 1976. (l to r) In back: Gordon Rowley, Dean Hubbard, Jim Schlickt.
The last two are not known. In front: Dick Snyder, Mark Teel and Curtis Lowe. You know who is
standing.

At the Harvey's Hotel at Stateline. ca 1976

WELSH & BRESEE, INCORPORATED ⬛ WHOLESALE BUILDING MATERIALS

March 8, 1976

Sal Carson Orchestra & Agency
127 Hardie Drive
Moraga, Calif. 94556

Dear Sal,

All I can say is well done, well done. Everyone seems
to know " The musical quarterback of the San Francisco 49'ers"
and our audience was no exception Sal.

When our guests were shouting for their Helen O'Connel
favorites, I knew you had also given us an excellent suggest-
tion.

When six hundred of our most influential customers are
involved, selection of our show becomes a very critical matter.

You achieved our objective......superbly. We just wanted
to take a moment to express our appreciation for an except-
ional performance.

J. Nelson

Appreciation letter. March 8, 1976

MASTHEAD

By GENE PERRY, EDITOR

BIG BAND BASH . . .

Enter: The Big Band Sounds of Sal Carson and his 17-piece Astro Recording Orchestra! Wow, a swingin' affair all the way from "Tower of Power" and "Chicago" renditions to the blazing arrangements of Goodman, Dorsey, Miller, Basie . . . yes, even a few Wayne King waltz-like tunes tossed in for the young-oldtimers. Watch out Lawrence!

As if you didn't already know, Sal is the director of the 45-piece S. F. 49er Band who was cited last season for his most outstanding rendition of "The Star Spangled Banner" at Kezar Stadium.

The Carson band is widely known for its versatility and ability to please in any age bracket. You see, Sal is not only a dedicated union musician, but he's a musical contractor as well, heading, along with his big band, numerous combos of various sizes and mixed talents.

"San Francisco's Music Man," as he is known, has a "thing" about him. He is a firm believer in having a beautiful girl front his band as vocalist. He's had some beauties, too. Barbara Eden ("I Dream of Jeannie"), Donna Theodore ("Oklahoma," with John Raiit), Julie Mason (Don Sherwood TV Show), Gloria Craig, who left Sal to join the Ray Anthony band, and his current group of lovelies, i.e., Sharon Carnes, Sylvia Gaylord and Joan Blackman.

No stranger to Union functions, Carson boasts of playing Anthony Ramos' California State Council of Carpenters' Ball at the S. F. Sheraton Palace, Joe O'Sullivan's 90th Anniversary of Carpenter's Union Local 22 at the S. F. Hilton, and Joe Belardi's Culinary Workers, Bartenders and Hotel Employees party, which included George Raft as MC, featured Comedian Shecky Greene, with Vocalist Keely Smith, at the Hyatt Regency.

Masthead" by Gene Perry, Organized Labor, March 8, 1976

It's nice to have friends. Keep reading. He got the gig

★ ★ ★

THEY NETTED ANDY RUSSELL, the singer, to entertain at the March 31 "big band" dinner dance of Capella Auxiliary of Cerebral Palsy Center, to be at Hs Lordship with Sal Carson's orchestra and music only from the '30s and '40s ..... They're a cruel bunch in the Alameda County Sheriff's Dept. Deputy George Matzek was retiring after 28 years and they gave him a huge sendoff party at the Elegant Ranch with maybe 300 friends on hand, but instead of accolades it was a roast. Don Arnt caught a few of the printable comments. "Because George is clumsy, they gave him a Medic Alert bracelet and on the back the caution was, 'Falls down a lot.'" "George has done for law

Bill Fiset, in the Oakland Tribune, March 15, 1976

A word of our host, Phil. His title is Director of Customer Relations and Host Manager. You can't get much higher than that at Stateline unless you spell your name H-A-R-V-E-Y. An old Oaklander, Phil made it to the top (of the wheel) via Fremont High and the Oakland sandlots, i.e., the E. Bercovich & Sons semi-pros, Langendorf Royals, Melrose Merchants, Topaz Bar Nine, and later a "cup of coffee" with Lefty O'Doul's S.F. Seals in the Coast League. The top exec., Music Man Sal and your agent reminisced of Bay Area times into the wee hours. Our "hot stove league" was only broken by Sal's outstanding stage show, with orchestrations covering "Battle Hymn of The Republic" (truly a thriller), "Sugar Blues" (a la Clyde McCoy), his own "Honey Dear" (and believe it or not after 30 years of doing the number he forgot the words),

(Continue to Page 6) 8/16/76

The Top of the Wheel. August 16, 1976

Hi, Sal! Just wanted to let you know I'm thrilled that Capwell's followed through on my suggestion to call you. Look forward to seeing you on Dec. 4. Breen

1977

Harvey's Resort Hotel

Sal Carson Band to play in Tiki Lounge

Headline, Tahoe Daily Tribune, July 23, 1976

6/28/76   SCOOP

— Scoop Photo by Ken Arnold

PIANOBAR ENTERTAINMENT EVERY FRIDAY EVENING from five until seven o'clock makes the Press Club San Francisco's "most enjoyable spot to drop in for cocktails."

(L to R) Songstar Dee Parker, who has recorded with the big bands; Guy Cherney, a best-selling recording artist when he starred in major supper clubs; Drummer Bill Catalano; Accordionist Dino Binetti and Orchestra Leader Sal Carson, trumpet.

The musicians made an impromp-tu visit to the Club while Dee and Guy were singing at LeBaron's piano-bar and gave them great combo backing.

Thanks to Ken Gillespie's dynamic Entertainment Committee, the best talent in the major hotels and clubs are among the "Celebrity Hour" guest stars.

**Meet and Greet
Your New Members . . .**

June 28, 1976, Scoop the periodical of the San Francisco Press Club.

A UNIQUE seven-man band played at Board of Supervisors President Quentin Kopp's celebration last night. All leaders in their own right—Sam Stern, Sal Carson, Billy Catalano, Art Norkus, Joe Marcellino, Dino Benetti and Johnny Robinson. Everybody reached for the baton, but Stern won.

"My Town" by Jack Rosenbaum. San Francisco Examiner,
January 9, 1976

"all that glitters"
BOB TUTTLE

Reddy, Coniff In Nevada

Helen Reddy, the Australian singer who gave women throughout the world a song they could believe in ("She Is Woman"), comes to Del Webb's Sahara Tahoe Aug. 12-25. Appearing with her is comedian Barry Hugh Crocker. Ray Coniff brightens the Headliner Room stage with his "Happiness Is Music" beginning July 29 at Harrah's Reno. Showtimes for the two-week engagement are 8:15 and midnight. Eddy Arnold brings his unique blend of music to Harrah's South Shore Room for a two-week engagement beginning Friday, July 30. Sammy Davis Jr. closes Thursday night, July 29.

Conchita, an outstanding female vocalist who has appeared numerous times at Mabuhay Gardens in San Francisco, is appearing in the Entertainment Center at Harvey's Inn, South Lake Tahoe, through August 2.

RAY CONNIFF   **CONCHITA**

The Sal Carson Band featuring San Francisco vocalist Sylvia Gaylord will be appearing in the Tiki Lounge at the Top of the Wheel, Harvey's Resort Hotel at Lake Tahoe July 27 - August 2. Carson, an Orinda resident, is one of the top trumpeters in show business today. He was the musical director in the city for the Bob Hope, Roger Miller and Carol Channing shows. Miss Gaylord performs regularly at Paoli's and has done numerous commercials.

Down at Las Vegas, comedy star Bill Cosby started a three-week engagement July 13 at the Las Vegas Hilton. Co-star on the program is singer, dancer, actor Ben Vereen. Japanese singing star Hiroshi Itsuki debuts on the Hilton stage Aug. 1. Two newcomers to the Hilton entertainment lineup, singing great John Davidson and funnyman Norm Crosby, open a special two-week stand on Aug. 3.

SCOOP
Published Weekly by the Press Club of San Francisco

CHARLIE HUY, Editor;   8/9/76

Sal Carson and his band are back from their engagement at Harvey's Hotel, Top of the Wheel, Lake Tahoe, where beautiful Sylvia Gaylord was his featured vocalist.

Sal's trumpet solo of the National Anthem yesterday, marked his third season playing for the San Francisco 49'ers at Candlestick Park with his 45-piece band.

Scoop. August 9, 1976

Danny Kaye, the award receiver.

"All that glitters" by Bob Tuttle, July 23, 1976

–186–

Catholic Youth Organization
dinner, 1977

San Francisco Welcomes
The Most Reverend
John R. Quinn, D.D.
Archbishop of San Francisco

The Catholic Youth Organization
Salutes
Edward J. Daly
Recipient of the
1977 "Service to Youth" Award

AMERICAN FRIENDS OF THE HEBREW UNIVERSITY

SCOPUS AWARD DINNER AND BALL

Gold Room—Fairmont Hotel

Wednesday, May Eighteenth, Nineteen Hundred and Seventy-Seven

PROGRAM

DAIS INTRODUCTIONS . . . . .Jay A. Darwin

INVOCATION . . . . .Dr. Shimon Slavin

DINNER

TOAST . . . . .The Honorable Avraham Harman

WELCOME . . . . .Alfred Fromm

GREETINGS . . . . .Dr. Max M. Kampelman

GUEST ARTISTS . . . . .The San Francisco Boys' Choir
conducted by Dr. William J. Ballard

ADDRESS AND PRESENTATION OF
SCOPUS AWARD . . . . .The Honorable Avraham Harman
and Benjamin H. Swig

RESPONSE . . . . .Danny Kaye

CLOSING REMARKS . . . . .Alfred Fromm

Music By Sal Carson

Scopus Award
Dinner and Ball.
May 18.,1977

Green Grocer

JOE CARCIONE is among the produce experts who hold forth regularly at Yolanda's cafe inside the South San Francisco Produce Market. The KCBS Radio personality is among those who take advantage of the good food and reasonable prices at Yolanda's where complete dinner specials start at $2.95. Carcione's office is in the busy produce terminal and he enjoys regaling Yolanda regulars with his early morning stories. Carcione's first cousin, incidentally, is popular bandleader Sal Carson whose 45-piece band is the official San Francisco 49er musical group. You'll find large private room for parties at Yolanda's. For information and reservations, call 589-1161.

Sal's cousin Joe Carcione was known as the Green Grocer. San Francisco Progress May 27, 1977

A Home Body

SAL CARSON, popular Bay Area bandleader, has signed a contract to make commercials with Andy Russell, singer extraordinaire and one of the "in-house" celebrities working for Home Savings and Loan Association. Russell performed at the opening of the new West Portal Home office and he and Carson and band are busy performing at special events at other Home Savings locations in Northern California. Carson, whose 45-piece orchestra is the official San Francisco 49er band, will be opening June 21 for an engagement at the Top of the Wheel at Harvey's Resort, South Lake Tahoe. The engagement extends through July 3.

Weekly Voice. May 27, 1977

san francisco
chamber of commerce

CIVIC
AWARENESS

membership drive
1976

Cover of dinner dance program. October 21, 1976

MASTER OF CEREMONIES

MARVIN T. BENSON
Metropolitan Life Insurance Company
CHAIRMAN, MEMBERSHIP DRIVE

****

INTRODUCTION OF THE HEAD TABLE

****

RECOGNITION OF TOP SALES PERSON
and
TOP SALES TEAM

****

SELECTION OF PRIZES BY WINNERS
IN DESCENDING ORDER OF SALES VOLUME

****

ENTERTAINMENT

SAL CARSON BAND
Dancing 9-12

****

Inside of program

Oakland Tribune Thurs., Sept. 2, 1976

Robin Orr

The Big Band sound of Sal Carson's orchestra was "In The Mood" when Jim and Carol Yust of Walnut Creek (couple at left) and Kathy and Bob Dimond of Lafayette joined hands for a circa 1976 interpretation of the 1940's dance favorite. The scene was Saturday night at Castlewood Country Club, where Fir Branch of Children's Hospital staged its Big Band Ball, starring singer Andy Russell. See Robin Orr's column

—Organized Labor—Monday, March 8, 1976

MASTHEAD

By GENE PERRY, EDITOR

BIG BAND BASH . . .

Enter: The Big Band Sounds of Sal Carson and his 17-piece Astro Recording Orchestra! Wow, a swingin' affair all the way from "Tower of Power" and "Chicago" renditions to the blazing arrangements of Goodman, Dorsey, Miller, Basie . . . yes, even a few Wayne King waltz-like tunes tossed in for the young-oldtimers. Watch out Lawrence!

As if you didn't already know, Sal is the director of the 45-piece S. F. 49er Band who was cited last season for his most outstanding rendition of "The Star Spangled Banner" at Kezar Stadium.

The Carson band is widely known for its versatility and ability to please in any age bracket. You see, Sal is not only a dedicated union musician, but he's a musical contractor as well, heading, along with his big band, numerous combos of various sizes and mixed talents.

"San Francisco's Music Man," as he is known, has a "thing" about him. He is a firm believer in having a beautiful girl front his band as vocalist. He's had some beauties, too. Barbara Eden ("I Dream of Jeannie"), Donna Theodore ("Oklahoma," with John Raitt), Julie Mason (Don Sherwood TV Show), Gloria Craig, who left Sal to join the Ray Anthony band, and his current group of lovelies, i.e., Sharon Carnes, Sylvia Gaylord and Joan Blackman.

No stranger to Union functions, Carson boasts of playing Anthony Ramos' California State Council of Carpenters' Ball at the S. F. Sheraton Palace, Joe O'Sullivan's 90th Anniversary of Carpenter's Union Local 22 at the S. F. Hilton, and Joe Belardi's Culinary Workers, Bartenders and Hotel Employees party, which included George Raft as MC, featured Comedian Shecky Greene, with Vocalist Keely Smith, at the Hyatt Regency.

SAL CARSON BAND
TIKI LOUNGE
TOP of the WHEEL
Through Aug 12

Harvey's
RESORT HOTEL CASINO

SAL CARSON, popular Bay Area bandleader, has signed a contract to make commercials with Andy Russell, singer extraordinaire and one of the "in-house" celebrities working for Home Savings and Loan Association. Russell performed at the opening of the new West Portal Home office and he and Carson and band are busy performing at special events at other Home Savings locations in Northern California. Carson, whose 45-piece orchestra is the official San Francisco 49er band, will be opening June 21 for an engagement at the Top of the Wheel at Harvey's Resort, South Lake Tahoe. The engagement extends through July 3.

The Sal Carson Band will be appearing in the Tiki Lounge at the Top of the Wheel, Harvey's Resort Hotel, South Lake Tahoe, Tuesday through Aug, 2, alternating with Ron Rose and Lady D.

Sal Carson is one of the top trumpeters in show business today.

He was the musical director in San Francisco for the Bob Hope Show, the Roger Miller Show and the Carol Channing Show.

Sal and his band specialize in the popular Top 40 tunes of today and along with the great standard songs of the '40s, '50s, and '60s. They have the ability to round out their performance with everything from the Hora to the Hawaiian Wedding Song.

"My whole idea is to hit the people with nostalgia," says Sal, a man who has brought the sounds of Count Basie, Glenn Miller and the Dixieland greats.

This year will be the third season the Carson's 45-piece band plays for the San Francisco 49er's during their home games in Candlestick Park.

Starring among those members of the band to appear at Harvey's is Sylvia Gaylord, a beautiful and talented vocalist.

SAN FRANCISCO'S

MUSIC MAN

SCOOP
Published Weekly by the Press Club of San Francisco

CHARLIE HUY, Editor;   8/9/76

Sal Carson and his band are back from their engagement at Harvey's Hotel, Top of the Wheel, Lake Tahoe, where beautiful Sylvia Gaylord was his featured vocalist.

Sal's trumpet solo of the National Anthem yesterday, marked his third season playing for the San Francisco 49'ers at Candlestick Park with his 45-piece band.

Oakland Tribune   Thurs., April 6, 197

SINGER ANDY RUSSELL was excited that Claire and Lee Shaklee were at Capella Auxiliary's Friday night dinner dance at Hs Lordship's because he's a real health nut. Not only does he take all the Shaklee vitamins, his wife, Ginny, is a distributor for Shaklee Products. Besides, the Shaklees love to dance so much they scarcely ever left the dance floor. A compliment to orchestra leader Sal Carson and singer Andy, whose song hits of the 40s are among Claire and Lee's favorites.

Group of clippings, 1976 and 1978

Tiki Lounge performer

6/24/77

Sal Carson Band entertains at Harvey's

Sal Carson and his Band are in the Tiki Lounge, Top of the Wheel, Harvey's Resort Hotel through July 3, alternating with the Ron Rose Sound.

Appearing in the Theatre Lounge are: Chris Wade (through Sunday); Sounds of Brass (through July 12); Jamie (through July 5); Tunes Plus One (through Sunday); and Frankie Fanelli (through Sunday).

Opening in the Theatre Lounge Monday is the Philthy McNasty Show (through July 10); Jack Lox and the Big Country Express (through July 3) and the Ernie Menehune Show (through July 17).

Sal Carson has signed a contract to make commercials with Andy Russell, singer extraordinaire.

Carson's 45-piece orchestra is the official San Francisco 49er band. The band plays the old tunes of Dorsey, Miller, Basie and Goodman and even a few Wayne King waltz-like tunes tossed in for the young-oldtimers.

The band is widely known for its versatility and ability to please any age bracket. Carson is not only a dedicated musician, but he's a musical contractor as well, heading along with his big band, numerous combos of various sizes and mixed talents.

Carson has been an accompaniest to Bob Hope, Pat Boone, Ed Ames, Frankie Laine, Roger Miller, Kaye Stevens, Duke Ellington, Barbara Eden, Bobby Goldsboro, John Davidson and the Johnny Mann Singers.

Carson has a great talent for "feeling" the mood of the dancers and requests at the Top of the Wheel are always welcome. His own superb trumpet style and sound have been enjoyed by dancers and music lovers at the top hotels in the country.

Tiki Lounge gig. June 24, 1977

Joe Allen and Sal at a Bar Mitzvah. October 29, 1977

Robin Orr column,
Oakland Tribune,
June 7, 1977

... The Social Circle ...

SHADES OF GATSBY: There were lots of graceful floppy-brimmed hats and ladies carrying nosegays Saturday in the garden of Nancy Holliday's beautiful hilltop home in Lafayette, where "The Last of the Elegant Garden Parties" proved to be the epitome of elegance if not, it is to be hoped, the last. The weatherman couldn't have served up a more perfect evening for the East Bay Center for the Performing Arts benefit, which got underway with cocktails and flute music in the pool area, where guests could enjoy the spectacular view of the valley below. Later there was dinner and celebrity entertainment served up under a tasseled white tent, and still later there was dancing around the pool to the music of Sal Carson's orchestra. Topping it all off was the unscheduled moonlight swim led by hostess

ROBIN ORR

Nancy, who doffed her pearls, gold jewelry and antique satin pumps, placed them in a neat little pile and proceeded to make a perfect Esther Williams dive into the pool, wearing her yellow and white chiffon dress. Her daughter, Brett Holliday, followed suit. Then a guest jumped in, then another and another, until pretty soon they had a regular aquacade. And the band played on.

Afterward, the pretty and elegant hostess told friends, "You know I'm just really glad I did that." She was so pleased over the party's success it seemed an appropriate way to celebrate.

There was ample reason to be jubilant. The party was eminently good show all around. Besides all the beautifully dressed women there were some spiffy gentlemen in the crowd. Some of them wore white trousers and blue blazers, some Gatsby type shirts (Hal Ellis wore a blue and white striped one with white collar) and Gatsby type hats (Rodger Dobbel looked marvelous in his)

Sal Carson Band entertains at Harvey's

Sal Carson and his Band are in the Tiki Lounge, Top of the Wheel, Harvey's Resort Hotel through July 3, alternating with the Ron Rose Sound.

Appearing in the Theatre Lounge are: Chris Wade (through Sunday); Sounds of Brass (through July 12); Jamie (through July 5); Tunes Plus One (through Sunday); and Frankie Fanelli (through Sunday).

Opening in the Theatre Lounge Monday is the Philthy McNasty Show (through July 10); Jack Lox and the Big Country Express (through July 3) and the Ernie Menehune Show (through July 17).

Sal Carson has signed a contract to make commercials with Andy Russell, singer extraordinaire.

Carson's 45-piece orchestra is the official San Francisco 49er band. The band plays the old tunes of Dorsey, Miller, Basie and Goodman and even a few Wayne King waltz-like tunes tossed in for the young-oldtimers.

The band is widely known for its versatility and ability to please any age bracket. Carson is not only a dedicated musician, but he's a musical contractor as well, heading, along with his big band, numerous combos of various sizes and mixed talents.

Carson has been an accompanist to Bob Hope, Pat Boone, Ed Ames, Frankie Laine, Roger Miller, Kaye Stevens, Duke Ellington, Barbara Eden, Bobby Goldsboro, John Davidson and the Johnny Mann Singers.

Carson has a great talent for "feeling" the mood of the dancers and requests at the Top of the Wheel are always welcome. His own superb trumpet style and sound have been enjoyed by dancers and music lovers at the top hotels in the country.

Same article, another newspaper, June 24, 1977

POPULAR BAND LEADER Sal Carson, one of the top trumpeters in show business, is appearing with his band in the Tiki Lounge, Harvey's Resort Hotel through July 3. He alternates in the lounge with the Ron Rose Sound, which continues through Oct. 16.

Della Reese was at the benefit and backed by Sal. Remember, "Don't You Know?"

MEANWHILE, a record crowd of 550 Caucasians and Chinese whooped it up Friday night, on Big Game eve, at the Empress of China in San Francisco, the occasion being the annual dinner dance and football rally given by the Chinese Chapter of the U.C. Alumni Association.

"We had a ball and danced to Sal Carson's 12-piece orchestra until 1 a.m.," reports beauteous Carolyn (Mrs. Paul) Gan of Albany. "We felt especially honored because the university president, David Saxon, and Berkeley chancellor, Albert Bowker, and their wives spent the entire evening with us."

The U.C. Marching Band, Cal Glee Club and lovable Oski made their rounds, as usual, and most of the ladies wore blue and gold, according to Carolyn, "although a few — Stanford sympathizers, or else they had a sense of humor — wore red."

The Flying Tigers Club bid $500 on the Cal football that was auctioned off, and then turned the money and ball back for a second auctioning. This time around, Yuen Gin, an El Cerrito CPA-attorney, was the high bidder at $600. He kept his loot. Laura Lee, wife of Oakland dentist Ted Lee, won three hard-to-get Big Game tickets for $100 (a steal)

Genevieve Ong of Oakland was mistress of ceremonies. Others in on the act were Diana Chiao, Bert Mah, Jennie and Milton Louis, Mabel Hom, Roy and Ellen Gock and Karen and Steve Chin.

Robin Orr is on vacation

After the Big Game. November 21, 1977. Oakland Tribune. Louise Wright in the absence of Robin Orr

'Evening on Broadway' for Oakland Symphony

"An Evening on Broadway," a gala celebration to benefit the Oakland Symphony and to premier Capwell's newly refurbished first and second floors, is planned at Capwell's Oakland for Sunday, Dec. 4 from 6:30 to 9:30 p.m.

Some of the evening's events will be a choreographed fashion show, dancing to Sal Carson and his orchestra; gourmet hors d'oeuvres, wine, and a guest star performance by Della Reese.

The theme, "An Evening on Broadway," was chosen because both Capwell's and the Oakland Symphony home, The Paramount, are located on Broadway. Broadway is also synonymous with New York, which is the fashion, theatre and music capital.

Tickets at $12.50 each may be reserved with Mrs. Vernon Tudor, 220 Estates Dr., Piedmont, 547 - 4629. All proceeds will go directly to the Oakland Symphony.

Benefit for the Oakland Symphony. Midweek Sun, November 23, 1977. Sal had a 17 to 18 piece band.

A Gala on Broadway

The countdown has started, and there are only seven more days until —

No, no...not Christmas. (So relax).

There are only seven more days until — the big party to celebrate completion of the refurbishing of the first and second floors of Oakland's Capwell's store.

The gala, themed "An Evening On Broadway," will be a benefit for the store's neighbor on Broadway, the Oakland Symphony (whose "home" is the nearby Paramount Theater), in addition to a celebration of the updated new look of the store.

The 6:30 to 9 p.m. affair will include a choreographed fashion show, wine and hors d'oeuvres, dancing to the music of Sal Carson and his orchestra and a special guest appearance by entertainer Della Reese.

Tickets may be reserved with Mrs. Vernon Tudor, 547-4629.

Benefit for the Oakland Symphony. Midweek Sun, November 23, 1977.

An Evening on Broadway

Capwell's invites you to our Gala Benefit for the Oakland Symphony. Join us in the dramatic celebration, premiering our newly refurbished First and Second Floors

SUNDAY,
DECEMBER 4, 1977
6:30 p.m. to 9:00 p.m.
Capwell's Oakland
20th & Broadway

ENTERTAINMENT:
Special Guest Star:
Della Reese
A Fashion Celebration

DANCING
to Sal Carson
and his Orchestra
Hors d'Oeuvres
Complimentary Wine
No Host Bar
Black Tie Optional
Special Drawing:
'Invitation to Broadway'
Seven-day Trip
for two to Manhattan,
including Theatre tickets and dinner at New York's famed Sardi's Restaurant.
Courtesy of Capwell's/
Ask Mr. Foster Travel Service.

Broadway Gala invitation

Mr. Music

SAL CARSON and his orchestra will play for dancing New Year's Eve at Bimbo's 365 Club. Headlining the show this New Year's Eve will be Italian song star Nilla Pizzi and famed comedian Allan Drake. Advance reservations point to an early sellout.

Mr. Music. December 16, 1977

Weekly Voice, December 29, 1977

The Place To Be New Year's Eve

Bimbo's 365 Club has long been considered "the place to be" on New Year's Eve. Mr. Bimbo always seems to have the most exciting entertainers, the most elegant setting and the best food around. And this New Year's Eve is no exception. Famed Italian song star Nilla Pizzi headlines the show, along with comedian Allan Drake. The popular Sal Carson Orchestra will play for dancing. Also included are a gourmet dinner and lots of party favors. Tickets are still on sale at Bimbo's, but hurry!

"LIVE" from BIMBO'S
in San Francisco

VIC DAMONE

And

THE SAL CARSON ORCHESTRA

Vic Damone recording 1978 and photo. Damone was born June 12, 1928 in Brooklyn, NY

Donation to the March of Dimes by Home Savings & Loan Association February 3, 1978. Photo by George Kruse. Chuck Hess, an executive of the S & L is next to Sal. Hess was responsible for many gigs.. Fifth from the left is Frank Dill, a radio personality.

Robin Orr

Oakland Tribune Thurs., April 6, 1978

SINGER ANDY RUSSELL was excited that Claire and Lee Shaklee were at Capella Auxiliary's Friday night dinner dance at Hs Lordship's because he's a real health nut. Not only does he take all the Shaklee vitamins, his wife, Ginny, is a distributor for Shaklee Products. Besides, the Shaklees love to dance so much they scarcely ever left the dance floor. A compliment to orchestra leader Sal Carson and singer Andy, whose song hits of the 40s are among Claire and Lee's favorites.

Robin Orr Column, Oakland Tribune, April 6, 1978

As if you didn't already know, Sal is the director of the 45-piece S. F. 49er Band who was cited last season for his most outstanding rendition of "The Star Spangled Banner" at Kezar Stadium.

The Carson band is widely known for its versatility and ability to please in any age bracket. You see, Sal is not only a dedicated union musician, but he's a musical contractor as well, heading, along with his big band, numerous combos of various sizes and mixed talents.

"San Francisco's Music Man," as he is known, has a "thing" about him. He is a firm believer in having a beautiful girl front his band as vocalist. He's had some beauties, too. Barbara Eden ("I Dream of Jeannie"), Donna Theodore ("Oklahoma," with John Raitt), Julie Mason (Don Sherwood TV Show), Gloria Craig, who left Sal to

Partial clipping, 1978

Del Courtney was born September 21, 1910 in Oakland, CA. He died February 2, 2006 in Honolulu, HI

San Francisco Examiner & Chronicle, April 16, 1978. "The Cocoanut Grove Presents". Sal's band May 13. Del Courtney's band June 17. Sal and Del were long-time friends. When the 49'ers were out of town the Raiders were at home so almost all the musicians played in both bands.

At home in Moraga. 1978

"**WE'VE SPENT** our last two anniversaries (Jan. 15) on Maui," **Kathleen** and **Sal Carson** postcard from an idyllic-looking (on the postcard) beach in Hawaii. "Last year fantastic weather, this year rain, wind and cold for seven straight days and nights. Worst weather, ever, they say."

See? All of you who couldn't afford a winter vacation in the Islands can now be pleased as punch that you just stayed home. You got the same thing for nothing on the mainland.

At postcard time, the Carsons were planning to put down at the Kona Surf before winging their way home. They'll definitely be here by Saturday night, when Sal and his orchestra will play for the Oakland Symphony's Winter Sonata Ball at the Paramount Theatre.

Sal and his orchestra have also been engaged to play for the Alameda County Easter Seal Society's Man of the Year Dinner honoring Clorox president **Bob Shetterly** ("The Man with the Big Heart") on Feb. 14 at the Oakland Hilton.

By the way, Oakland Symphony Guild president **Noreen Quan** is elated because three golden baton donations (the $500 variety) have been received for Saturday's ball. The **Stephen Bechtels** of Oakland and the **Frank Dorothys** of Walnut Creek, sent the first two, and that old standby, Anonymous, sent the third.

OAKLAND Symphony Guild drum-beater **June Casey** tells us that, at the ball, **Joyce Dobbel** will be modeling "oodles and oodles" of diamond necklaces, earrings, braclets and rings "flown out from New York especially" for the occasion by Montclair jeweler **Alan Dreher.**

Alan had better not overdo it. Joyce is so slim and willowy she might just collapse under the weight of all those rocks.

Nancy Buono of Alameda, **Cici Brown** of Oakland, **Dottie Ironson** of Piedmont and **Janet Koss** and **Betty Jo Olson** of Berkeley are other local beauties who will be modeling at the symphony benefit. They'll be wearing lingerie and furs from I. Magnin.

The Carsons aren't the only ones coming home from afar for Saturday's party, by the bye. **Rosemary** and **Ed Mein** of Lafayette, who went east to pick up their yacht, are sailing home through the Panama Canal just in time to attend.

Then there are **Gwen** and **Everett Comings,** who are coming (what else?) from Seattle for Friday's Lincoln Child Center opening day event at Golden Gate Fields.

Robin Orr's column. Oakland Tribune.
January 23, 1979

February 28, 1979 at Walnut Creek Regional Center.

S. F. PRODDES
Oct 29, 1978

BMI award, October 29, 1978. San Francisco Progress

SOMETHING TO SING ABOUT — Bill McCoy, organist for the Golden Gaters, Shamrocks and Warriors, belts out a tune for, from left: Sal Carson, head of the San Francisco 49ers band; George Cerruti, organist at Candlestick Park and Al Smith, vice president of Broadcast Music, Inc. BMI honored Bay Area sports musicians at special luncheon recently.

BMI award, different photo, at the Fairmont Hotel (l to r) Bill McCoy, George Cerruti, Al Smith (BMI), Sal.

1979 Press Club. Dino Benetti, Charly White, Sam Stern and Sal. Photo by Ken Arnold.

Special Olympics. San Francisco Chronicle. June 8, 1979

SAL CARSON and His Big Band will headline the entertainment during a benefit for the Special Olympics, Friday at Bimbo's 365 Club.

THE SAN FRANCISCO CIVIC COMMITTEE PRESENTS SPECIAL OLYMPICS

ANNUAL DINNER DANCE

At

BIMBO'S 365 CLUB
1025 Columbus Avenue

Friday, June 8, 1979

7 p.m.–Cocktails	$25.00
8 p.m.–Dinner	Per Person

Music By
SAL CARSON'S BIG BAND

Civic Committee

Joe Allen	Debbie Hoffman	K. D. Sullivan	Sal Carson
Chuck Hess	Terry Lowry	Mike Cleary	Babe Zanca
	Allen Gehrig	Dennis Ranahan	

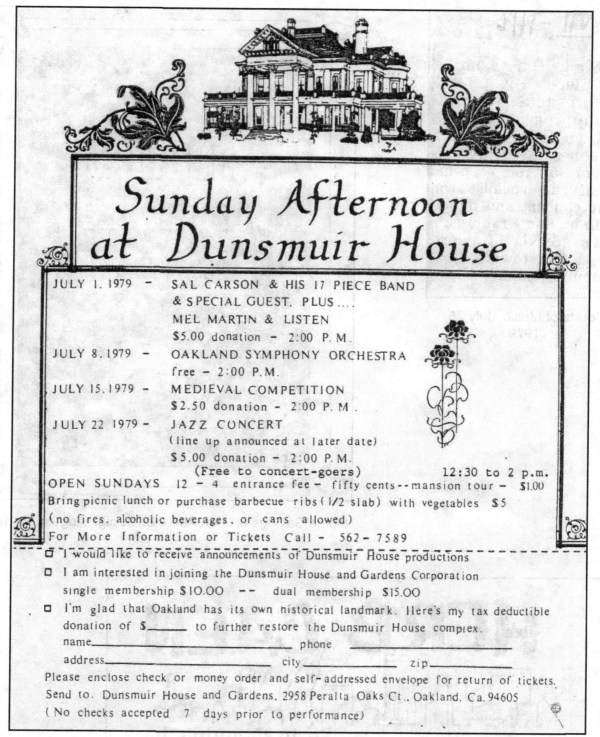

Dunsmuir House, Oakland. July 1, 1979

(opposite page)

(Far left) Special Olympics dinner dance. June 8, 1979

(Near left) Award to Sal from the Special Olympics
groups Allen Gehrig (left) and Ralph Johnson

Sound Of Music

Sal Carson's 14-piece Big Band returns to Serramonte Shopping Center's Fountain Court Wednesday, July 25 from 5 to 7 p.m. Featured vocalist for the concert and dance will be San Francisco's own Sylvia Gaylord . . . this town's most popular "canary."

Sound of Music, July 25, 1979

Home Savings & Loan Association gig. August 25, 1979

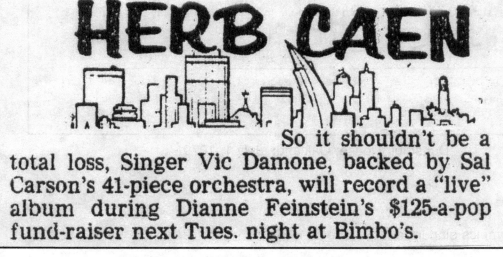

So it shouldn't be a total loss, Singer Vic Damone, backed by Sal Carson's 41-piece orchestra, will record a "live" album during Dianne Feinstein's $125-a-pop fund-raiser next Tues. night at Bimbo's.

Herb Caen, San Francisco Chronicle, 1978

Sal flyer for his band and contract performers, page 1

Same as above, page 2.

49'ers logo

"My Town" by Jack
Rosenbaum. .San
Francisco Examiner.,
May 31, 1974

S.F. Examiner
5/31/74

MY TOWN

Jack Rosenbaum

Nude encounter

Backfire: The executives Association luncheon at the Sheraton-Palace yesterday turned out to be more exciting than anyone anticipated. It honored retiring president Ed Snow, and some of the fun-loving got up a surprise. A box was carried in and out stepped a beautiful blonde who was wearing only earrings. Laughter — until one dignified member stood up and announced, "My wife and I didn't come here to be insulted" — and both stomped out.

There'll be a new musical look at 49er football games this fall. The strolling units will be replaced by a 45-piece band, led by Sal Carson . . . Some prices are still low in other countries. SF's Howard Young postcards from Bogota, Columbia, that modern cabs cost $2 — per hour.

Chapter 8
Go 49'ers

Sal was at a dinner party for the San Francisco Giants at the Omega Hotel where also attending was Robin Sequeiria who came over to Sal's table and asked "How would you like to be the 49'ers Band leader?" Wow! Sal's response was "I would be very happy to". Jack Duper a banjo player and leader of the Red Garter Band preceded Sal. They played at the 49'ers games for a period of about two years.

In a few days Sal was introduced to Lou Spadia and they hit it off very well. So a contract was signed specifying the band would consist of forty-five musicians. Forty pieces at the stadium for games and five musicians for Friday night parades preceding Sunday's games. The "parade" consisted of a small group in a convertible playing jazz type tunes down Market Street to promote the 49'ers. This was about an hour gig. All in all it was fun.

Sal would also go to the airport to greet returning football players with a four piece band. Dino Beneti on accordion, a banjo player, tenor sax and Sal on trumpet. This was the same combo he used on Fridays before the games.

The forty piece band played about forty-five minutes before the game and, of course, fanfares during the game for touchdowns, etc and at half time. There were times when they backed some name singers such as Lou Rawls and they always backed the person who sang the National Anthem. Sal wrote the Anthem music in two different keys so it was appropriate for a man or a woman. On four occasions the singer failed to show up so there was Sal in the middle of the field playing the "Star Spangled Banner".

"That was quite an experience, especially the first time, we were playing Chicago". I asked if he forgot the tune (laughed). "No, I would never do that".

Chico Norton was the 49'er equipment manager for about thirty years, popular with the players and coaches. He was married to Sal's sister Sylvia so it was a big personal loss to the family and the 49'ers when Chico died.

Sal got to know the Morabito's very well especially Jane Marabito who hired Sal for some parties.

When Bill Walsh was hired as head coach , the 49'ers improved considerably His so called "Western Style" was perfectly suited for Joe Montana, my favorite quarter back. Walsh also had superb assistants, George Siefert and Mike Holmgren to name two..

Back to the musical side. Sal knew of and personally selected the musicians who were formerly members of some of the big name bands. One in particular that I knew was Vernon Alley a bass player who worked with everyone. The excellence of the musicians was the reason Del Courtney used the same players. This was practical because when the 49'ers were away the Raiders were at home. One very "important point is the professionalism of the musicians with superior reading skills. They had no need for rehearsals". If Sal had some new arrangements they ran through them before the game. "that's all it took". Many of the musicians had years of experience in the Big Band era playing in such bands as Basie and Goodman.

"The spirit and comradely of the group was such we really enjoyed ourselves. Howard Cosell once said the 49'er band was superior to all the other teams". Cosell enjoyed music and would drop by Turk Murphy's Earthquake McGoons.

Well, a six year gig is very rare and I suspect the costs could be reduced by a small rock band and perhaps that was the reason the relationship came to an end. Sal is still invited to 49'er picnic reunions and a 49'er fan. His memory of the relationship he had is still positive and a source of pride.

San Francisco Progress   Sat., Dec. 14, 1974 ★ Weekly Voice—13

Sal Carson Plays To '49er Fans

By Bob Tuttle

WHEN SAN FRANCISCO LOVES YOU, the whole world is at your feet, a phenomenon which is very much the case when the city speaks of Sal Carson, the band leader for the San Francisco 49ers. Sal, who in addition to playing for the team and its fans, entertains at private parties, receptions, luncheons, conventions and Bar Mitzvahs, in addition to running an agency, has been on the Bay Area musical scene for a quarter of a century. He began at Hoberg's Resort years ago and from there went to the St. Francis Hotel for the famous "Battle Of The Bands" in the fifties. Since then his career has taken him to the Fairmont, the Hilton, The Mark Hopkins, and off to Nevada to the "Top Of The Wheel" at Harvey's Resort Hotel, The Ponderosa Hotel in Reno, and many other places all the way from Portland, Oregon to Salt Lake City, Utah. He currently lives across the bay in Moraga with his wife Kathleen. Naturally, that town has fallen in love with his music as well, and to demonstrate it they are staging a "Salute to Sal Carson" on January 23. He'll be seen on local television at that time before being the guest of honor at a luncheon that will be shared by his admirers.

Column by Bob Tuttle, December 14, 1974. San Francisco Progress.

Scoopetts

By Charlie Huy

Vivian Duncan, whose birthday will be celebrated at the Press Club Thursday of this week (June 20) with a luncheon in her honor and a show, chalked up another show business "first" last week. She was the first celebrity guest on Cablevision's new show titled "Coming Out".

"ANNALS OF ALLERGY" Editor **M. Coleman Harris, M.D.** has moved back to San Francisco, from Santa Cruz, and is again a frequent Club visitor. Librarian **Jack McDermott** extends thanks to **Dr. Harris** for his donation of books to the Club Library. Also to **Dan Bohne**

for his generous contributions.

NEW LITERARY CRITIC at the Oakland Tribune whose byline is **Clay Roberts** is actually **Helen Knowland,** first wife of the late Senator. And mother of the paper's publisher, **Joe Knowland.**

MEMBER **Sal Carson** will conduct a 45-piece band at the 49er football games this fall. Replaces former strolling units.

"DATING GAME"s **Jim Lange** has moved to afternoon time on Radio KSFO since **Don Sherwood** has returned to the station in his previous early hour morning slot.

DUAL BIRTHDAY celebration is being planned by **J.B. "Jabe" Casaday,** 87, and his daughter **Patty Casaday Marchetti** at the Pig'N Whistle Hotel, 4801 West Colfax ave., Denver, Colo. on Sunday, June 23. Cards from their many

Beat the Band

Editor — Sal Carson's band is outplaying the 49ers at Candlestick Park. Unfortunately I attended the 49er-Cardinals game, I noticed that when Dennis Morrison was told he might go into the game, a water boy warmed him up. The 49ers have 35 other players on the bench, and one of them might have wanted some action. You don't see the bat boy warm up the Giant's relief pitchers.

STAN WALKER
San Mateo

San Francisco Chronicle,
October 12, 1974

"Scoopetts" by Charlie Huy.
Scoop, June 17, 1974

Sal Carson, whose Big Band began at Hoberg's esort and jumped to St. Francis Hotel, along the way acquiring a strong Sacramento following, is the new leader of the 49er band.

Born Salvatore Carcione, the maestro is a native of SF, an accomplished trumpeter, composer and vocalist. His record album "Honey Dear" is on Astro label.

New leader of the
49'er band.

Man For All Musical Seasons

PLAYING FOR LARGE CROWDS is nothing new for Sal and his group (which incidentally boasts of a female trombonist), although this is the first year he's backed up the great '49er show. In the past he's played to somewhat smaller audiences as an accompaniest to Bob Hope, Pat Boone, Ed Ames, Frankie Laine, Roger Miller, Kaye Stevens, Duke Ellington, Barbara Eden, Bobby Goldsboro, John Davidson and the Johnny Mann Singers. In the picture to the left he sings out and plays his famous trumpet along with the talented Country Western vocalists, the Whittington Sisters. Sal and his band may specialize in the sound of the '40's and '50's, but they have the ability to round out their performance with everything from the Hora to the Hawaiian Wedding Song. May we suggest that you arrive at this Sunday's game against the New Orleans Saints early. You'll be treated to a pre-game show for one hour that will boast of musical accompaniment to the warm-up scrimages. — One thing is certain: although the season is nearly over, the band plays on.

Man For All
Musical Seasons,
December 14,
1974.

art Rosenbaum S.F. Chronicle 3/24/75

UP, **MAESTRO:** Sal Carson & band have been rehired for 1975 by the 49ers. The announcement offers a chance to correct a rumor started in Oakland that Sal struck up the band once just as the quarterback started to bark signals, forcing the 49ers to call a time out and get back in rhythm.

"Untrue," said Coach Dick Nolan. "Never heard of it," said Pres. Lou Spadia, signing the contract.

Art Rosenbaum article. March 24, 1975. <u>San Francisco Examiner.</u>

Band rehearsal. ca 1970's

Wining & Dining by Bob Tuttle. <u>West Bay Today.</u> November 28, 1976

Bob Tuttle *Wining & Dining*

Carson Band Eyes New Disc

The San Francisco 49'ers are not moving their franchise to Manila where they will be called the Manila Folders and they are not changing their official band, either. But for Sal Carson and his 42 - piece band who play at 49'er games at Candlestick, the Monday, Nov. 29 game with Minnesota will be the end of the musical football season. Carson, who incidentally, is a first cousin to "Green Grocer" Joe Carcione, has a new record coming out soon. One of the busiest band and band agencies on the West Coast, interested persons may contact Carson at 254-1881. The Carson band is completing its third year as official music maker at Candlestick Park for 49'er games.

A warm day, ca 1970's

Music Sport Award. October 24, 1978

Jim McGee's "Mail Bag". ca 1970's, San Francisco Examiner

Sal Carson Plays To '49er Fans

By Bob Tuttle

WHEN SAN FRANCISCO LOVES YOU, the whole world is at your feet, a phenomenon which is very much the case when the city speaks of Sal Carson, the band leader for the San Francisco 49ers. Sal, who in addition to playing for the team and its fans, entertains at private parties, receptions, luncheons, conventions and Bar Mitzvahs, in addition to running an agency, has been on the Bay Area musical scene for a quarter of a century. He began at Hoberg's Resort years ago and from there went to the St. Francis Hotel for the famous "Battle Of The Bands".   Since then his career has taken him to the Fairmont, the Hilton, The Mark Hopkins, and off to Nevada to the "Top Of The Wheel" at Harvey's Resort Hotel.

Bandleader Sal Carson

"San Francisco's Music Man"

Reprinted from a San Francisco Progress article by Jack Rosenbaum.

Known as "San Francisco's Music Man," Sal Carson is an accomplished trumpeter, composer, and vocalist. His band has a reputation for being able to please every type of audience.

For six years, Carson led the 49'er Band. He composed the official team song, "49'ers So Proud and Bold."

A first cousin of Joe Carcione, local radio and television's Green Grocer, Carson has backed such outstanding performers as Bob Hope, Barbara Eden, Della Reese, and Shecky Greene. Home Savings of America is sponsoring the band's appearance at this year's dinner dance.

HERB CAEN

So it shouldn't be a total loss. Singer Vic Damone, backed by Sal Carson's 41-piece orchestra, will record a "live" album during Dianne Feinstein's $125-a-pop

49ers lead league in music

Mail Bag — I think it's about time someone wrote in and said what a great band Sal Carson has brought to the 49er fans. It is not very often one gets to hear a Big Band playing Count Basie tunes along with rock tunes with that great Big Band sound these days.

★ ★ ★

SAL CARSON'S fine band began playing old tunes. The old-timers danced cheek to cheek, eyes closed, either asleep on their feet or dreaming of the glory nights. David Allen, whose Boarding House night club a block away has a tough time staying open, looked at the

A grouping of clippings.

Two close-ups of Sal. ca 1970's

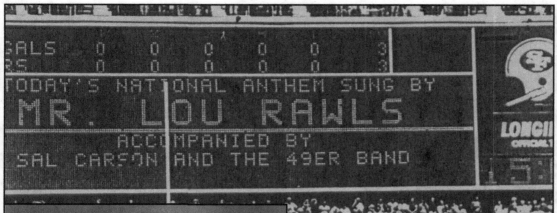

Lou Rawls at the 49'er game. ca 1970's

Publicity photo of Lou Rawls. What a voice.

Art Rosenbaum column. Letter to the editor.

Two Sal photos, ca 1975

Band before the game. ca 1970's

Sal, ca 1975

45 recording. 1979

sal carson
mabelle e. defer

49ers, SO PROUD AND BOLD

ARR: R. PALADINI

"49'ers, so Proud and Bold". The music was accepted into the Football Hall of Fame, 1979

Award to Sal. Fairmont Hotel, 1979. BMI Music Presentation.

Fairmont Hotel.
Tribute to Mayor George Moscone. "45 RMP!" How about rpm?

Sal Carson & His Big Band

Trumpet and Vocals

Swinging into a orchestra

18 Songs such as
-Satin Doll
-Cherry Pink and Apple
Blossom White
-SF 49'er's So Proud
and Bold is in Pro Foot-
ball Hall of Fame, Can-
ton, OH
-Memories
-Jersey Bounce
-After the love has gone
-As time goes by

Sal Carson (nee Sal Carcione), a Northern California and Nevada celebrity was dubbed San Francisco's Music Man by enthusiastic fans. Sal is an accomplished trumpet and flugel horn player, vocalist and composer. He keeps the dance floor packed with a repertoire of danceable music and has a reputation for being able to please every type of audience that runs a gamut from the Big Band sounds, Latin to 50's, 60's and popular songs of today. He definitely plays with dancers in mind and the arrangements are aimed at getting people onto the dance floor.

Sal started his band at Forest Lake Resort and also played at Hobergs Resort and the popular Konocti Harbor Resort & Spa in Lake County, CA, the Holiday Lodge & Casino Hot Springs, Reno, NV, and numerous Las Vegas hotels. For six seasons Sal and his Big Band played for the San Francisco 49ers at Candlestick Park. Sal and Mabelle Defer composed the song "49ers, So Proud and Bold" which is in the Pro Football Hall of Fame in Canton, OH.

In addition, Carson's band was featured at Harvey's Resort Casino, Top of the Wheel, Stateline, Lake Tahoe, NV, for four lengthy engagements. Sal Carson Orchestra and combos are always in demand for weddings, private parties, conventions, and political and labor union parties. His orchestra recorded an album with Vic Damone titled "Vic Damone in San Francisco - featuring *Christmas in San Francisco*."

Carson also backed Frankie Avalon, Bobby Rydell, Suzanne Somers, Sergio Franchi, Bob Hope, Mel Torme, Barbara Eden, Marvin Hamlisch, Shirley Jones and Vic Damone.

Sal Carson: featured on trumpet and vocals
Jerry Stucker: guitarist and consultant
Mike Vax: trumpet solo on *Song of India* and *I've Got My Love To Keep Me Warm*
Dean Hubbard: Solo trombone *Song of India*

Produced by **Sal Carson**
Recorded at Wally Heider Recording, San Francisco and Los Angeles, CA
Bert Schneider: Mastering engineer
"49ers, So Proud and Bold" composed by **Sal Carson** and **Mabelle Defer** (Carsal Music/BMI)
"San Francisco 49ers Superbowl Win #5" composed by **Sal Carson** and **Jerry Stucker** (Carsal Music/BMI)
Rudy Paladini: arrangements on songs 9, 11 and 13

CD Cover. ca 70's   CD liner notes.

SAN FRANCISCO FORTY NINERS

John Ralston

April 21, 1980

Mr. Sal Carson
127 Hardie Drive
Moraga, California 94556

Dear Sal:

On behalf of the entire San Francisco Forty Niner organization, I want to extend my heartiest thanks and appreciation for the tremendous job you have done for us over the past few years.

I am sure that we will have many opportunities to get together in the future, and trust that good health and happiness continue for you and yours. If I can be of assistance in any way, please give me a call. With every best wish, I remain,

Most cordially,

John Ralston

:l

49'er thank you let-
ter. April 21, 1980

The big band. ca 1979. The bass player was the well-known musician, Vernon Alley. I wish I knew the other names because the band was great.

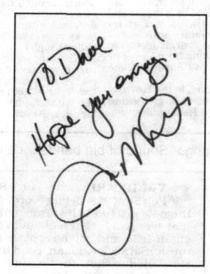

Joe Montana signed the inside of his book for Dave.

Joe Montana was co-author of the book "The Winning Spirit" and the primary speaker at a corporate session attended by my son-in-law, Dave D'Arrezo.

Sal Carson brings 'sound

By JEANNE TUCKER

The thing bandleader Sal Carson likes most about playing the New Year's Eve gala at St. Mary's College is it is one of the few nights of the year

SAL CARSON
'Old pro', a few years back

he gets to spend "at home" with his Moraga neighbors.

San Francisco - born and Oakland - bred, the musician has called Moraga home since 1966.

He moved here because "my wife Kathleen loved Moraga, and I do, too, but they promised Gateway Boulevard would be in so I could commute easily to San Francisco where most of my work is," he said.

In addition, the cityboy transplanted to a country home with a view of a walnut orchard sighed, "I just wish there were more going on in Moraga."

A superb trumpet player and vocalist, Sal appears with his band in the Bay Area at private parties, conventions, proms and weddings. "The music business has changed," he said. "Every situation is different. For instance at a wedding the bride will say 'I'm Italian and my husband's Jewish.' So you have to have music prepared for both."

And, prior to a party for a Frank Sinatra buff, Sal has to shuffle through his mental tune collection to prepare a swinging repertoire.

Each summer Sal's band plays Harvey's Hotel at South Shore, a road trip he greatly enjoys. And now for the past four years on autumn Sunday afternoons when most breadwinners are snoozing in front of their TV sets, Sal is at work leading his 45 - member Forty Niner band, usually doing a trumpet solo national anthem. "We have the greatest band in the National Football League, acclaimed by Howard Cosell," Sal proudly announced. "All we do is sit there in the stands and blow." It's a "hot band, according to Sal, along the lines of Buddy Rich or Doc Severinsen with "fine, accomplished" musicians who are skilled both in jazz and rock. The band always warms up Forty Niner spectators with a 45 - minute pre - game concert featuring the music of anything from Tower of Power to Chicago to Basie to Duke Ellington.

Sal is also involved in the business end of music, running a large booking agency in the City. He provides "top 40" (popular music charts) bands for proms all through the spring. "I have the best stable of rock musicians of anyone except perhaps for Bill Graham," he said. For convention and wedding crowds he is equally able to come up with veterans of the Glenn Miller or Tommy Dorsey bands as well as fine string instrumentalists.

In the days before his name appeared on marquees Sal's last name was Carcione. He is a first cousin to the Chronicle's and TV's Greengrocer, Joe Carcione. Sal's father, Guiseppi Carcione, sang with the San Francisco Opera and took his son to performances from the age of four. "Opera is my first love," Sal said, though his voice is more of a crooner's variety than dramatic tenor.

Originally, Sal started on the banjo when he was 11 and even had his own band at Oakland's Claremont Junior High School. At 16, he started to study trumpet with Oakland's Leo DeMers. In those years his idols were Harry James, Count Basie and Glenn Miller.

A three - year stint in the Army during WWII served as Sal's real opportunity to become a big band director. He was in charge of an Army - Air Corps band in Sioux City, Iowa which traveled the circuit of USO's, officer's and enlisted men's clubs in different cities. "I was very, very lucky to get that first break," Sal recalled happily.

One of the fondest memories of his career was the 20 summers his band played at Hoberg's in Lake County. "We'd have 2,000 people dancing under the stars, boy - meets - girl and families. Anyone who ever went to

(Top of pages 214 and 215) Sal Carson brings "Sound of big bands". ca late 1980's

Overheard".
July 24, 1988

OVERHEARD: Bandleader Sal Carson's 49er Pep Song has been recorded for release with the new pro football season, but Carson won't do it at 49er games. His band didn't survive the first cut of 1980, and will be replaced by rock 'n roll music. Sal's a good man, good lip. When a famous star failed to show for the singing of the National Anthem, Carson's solo trumpet drew the crowd's applause . . . Is this the age of hyperbole? In other times, 155-pounders were called "junior middle-weights." When Hope and Mattioli fought for TV, they were billed as "super welterweights." . . . To new Angel Ed Halicki's recent blast against Giants management for using him only in relief and advising him he had a bad arm, Gen. Mgr. Spec Richardson replies: "That man talks like he's a saint. He damn well isn't. If we thought he had a bad arm, why would he remain on our 25-man roster?"

# of big bands' to Moraga

Hoberg's in those days will never forget it," he said. Hoberg's closed in 1968.

And now Sal has hopes of reviving a little of the Hoberg's - type magic a lot closer to home. "If I get the time I would like to have three or four big band dances here in Moraga every year. The Moraga Rotary Club's New Year's Eve dance is a smash. And people are really starting to dance.

As he looked forward to more mu- sic - making, Sal also reflected on his career. No other profession or craft ever appealed to the bandleader - trumpeter - singer. "I just lived it," Sal said. "That is all I ever wanted to do — play music."

PLAYING FOR THE 49ers' DURING 45 - MINUTE PRE-GAME WARMUP
Moraga's Sal Carson leads his musicians in variety of tunes from classic to rock

Logo

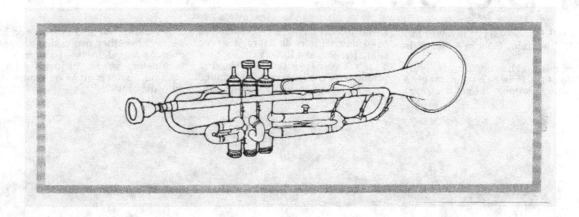

Sal Carson Orchestra

Swinging
in
San Francisco

Chapter 9
The 80's

Caroline Cartwright was Miss San Francisco in 1980. Besides being a beautiful woman, as was her mother, she enjoyed singing a few songs at parties with Sal's band. "She had a good voice".

Dottie was a socialite and married to Robert Cartwright a successful attorney. They hired Sal for parties held at their Hillsborough home. Sal's band played for their daughter Caroline's wedding and the Cartwright's' wanted the band for their son's wedding in Hawaii, but Sal already had a commitment. This important and friendly relationship led to playing for conventions and charity functions.

At a luncheon Dottie Cartwright told Sal she wanted to get Richard Burton to appear at the Doll Ball which was another charity function. At the time Burton was appearing at the Golden Gate Theater doing a show. Mrs. Cartwright went to the theater and somehow got into his dressing room to ask him to appear at the Doll Ball charity. "She followed up the visit with an elegant letter and he responded".

After his performance at the theater he walked into the Galleria with a group of people and walked right up to the bandstand. "You could have heard a pin drop. Never saw anything like it. He talked over the microphone and knew just what to say for three or four minutes. I could not do that. Dottie got Burton to show up. How about that".

The 80's also was the start of a pleasant relationship with Chuck Hess and the Home Savings and Loan Association. They picked up the tab for Sal's band at various charitable functions. They also paid for Helen O'Connell and/or Andy Russell as vocalists. Sal was everywhere. The major hotels, clubs and even the opening of a gas station where he used local jazz musicians Bob Mielke and Dick Oxtot.

On a sad note, here's what writer Herb Caen had to say: "....The 49'ers have bounced Sal Carson whose band has played the games a lot better than the team for the past six years". Sal understood the 49'ers were looking for a change and he still has a good relationship with the team's owners.

Sal worked a number of times with Sergio Franchi in the 80's, conventions, charity events and so on. "What a nice man, down to earth guy. I was heart broken when he passed away".

Sal was a sideman in a number of bands particularly in the early portion of his career. He worked with Howard Fredric, Maurice Anger and "Dutch" Kearns who had a big band at the Castlewood Country Club. "We are really good friends. He's a nice guy, good piano player and arranger. I worked with "Dutch" often and it was there that I met Donna Theodore who was the vocalist. "She was a beautiful young girl and a hell of a good singer. Johnny Carson loved her and she was on his show at least a dozen times. Was with Anthony Quinn at the Golden Gate Theater and went on to New York as a lead singer in big shows. Worked one summer with us at Hobergs and many other times. She's a good friend".

He continued to play gigs in prominent hotels in the Bay Area, Las Vegas and the Cocoanut Grove in Santa Cruz. Another pleasant memory was working with Vic Damone.

Joe Mazzola was another key player in Sal's career. In the 80's he was a labor leader, highly respected in the political end of it "He hired our band, generally a big band, for various events. Not just small parties". Mazzola, his wife Vera, came to Hoberg's with their children for many years so they were aware of Sal's band. Mazzola and Bob Costello were the big players in establishing Konocti Harbor Inn as an investment for the plumbers union. They hired Sal to play in Las Vegas with a big band when Mazzola ran for the National President of the Union. Sal thinks the world of Joe and Bob.

Sal on a
cable car.

Richard Burton was born in Wales, November 10, 1925. He died August 5, 1984. in Switzerland

Valentine Celebrity Doll Ball. ca 1980

Burton to appear at Doll show

The star of Camelot, Richard Burton, will be a 'Valentine Surprise' February 14th at the Celebrity Doll Show to be held at the Galleria, according to Mrs. Robert Cartwright, chairperson of the Little Jim Club of San Francisco Children's Hospital.

The benefit show will also feature Frankie Avalon and Alan Drake.

Sal Carson's Big Show Band will provide the music, courtesy of Home Savings and Loan Association.

Prizes to be offered are a round trip air fare to Hong Kong courtesy of O.C. Tours and a Delta Steamship Cruise to Los Angeles courtesy of Delta Steamship Lines.

Reservations for the Valentine night affair, which includes cocktails and doll show at 6:30 p.m., dinner at 8:30 p.m., may be made by calling 347-1275. Donation is $50 per person, reservations limited.

The Galleria is located at 101 Kansas Street in San Francisco.

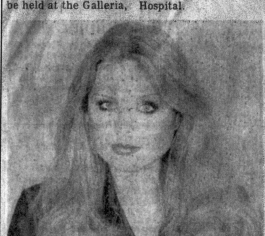

Caroline Cartwright, Miss San Francisco, USA 1980, will be on hand February 14 at the Galleria for the Valentine Celebrity Doll Ball and Doll Show.

Burton to appear at the Doll Show. Ca 1970. Caroline Cartwright, the daughter of Dottie and Robert Cartwright.

Borg denies sour note in wedding band

By Bucky Walter

He's recently lost matches — surprise! — but tennis' No. 1 Bjorn Borg pooh-poohs the notion it's because marrying Mariana Simionescu has affected his game.

"Not yet, anyway," he says.

"I don't think it should. Before we were married, I was living with her four or five years, and the only thing different is that we got married."

Love that match.

• • •

Chunk of irony: For leading the Raiders to the Super Bowl, Jim Plunkett was paid $190,003 — or $178,599 less than Dan Pastorini, whose record was 2-3 when he busted a leg.

Plunkett's contract is coming up for renegotiation. The Raiders have the highest payroll in the NFL and hardly ever get into salary disputes. Expect the gap to close.

• • •

Perhaps we're overly optimistic — reading reports of hopeful prognosis — that James Rodney Richard will be able to pitch for the Houston Astros this year.

The other day the Chicago Sun-Times' Ron Rapoport solicited advice from a leading neurosurgeon, who told him, "One thing they (stroke victims) don't do is go out and play professional baseball."

"Miracles can occur in medicine, but this would be the greatest one since Lazarus."

A melancholy opinion. Let's pray J.R. beats the odds.

The Evening Muse

To commemorate the University of Georgia's 1980 football championship, the Coca-Cola folks have struck more than a million special 10-ounce bottles emblazoned with a Bulldog and the slogan: "Coke and Bulldogs No. 1."

Sorry, collectors, they're available only in Georgia. Regular 10-ounce bottles of Coke cost about 35 cents. The commemorative bottles are selling for 60 cents.

• • •

Baseball Hall of Famer Ty Cobb became a millionaire by buying Coca-Cola stock in the potable's early days. (He tipped off other baseballers — and jockscribes, too.)

Addendum: Ty Cobb, a distant cousin of the Georgia Peach, recently was appointed an assistant U.S. attorney for Maryland. Says Maryland's Ty: "I played high school, college and semipro ball, but not with distinction."

• • •

Until now, it hadn't been reported — that NBA deputy commissioner Simon Gourdine found the Warriors' Bernard King innocent of intentionally hitting Dallas' Jim Spanarkel in a Jan. 7 game at Oakland. Coliseum fans were outraged when ref Mike Mathis ejected King. Gourdine, after studying videotapes: "I could not conclude in any way that he intended to hit Spanarkel." The automatic $250 fine for ejection stands. But had King been found guilty, the fine would have increased dramatically and King likely would have been suspended.

• • •

Pitcher Matt Keough of the A's tells it as it is: "Winning isn't everything, but losing sucks."

• • •

GM Jack McKeon of the Padres lists the Astros, Reds, Giants and Dodgers as "teams that may cause us problems" in NL-West, somehow overlooking the Braves, sixth team in the division.

• • •

Mail Box: "Did you know that in our youth, Dom DiMaggio sold newspapers in front of the Golden Pheasant on Powell and Geary streets? A classy kid later stepped up in class."

• • •

Name Dropping: They anticipate that Richard Burton, here in "Camelot," also Frankie Avalon and Alan Drake, will be Valentine surprises at tomorrow night's Celebrity Doll Show at the Galleria, a benefit for the Little Jim Club of S.F. Children's Hospital. Sports angle: Sal Carson's 49ers' band will provide the music.

• • •

GG Fields' advertising manager, Norm Hershon, thought up this year's theme, "Escape to Golden Gate Fields," which has been appearing in newspaper ads.

Irrepressible Bob Wuerth, Bay Meadows' publicist, rose nobly to the occasion.

"You should run the ad in the San Quentin News," he advised Hershon.

"The Evening Muse" by Bucky Walter, ca 1978

MUSIC & ENTERTAINMENT CONSULTANTS • TALENT AGENCY

SAN FRANCISCO'S

SAL CARSON
ORCHESTRAS & PRODUCTIONS

MUSIC MAN

(415) 254-1881

127 HARDIE DRIVE • MORAGA, CA 94556

Business card

Hi Sal
Here are some pictures and a few bios..Hope we can do some things in Reno or Tahoe together

Andy

Andy Russell's business card and note to Sal. I always enjoyed his version of "Besame Mucho", "Magic is the Moonlight" and "Amor".

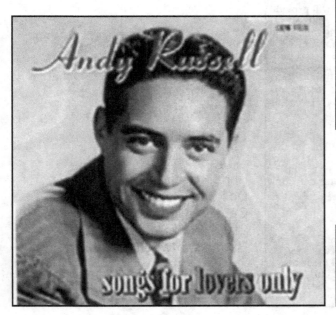

Andy Russell (Andres Rabago) was born September 16, 1919 in Los Angeles. He died April 16, 1992 in Phoenix, AR

"San Francisco's Music Man"

Reprinted from a San Francisco Progress article by Jack Rosenbaum.

Known as "San Francisco's Music Man," **Sal Carson** is an accomplished trumpeter, composer, and vocalist. His band has a reputation for being able to please every type of audience.

For six years, Carson led the 49'er Band. He composed the official team song, "49'ers So Proud and Bold."

A first cousin of **Joe Carcione**, local radio and television's Green Grocer, Carson has backed such outstanding performers as **Bob Hope**, **Barbara Eden**, **Della Reese**, and **Shecky Greene**. Home Savings of America is sponsoring the band's appearance at this year's dinner dance.

Jack Rosenbaum column, <u>San Francisco Progress</u>. ca 1980

Bill Fiset

A REALLY NICE dinner dance out at Hs Lordships as a Cerebral Palsy benefit the other night, with Sal Carson making a "big band" sound with only 14 pieces, and entertainment by singer Andy Russell, who's been around a few years and is a total professional. He's never been in better voice (and his "Besame Mucho" is better than ever.)

Bill Fiset's column <u>Oakland Tribune</u>, ca 1980's

SINGER ANDY RUSSELL was excited that Claire and Lee Shaklee were at Capella Auxiliary's Friday night dinner dance at Hs Lordship's because he's a real health nut. Not only does he take all the Shaklee vitamins, his wife, Ginny, is a distributor for Shaklee Products. Besides, the Shaklees love to dance so much they scarcely ever left the dance floor. A compliment to orchestra leader Sal Carson and singer Andy, whose song hits of the 40s are among Claire and Lee's favorites.

Bill Fiset's column <u>Oakland Tribune</u>, ca 1980's

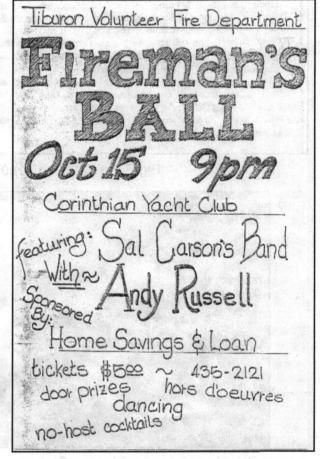

Fireman's Ball. October 15, 1980

Sal Carson—Andy Russell at the 'Big Band Ball'

PLEASANTON — You can re-live the days of romantic songs and touch-dancing by attending the "Big Band Ball" sponsored by Fir Branch of Children's Hospital Medical Center, Saturday, at Castlewood Country Club in Pleasanton.

Star of the evening will be Andy Russell, handsome singer who gained fame in the 40's with bi-lingual hits such as "Besame Mucho" and "Amor." Russell went on to earn six more gold records, including "Magic is the Moonlight," "What a Difference a Day Makes," "I Can't Begin to Tell You," and Laughin' on the Outside, Cryin' on the Inside."

He'll sing them all, plus some contemporary tunes accompanied by Sal Carson's big orchestra who will provide music for dancing until midnight. Carson, bandleader for the San Francisco 49ers, has just returned from a tour of the Nevada night club circuit.

Andy Russell, who took over Frank Sinatra's spot as lead singer on the Hit Parade in 1947, left his native Los Angeles in the 50's to extend his career into Latin and South America.

Since then, he's become a film and television star in Argentina, Mexico and Spain, garnering awards as an unofficial good-will ambassador for the U.S.

Now, Russell has returned to his own country under the aegis of Home Savings and Loan, the association sponsoring his appearance at Castlewood next week.

Carson, the 49ers band leader, opened the team's season with a trumpet solo of the National Anthem, then flew to Harvey's at Stateline for a two week engagement at the Top of the Wheel. The band leader is back home in the Bay Area this week.

"I became involved in this through Home Savings and Loan," Carson said. "They're sponsoring the party for the medical center in Oakland. I think it's a great cause."

Carson and his band will back up Russell and provide their own renditions of songs from the 40's. But the band isn't limited to nostalgia from the past.

"We're doing a lot of the modern stuff," Carson added. "We play the better tunes of today. Songs like "Love Will Keep us Together," "Tequilla Sunrise," and "Laughter in the Rain," along with the great Miller and James hits."

The band leader said he has worked with Russell before. "We did one of these benfits with Andy Russell at the Oakland Hilton last July 4," he recalled. The Oakland benefit ball was also sponsored by Home Savings and Loan.

Sports fans can catch Carson's band the following day when the 49ers play the Oakland Raiders or at several local clubs. "We'll be in the Bay Area until spring," he said.

Carson and his big band will return to the Nevada circuit when they leave the Bay Area next year.

The Aug. 28 party gets underway with cocktails at 7 p.m., followed by a dinner of filet mignon, shrimp salad, stuffed potato, and vegetables with white or red wine on each table and Grand Marnier souffle for dessert, according to members of the hospital branch.

Barbara Linse of Danville, chairwoman of the Big Band Ball at Castlewood is asking for early reservations. Tickets are $12.50 per person and may be made by calling 339-9335. Checks should be made payable to the Children's Hospital Branches, Inc.

"Big Band Ball", ca 1980's. <u>Tri-Valley Herald & News</u>

Grand opening of a Chevron Station in Pinole, early 1980's. (l to r) Rick Elmore, Bob Mielke, Sal and Dick Oxtot

ca 1980's mailer

The Hiring Hall (ILWU), March 22, 1980. Nice looking poster, but it never happened

Second photo of the opening. Sal loved jazz, enjoyed playing it, "But I just could not make enough money playing jazz".

Tribute to Guy Cherney, June 5, 1980

Drawing of Bob Mielke by Nancy Tapscott Conzett

Tribute to Guy. (l to r) Guy Cherney, Mel Torme, Bill Soberanes (newspaper writer) and Sal

ROSALYNN CARTER

February 13, 1980

To Sal Carson

I want you to know how much I enjoyed your beautiful music during my trip to San Francisco last week. Thank you so much for making my visit such a pleasant one.

Thank you, too, for the Vic Damone records. I am pleased to have them.

Sincerely,

Rosalynn Carter

Mr. Sal Carson
127 Hardie Drive
Moraga, California 94556

Letter from
Rosalynn Carter,
February 13, 1980

Jack Rosenbaum

7-2-80

Musical move

Seven (as in touchdown and extra point) isn't Sal Carson's lucky number. He had looked forward to his seventh season as the 49ers bandleader and to present a new version of the team's fight song which he had recorded and introduced at a Hallidie Plaza concert. But all

for naught. The 49ers are bringing in a new band, apparently to feature more disco and rock. But will it score those needed touchdowns?

Jack Rosenbaum article in the San Francisco Chronicle. July 1, 1980

★ ★ ★

WASHINGTON JOKE: "If Reagan is elected, there'll be a First Lady and a Second Lady"—the last being a reference to Nancy's *tres gai* and highly amusing chum who will be all OVER the White House. Still, he's more fun that Ham Jordan but he's never still . . . Pat Simmons reportedly wants half of Pier 39—Pier 19½? — plus the Silverado (Napa) showplace as a divorce settlement from Warren. He gets to keep the Sony . . . A maternity dress is about to produce a paternity suit for one of the town's more swinging restaurateurs, famous for fresh fish . . . There they go: After six years of long nights, Bandleader Jimmy Diamond has left the Fairmont's New Orleans Room "by mutual consent" and is now working in Atlantic City. His replacement: Trumpeter Buddy Powers, who also plays those Fri. tea dances at the Hyatt Regency . . . As if that weren't enough, the 49ers have bounced Sal Carson, whose band has played the games a lot better than the team for the past six years.

★ ★ ★ 7-14-80

Herb Caen, July 14, 1980. San Francisco Chronicle

Art Rosenbaum

OVERHEARD: Bandleader Sal Carson's 49er Pep Song has been recorded for release with the new pro football season, but Carson won't do it at 49er games. His band didn't survive the first cut of 1980; and will be replaced by rock 'n roll music. Sal's a good man, good lip. When a famous star failed to show for the singing of the National Anthem, Carson's solo trumpet drew the crowd's applause . . . Is this the age of hyperbole? In other times, 155-pounders were called "junior middleweights." When Hope and Mattioli fought for TV, they were billed as "super welterweights." . . . To new Angel Ed Halicki's recent blast against Giants management for using him only in relief and advising him he had a bad arm, Gen. Mgr. Spec Richardson replies: "That man talks like he's a saint. He damn well isn't. If we thought he had a bad arm, why would he remain on our 25-man roster?"

San Francisco Chronicle, Art Rosenbaum, July 25, 1980

By Daniel DeLong

Published Weekly by the Press Club of San Francisco

Sal Carson, the man with a big horn, is happier than usual these days. And it isn't simply because the Club's Black Cats orchestra sounds so well, either.

His new album with **Vic Damone** is out and doing well. And, he has a letter from the First Lady, who was here in February. **Sal** played the event and **Roz** was duely impressed.

5/26/80

San Francisco Chronicle, Art Rosenbaum, July 25, 1980

Carson Band To Play S.F. Convention

Sal Carson, popular San Francisco orchestra leader who directs the San Francisco 49er forty-five piece swing band at Candlestick Park, has been engaged by AFL-CIO headquarters, Washington, to play the upcoming AFL-CIO Eleventh Constitutional Convention, opening in San Francisco Oct. 2.

Article about Sal at the S.F. Convention, mid 80's.

–225–

scoop

published weekly by the Press Club of San Francisco

DANIEL DeLONG, Editor

MARK RODMAN, Business Manager

Monday, May 26, 1980

(415) 775-7800

Club's Table Tennis finals are Saturday

Press Club members and friends are invited to cheer their favorites in the finals of the 25th Annual Table Tennis Tournament, Saturday, May 31, beginning at 11 a.m. in the second floor lounge.

Featured in the Championship Class will be defending champion Bassem Moussa, who will meet the winner of a match between Dan Chu and Bill Brauer.

In the Intermediate Class, either Mark Edwards or Lou Felder will meet the winner between Allan Schuman and Tom Ellis.

Finalists in the Novice Class are George Shistar and Gene Newman.

Press Club members swing into high gear to the Black Cats orchestra of Sal Carson after Wednesday dinner. More than 130 members ate the Wednesday night buffet and then danced until 10 p.m. Dick Osborn photo.

Scoop, May 26, 1980

Carson Band To Play S.F. Convention

Sal Carson, popular San Francisco orchestra leader who directs the San Francisco 49er forty-five piece swing band at Candlestick Park, has been engaged by AFL-CIO headquarters, Washington, to play the upcoming AFL-CIO Eleventh Constitutional Convention, opening in San Francisco Oct. 2.

The Carson Band will initiate the first Business Session of the Convention at San Francisco Auditorium with the playing of the National Anthem, to be sung by Vocalist Gloria Craig. Miss Craig began her singing career with an earlier Carson orchestra at Hoberg's Resort, Lake County, later moving to the Ray Anthony orchestra where she gained national stardom.

Another article about Sal at the S.F. Convention, mid 80's.

"An Evening With Jim Scatena". September 27, 1980

Scatena Night

Prominent San Francisco businessman *James Scatena*, who has devoted his energies and talents to a long list of charities and civic causes, will be honored at *"An Evening With Jim Scatena"* on Saturday, Sept. 27 at *Bimbo's 365 Club*. Cocktails, a gourmet dinner and dancing to the *Sal Carson Orchestra*

SENATE OF CALIFORNIA

———

SENATOR MILTON MARKS
OF
SAN FRANCISCO

ROOM 2070
STATE CAPITOL
SACRAMENTO 95814

August 13, 1980

Mr. Sal Carson
127 Hardie Drive
Moraga, California 94556

Dear Sal,

I was so pleased to learn that you have been selected to receive the Irish-Israeli-Italian Society's "Certificate of Appreciation". It is a well-deserved honor for someone who has done so much for our community.

My best wishes always,

Cordially,

MILTON MARKS

MM:pc

Letter from Milton Marks, August 13, 1980

"Laughing Sal" at the beach with our Sal and Carolyn Cartwright (Miss San Francisco). Mid 1980's. "Laughing Sal" was a big attraction in the 80's and was Dottie Cartwright's brother.

O. J. SIMPSON ENTERPRISES
11661 SAN VICENTE BLVD.
LOS ANGELES, CALIFORNIA 90049
(213) 820-5702

August 21, 1980

Mr. Sal Carson
127 Hardie Drive
Moraga, California 94556

Dear Sal:

Thank you for your kind letter and information regarding your property in Reno.

Unfortunately, with several other ventures going on at this time, it is not possible for me to invest in property of this magnitude. I trust you will understand and appreciate my dilemma.

I was sorry to hear that your band will no longer be at the 49'er games. It won't seem the same -- however, I want to wish you every future success and thank you for thinking of me in this regard.

Best personal regards,

O. J. SIMPSON

OJS:cr

Letter from O.J. Simpson,
August 21, 1980

Photo of Carmen
Ortiz. Musicians
who double normally
get paid more. Sal
just paid for singing
or playing the guitar.
ca 1980's

September 10, 1980

Dear Sal:

The 1980 Jerry Lewis Telethon is over, and it was the most successful in the 15 year history of these events. Over 31 million dollars was raised nationally, and the Muscular Dystrophy Association is proud to report that over $943,000.00 of that figure came from the Bay Area.

The generous contribution of your time and talent to this year's Telethon was one of the reasons that it was so successful. The presence on our phone banks of so many prominent figures from the arts, government, sports and media helped to convey to our viewers that the battle to defeat the 40 diseases covered by the Muscular Dystrophy Association is a genuine community effort.

The gift of your time was a real contribution to the M.D.A., and we want you to know that your gift was appreciated.

We truly hope that the experience was a positive one for you in every respect.

Sincerely,

Helen Jones
District Director
MDA, San Francisco, Ca.

Bud Spangler
Talent Coordinator
1980 Jerry Lewis Telethon

September 10, 1980 letter regarding the Jerry Lewis Labor Day Telethon coordinator was Bud Spangler who did many jazz shows for See's Candy (Chuck Huggins, president)

–229–

AMC
Cancer Research Center
and Hospital

West Coast Development Office

February 19, 1981

Mr. Sal Carson
127 Hardie Drive
Moraga   CA 94556

Dear Mr. Carson:

Thank you for your performance at the February 5th Chinese
New Year dinner dance at the Fairmont Hotel.

It was thrilling to celebrate the beginning of the Year of
the Rooster with the Chinese community. You and your
orchestra were a wonderful part of a very fine evening.

On behalf of our Executive Committee and the AMC Cancer
Research Center and Hospital, we thank you for your
participation.

Warm regards,

Cyril Magnin
Chariman

J. Gary Shansby
Chairman

s

Letter dated February 19, 1981. One of the signatures was by Cyril Magnin who was very
well known and highly regarded in San Francisco.

LABOR VICTORY DINNER
Honoring Joe Mazzola

Tuesday Evening, May 5, 1981

Grand Ballroom — Fairmont Hotel

San Francisco, California

Joe Mazzola. Fairmont Hotel, May 5, 1981

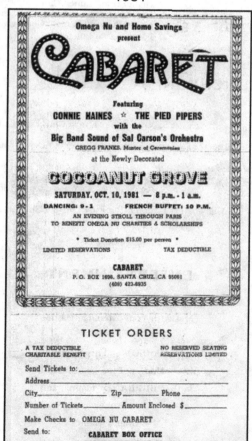

Omega Nu and Home Savings present

CABARET

Featuring

CONNIE HAINES ☆ **THE PIED PIPERS**

with the

Big Band Sound of Sal Carson's Orchestra

GREGG FRANKS, Master of Ceremonies

at the Newly Decorated

COCOANUT GROVE

SATURDAY, OCT. 10, 1981 — 8 p.m. - 1 a.m.

DANCING: 9 - 1   FRENCH BUFFET: 10 P.M.

AN EVENING STROLL THROUGH PARIS
TO BENEFIT OMEGA NU CHARITIES & SCHOLARSHIPS

• Ticket Donation $15.00 per person •

LIMITED RESERVATIONS   TAX DEDUCTIBLE

CABARET

P.O. BOX 1698, SANTA CRUZ, CA 95061

(408) 423-8935

TICKET ORDERS

A TAX DEDUCTIBLE
CHARITABLE BENEFIT

NO RESERVED SEATING
RESERVATIONS LIMITED

Send Tickets to: _____

Address _____

City _____ Zip _____ Phone _____

Number of Tickets _____ Amount Enclosed $_____

Make Checks to OMEGA NU CABARET

Send to: **CABARET BOX OFFICE**

"Cabaret", Cocoanut Grove, Santa Cruz. October 10, 1981

PROGRAM

Joseph Alioto, *Toastmaster*

Welcome .... Larry Mazzola

Invocation .... Bishop Mark J. Hurley

Remarks .... Marvin E. Lewis

Remarks .... John F. Henning

Honored Guest .... Joseph P. Mazzola

Dancing to the music of

Sal Carson

MENU

Papaya Boat with Marinated Bay Shrimp on Bed of Shredded Lettuce
Garnished with Cherry Tomatoes, Sliced Eggs, Asparagus Tips,
Hearts of Artichoke, French and Thousand Island Dressings

Roast Filet of Beef Bourguignonne
Pass Bearnaise Sauce
Broccoli Polanaise
Artichoke Bottom with Glazed Carrots
Rissole Potatoes

Macedoine of Fruit Flambe over Vanilla Ice Cream
Candy Baskets with Fairmont Confections
Coffee

Cheese Sticks   French Rolls

Program for Mazzola tribute.

Connie Haines was born January 20, 1922 in Savannah, GA. She won an amateur contest on Fred Allen's NBC Radio Show when she was only thirteen. Later in life she was the vocalist for Harry James, Tommy Dorsey and others.

WESTERN SHRINE ASSOCIATION
LADIES DAY LUNCHEON

Honoring

The First Lady of Shrinedom

JOAN H'DOUBLER

Imperial Sir F.T. H'Doubler, Jr.'s Lady

Friday
May 22, 1981
Continental Ballroom
Hilton Hotel
San Francisco

Western Shrine Association
Luncheon, May 22, 1981

PROGRAM

.... Noble John Mord, President
Islam Shrine Lunch Club

Colors......................... Islam Patrol

.... Noble Jim Bouick, Vice President
Islam Shrine Lunch Club

.... Noble Burton Graham, Chaplain
Islam Shrine Lunch Club

LUNCHEON

Introduction of Mrs. Marion Mord .... Lunch Club First Lady

Introduction of Mrs. Fran Haun ...... Director General's Lady and Mistress of Ceremonies

Introduction of the Mayor of San Francisco..................... Hon. Dianne Feinstein

Introduction of Mrs. Helen Busse .... W. S. A. President's Lady

Introduction of our Guest of Honor .... Mrs. Joan H'Doubler, the First Lady of Shrinedom

Introduction of Distinguished Guests

Program for
Shrine luncheon.
Miss Connie
Haines was
backed by Sal's
band. May 22,
1981

ENTERTAINMENT

Music for your listening pleasure
by
SAL CARSON and his orchestra
with melodies of the 50's and 60's
in the "BIG BAND" manner and
starring
Miss Connie Haines
in concert

(Top left) A Las Vegas gig. August 1981.

(Top right) The Grove has a large ballroom. Photo by Jim Goggin

Santa Cruz postcard.

Headdress Parade, October 18, 1981. Seated is Connie Torretta, (l to r) Jackie Bell, Cal Moore, Sal. Not in photo, Pat Fuller.

Sal Carson sends out a few notes as Connie Torretta, seated, tries on hat for headdress parade. Looking on are Jackie Bell, left, Cal Moore, right, Pat Fuller.

About People

Dance to the Carson sound

Sal Carson and his band, will be on hand to play his great music at Hemlock Branch's annual event "You the Night and the Music." The benefit for Children's Hospital Medical Center will be held Saturday from 9 p.m. to 1 a.m. at Hilltop Mall and has been themed "Stairway to the Stars." Home Savings and Loan is underwriting the cost of the band.

In San Francisco, Sal Carson (born Salvatore Carcione) and his music, are almost a civic institution. Sal is a master of both the Big Band sound and todays newest beat. For many years he was official Band Leader at all 49'er home football games and has backed many outstanding performers such as Bob Hope, Pat Boone, Roger Miller, Bobby Goldsboro, Della Reese, Shecky Green, Barbara Eden, Vic Damone and the Johnny Mann Singers.

Tickets cost $19 per person for the evening and are available at the Hilltop Office, Mechanics Bank, or by contacting Bessie Anton at 223-1258 or Opal Harcourt at 724-0129.

Jackie Bell is coordinating a headdress parade for the evening event.

"Stairway to the Stars". October 18, 1981

December 29, 1981

Mr. Sal Carson
127 Hardie Drive
Moraga, CA 94556

Dear Sal:

My sincere thank you for the "Hello Dolly/ 49ers" records.

I appreciate your thinking of me during this holiday season.

With best wishes for the New Year, I am

Sincerely,

Sam J. Sebastiani

SJS:aa

Letter from Sam J. Sebastiani. December 29, 1981

Tower Records ad. January 20, 1982

Donna Theodore was the vocalist on numerous Sal gigs. Her career consists of awards and a Tony nomination, plus stage and TV appearances.

–234–

HERB CAEN

Feb. 82

SAL CARSON'S fine band began playing old tunes. The old-timers danced cheek to cheek, eyes closed, either asleep on their feet or dreaming of the glory nights. David Allen, whose Boarding House night club a block away has a tough time staying open, looked at the mob and sighed "I get it. Sell drinks for two bits and a dinner for two six bits and you pack 'em in." Bimbo stood in the lobby, surrounded by his doting children and grandchildren. He always gave a sucker an even break, and you

Mr. and Mrs. Tommy Harris stopped to cha with bandleader Sal Carson (right)

scoop
publishe
press cl

BETTY NICHOLAS, Editor

Volume 31, Number 13   Monday, March 29, 1982   (415) 775-7800

Music of Sal Carson at President's Ball

SAL CARSON

The third annual President's Ball, calendared for Thursday evening, April 15th, promises to be a memorable and gala evening of dining and dancing in the Club's Tapestry Dining Room.

Artist Member Sal Carson and his Black Cat Orchestra — 14 members strong — will be on hand to provide the danceable music Sal is so rightfully famous for. Dancing will begin at 8:00 p.m. following the sit-down dinner.

Press Club artist members Sam Stern, violinist; Jimmy Moore, double bass player and accordionist Dino Benetti will entertain during the cocktail hour from 6 – 7:00 p.m.

Chef Stig Filbig's special dinner menu will include Fresh Asparagus Vinaigrette, Roast Fillet of Beef Bordelaise and Strawberries Romanoff.

Early reservations are suggested; call the Front Desk — 775-7800. Price of the evening is $15.00 per person.

Fri. April 9th
Luncheon To Honor Senator Hayakawa

U. S. Senator S. I. (Sam) Hayakawa will be the guest of honor at a special luncheon on Friday, April 9th, here at the Press Club.

Senator Hayakawa, whom localites will recall as the feisty fellow in the tam-o-shanter who, as president of San Francisco State University, stood up to rebellious students and by means of semantics restored peace and order to the campus, will complete his 6-year term in the U.S. Senate in January, 1983. He is not seeking reelection.

Senator Hayakawa was elected November 2, 1976 in his first bid for political elective office, defeating incumbent Democratic Senator John V. Tunney. He had been a life-long Democrat until 1973 when he broke away and registered as a Republican.

Pre-luncheon cocktails are scheduled for 11:30 a.m., followed by lunch in the Tapestry Dining Room
— See page 2

SENATOR HAYAKAWA

Celebrity Hour To Showcase Singer Julie Shannon

The sparkling combination of beautiful and talented pop singer Julie Shannon and our own brilliant pianist, artist member Jimmy Diamond, will brighten the Friday, April 2nd Celebrity Hour in the Second Floor Clubhouse. Downbeat will be at 6:00 p.m.

Julie is a long-time favorite in the big-band circuit, having performed with Jimmy Diamond at the Fairmont Hotel, with Sal Carson's band at the Claremont Hotel in Berkeley, at San Francisco's "Dis-
— See page 2

JULIE SHANNON

(Top left) Herb Caen article. San Francisco Chronicle, February 18, 1982

(Top right) Black Tie Party at the 50th anniversary of Bimbo's 365 Club. 1932 prices. February 18, 1982. Tommy Harris was a popular performer in the 1930's and later the owner of Tommy's Joynt, an "in" place to go.

Scoop, March 29, 1982. Senator S.I. Hayakawa was quite knowledgeable about jazz and was often at Earthquake McGoon's.

GANNETT NEWSPAPERS

Greater Buffalo Press, Inc.
302 Grote St., Buffalo, NY 14207
716-876-6410

John P. Doelman, III
Director of Newspaper Relations

May 12, 1982

Mr. Sal Carson
127 Hardie Drive
Moraga, CA. 94556

Dear Sal,

Last month's party at the North Beach Restaurant was our most successful
ever and I must say a large part of that success was due to you. We have
had music at all of our American Newspaper Publisher Convention parties
from New York, to Atlanta, to Chicago etc. but never has a group been so
in tune with our guests—you were super!

The convention is being held in N.Y.C. next year and if there is any
practical way you could get to the 'Big Apple' and play for us the booking
would certainly be your's.

Sal, the Koessler's join me in sending you a warm Thanks for a job
beautifully done.

Best Regards,

JOHN P. DOELMAN, III

JPD/lml

P.S. Enclosed is our guest list.

Party at North Beach Restaurant. May 12, 1982

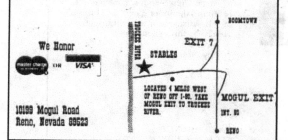

Sal's ranch, 1983

A home built in 1906 with walls 32 inches thick is on Sal's forty-three acres near Reno

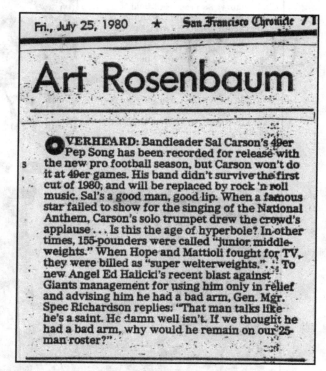

Fri., July 25, 1980   ★   San Francisco Chronicle 71

Art Rosenbaum

OVERHEARD: Bandleader Sal Carson's 49er Pep Song has been recorded for release with the new pro football season, but Carson won't do it at 49er games. His band didn't survive the first cut of 1980; and will be replaced by rock 'n roll music. Sal's a good man, good lip. When a famous star failed to show for the singing of the National Anthem, Carson's solo trumpet drew the crowd's applause . . . Is this the age of hyperbole? In other times, 155-pounders were called "junior middle-weights." When Hope and Mattioli fought for TV, they were billed as "super welterweights.". . To new Angel Ed Halicki's recent blast against Giants management for using him only in relief and advising him he had a bad arm, Gen. Mgr. Spec Richardson replies: "That man talks like he's a saint. He damn well isn't. If we thought he had a bad arm, why would he remain on our 25-man roster?"

Art Rosenbaum, San Francisco Chronicle, July 25, 1980

BANDLEADER SAL CARSON has taken over the Mogul Stables off Mogul Road six miles west of Reno. When he's not leading his band, Sal takes care of 22 riding horses. The stables offer horseback trail rides from a half-hour to two-day pack trips. Oct 17th 82

"High Ho Silver, Away", October 17, 1982

the centerpiece

February-April 1983   Volume II, Issue 1

Newsletter for the Cerebral Palsy Center for the Bay Area

CAPELLA DINNER DANCE MARCH 19
Music Man, Sal Carson, to Play

The renowned Sal Carson Band will provide the music for Capella Auxiliary's benefit dinner dance, "Down Mexico Way."

Scheduled for Saturday, March 19, at the Cerebral Palsy Center, this year's event will feature a charming south of the border atmosphere. Guests are invited to wear casual dress or traditional Mexican attire.

Known as "San Francisco's Music Man," **Sal Carson** is an accomplished trumpeter, composer, and vocalist. His band has a reputation for being able to please every type of audience.

For six years, Carson led the 49'er Band. He composed the official team song, "49'ers So Proud and Bold."

A first cousin of **Joe Carcione**, local radio and television's Green Grocer, Carson has backed such outstanding performers as **Bob Hope**, **Barbara Eden**, **Della Reese**, and **Shecky Greene**. Home Savings of America is sponsoring the band's appearance at this year's dinner dance.

Cocktails will be served at 6:30 p.m. with dinner at 8:00 p.m. Reservations are $25.00 per person and may be made by calling the Center at (415) 531-3323.

Don't miss out on the fun!

Bandleader Sal Carson

Message from the president . . .

The beginning of a year is traditionally a time to pause and reflect on events which occurred during the "old" year and to plan and resolve to improve or to accomplish more in the "new" year.

At the Cerebral Palsy Center, we can look with pride on our 1982 accomplishments. Thanks to all our volunteers and contributors, we provided *more* services to *more* clients and raised *more* funds than any year in our history.

So, you might say, what could possibly be our problem in 1983? My friends, each year brings new challenges, and 1983 will be no exception. However, our biggest problem, following an extremely successful year, can surely be COMPLACENCY.

Let us not sit back and revel in our past successes. Instead, let us reaffirm our commitment to the Center and its clients and dig deeper in our pockets and strive for a bit more energy to devote more time to Center activities.

You will not only be providing the means for a program unmatched in the Western United States, but you will be receiving the inner glows and blessings of self satisfaction that will brighten your year throughout 1983.

Happy New Year,

Larry Rodriggs

DOLL HOUSE WINNER WALNUT CREEK'S YOUNGEST HOMEOWNER
*4-1/2-month old **Gina Jenkins'** name was on the winning ticket of the Victorian doll house raffle at the annual Christmas Bazaar. Here she gets ready to move into her new home. Gina's mom, **Bobbie Jenkins**, and Mercury Auxiliary President **Lin Barker** offer their congratulations. Members of the Contra Costa Auxiliary constructed and custom-furnished the model farm house.*

Capella dinner, <u>The Center Piece</u>, February, 1983

March 21, 1983

Mr. Sal Carson
127 Hardie Drive
Moraga, CA 94556

Dear Sal:

Just a note to thank you once again for your great
cooperation prior to our Spring Event. And your
music was just perfect for our crowd -- varied and
quite "danceable."

My wife, Esther, enjoyed meeting you and asked me to
thank you for playing her favorite song.

Best wishes in all your endeavors.

Sincerely,

Alfred J. Garrotto
Public Relations Director

Letter from Cerebral Palsy Center.
March 21, 1983

☆ ☆ ☆

THE OMELETTE HOUSE in San Mateo will show mothers just how special they are by presenting a carnation to each of the lovely women on their special day (May 8) ... Making plans for a special dining event? ELIAS LOWELL and his staff can accommodate up to 300 people for banquets, receptions, meetings and other gatherings in the spacious party facilities. Ample lighted parking is also available ... PAT COLLINS, the "Hip Hypnotist" who has been entertaining people with her combination of hypnosis, humor and song for over 20 years, is currently appearing in the Lion's Den at the MGM Grand Hotel-Reno. Miss Collins appears twice nightly, except Mondays, through May 24 ... On Friday, April 22, the Tapestry Room at the Press Club of San Francisco will be filled with "Big Band" sounds recalling Goodman, Dorsey and Miller when the renowned SAL CARSON BAND will entertain for "Tea Dancing" 5 to 8 p.m. Carson, talented trumpeter, composer, and vocalist (he led the 49er Band for six years) will present music to please any age group. Tickets are $5 per person. For further information, call 775-7800 ... NINO FREDIANI, billed as "the world's fastest juggler," performs twice nightly in the FLAMINGO HILTON and TOWER stage production, "City Lites." Frediani's act is based on speed and audience participation.

San Mateo Times. April 21, 1983

–239–

THEY COULD HAVE DANCED ALL NIGHT — AND ALMOST DID!

We gave a Tea Dance and *everybody* came!

It started out as an experiment and ended up as an immediate success. "Friday Night Tea Dancing" in the Tapestry Room made its debut on April 22 and a very large turnout insured a repeat on May 13.

Stunning ladies and debonair gentlemen crowded the dance floor and moved with ease to the 'big band' sounds of Sal Carson and his *terrific* Orchestra. (And all for a ridiculously low $5 per person.)

The 'first nighters' want more and more they will get when "Friday Night Tea Dancing" returns mid-May to the Tapestry Room. It looks like an idea whose time has come and we are hoping that it will become a major monthly event.

Spread the word, get out your dance card and call the Front Desk at 775-7800 to book for the "Tea Dance" on Friday, May 13.

THE SOUNDS OF SAL CARSON

TEA DANCERS

Tea Dancing. <u>Scoop</u>. May 2, 1983

SCOOP

published weekly by the
press club of san francisco
• established 1888 •
2,198 members
150 reciprocal clubs, world-wide

RON LENT, Editor

MARION RODMAN, Business Manager

Volume 32, Number 33

Monday, August 15, 1983

(415) 775-7800

Charles Huy Named Chairman of Nominating Committee

Press Club President Dave McElhatton has announced the list of names of the nominating committee for the Fall, 1983 Club election.

McElhatton named Charles Huy as chairman of the seven-member committee. Other nominating committee members are: Richard E. Cruikshank, Dr. Stanley Diamond, Richard Lippke, Charles Phillips, Ernest Rosenthal, and Marcylyn Voth.

The committee will interview candidates for nomination to the Club's board of directors on Tuesdays, August 23 and 30, 1 p.m. to 3 p.m., in the Board Room on the second floor.

For further information, contact Charles Huy at 775-7800.

Golf Tournament Celebrity List Continues to Grow

A spokeswoman for the upcoming Press Club benefit golf tournament has announced the addition of "Green Grocer" Joe Carcione of KGO-TV Ch. 7 and KCBS radio to the list of celebrity participants.

Vickie Jenkins says that 11 other Bay Area media and sports personalities have signed up for the Press Club's benefit Celebrity Golf Tournament at San Ramon on Sunday, Sept. 11. Teeoff time is 11 a.m. at the San Ramon National Club.

In addition to Co-chairmen Dave McElhatton, Frank Dill and Herb Caen, early celebrity sign-ups include: Joel Bartlett, Ch. 5 meteorologist; Don Bleu, KYUU disc jockey; Pete Giddings, Ch. 7 meteorologist; Jan Hutchins, Ch. 36 news anchorman; Bill Moen, KABL; and Mark Soltau, S.F. Examiner golf writer.

Stan Seaman, president of California Trophy and Engraving Co., Inc., will donate a perpetual trophy that will have the names of the winning Best Ball Team and celebrity inscribed on it. Tom Ripp, president of Tom Ripp Co., Inc., will donate a complete stereo set as a major prize.

Assisting Sandy Kahn in coor-

-See page 3

SAL CARSON

Sal Carson Band To Perform At Tea Dance on Friday at 5

The "Big Band" sound will fill the air in the Tapestry Room on Friday, August 19 when the Sal Carson Band performs during "Tea Dancing." The three-hour event begins at 5 p.m.

Carson said Club members are invited to "join us for an evening of fun and dancing to 'Big Band' sounds like Goodman, Dorsey and Miller. There will be music to please any age group."

Carson, known as the man with the great trumpet, has been a Bay Area music scene mainstay for more than 20 years.

Admission is $6 in advance and $7 at the door. For reservations, call the sponsoring Press Club at 775-7800

In a related development, San Francisco FM radio station KALW taped Carson's "Tea Dancing" sounds on July 29 for later broadcasts. Two half-hour shows will be made on Carson for the station's Big Band show later this summer, said KALW Producer-Announcer Ward Glenn.

More Tea Dancing. Scoop. August 15, 1983

Marine Firemen's Union
AFFILIATED WITH THE SEAFARERS INTERNATIONAL UNION OF N. A.
AFL-CIO

BRANCHES
Seattle, Washington
San Pedro, California
Honolulu, Hawaii

240 Second Street
San Francisco, California 94105
(415) 362-4592
Dispatcher: (415) 362-7593

PORTS SERVICED
Portland, Oregon
New York, N.Y.
New Orleans, La.

December 6, 1983

Mr. William Catalano, President
Musicians' Union, Local 6
230 Jones Street
San Francisco, CA 94102

Dear Bill:

On behalf of the officers and membership of the Marine Firemen's Union, I would like to thank you for your assistance in making our October 28 Centennial Celebration a huge success.

Mr. Sal Carson, who was referred by you, and his orchestra were a main attraction at the Sheraton Palace Dinner-Dance and everyone enjoyed the music tremendously.

As mementos of the wonderful occasion, I am sending you our commemorative coaster, an MFOW cap and jacket and our booklet high-lighting the Union's history. I hope you enjoy these small tokens of our appreciation.

Best wishes and warmest personal regards.

Sincerely and fraternally,

Henry "Whitey" Disley
President

HD:sds
Enclosures
cc: Treasurer Joel McCrum

ope-3-afl-cio (76)

Letter from Marine Fireman's Union. December 6, 1983

SAN FRANCISCO'S FESTA ITALIANA

FISHERMAN'S WHARF
PORT TENANTS ASSOCIATION

Michael Geraldi
President

Tony Caselli
Vice President

Pat Flanagan
Vice President

Vic Simi
Secretary

CO-CHAIRMEN
Nunzio S. Alioto
Steve Giraudo

COMMITTEE
Joseph Alioto
Al Baccari
Joe Bonetti
Gary Burns
Steffanie Cincotta
Paul Capurro
Virginia Cresci
Chadwick Ertola
Michael Gallette
Michael Geraldi
Nino Geraldi
Louis Giraudo
Paul Guardino
Lu Hurley
Gloria Pardini
Chuck Podesta
Frank Pompei
Al Scoma
Vic Simi
Tom Traverso

ARCHITECTS
Kotas/Pantaleoni

PUBLIC RELATIONS-
ADVERTISING
Ford Worthing

FISHERMAN'S WHARF, PIER 45 · OCT. 7, 8, 9, & 10 1983

Cabaret Stage

Fri-Sat-Sun

12 - 4	Tony Hall
4:15 - 5:15	Christine Corelli - Carson Band
5:15 - 6:15	Sal Carson Band
6:15 - 7:15	Corelli - Carson Band
7:30 - 11:30	Jimmy Dorsey Band - Lee Castle

Monday

12 - 4	Tony Hall
4:15 - 5:15	Corelli - Carson Band
5:15 - 6:15	Sonny King - Carson Band
6:15 - 7:15	Corelli - Carson Band
7:30 - 11:30	Jimmy Dorsey Band - Lee Castle

Mr. ___
Bud Bunnel
673 -3782

(984) 673-3782

673- 0183

correspondence mailing address: FESTA ITALIANA, PIER 45 SHED A, FISHERMAN'S WHARF, SAN FRANCISCO CA 94133 (415) 474-4825

Festa Italiana. October 7-10, 1983

The Little Jim Club
of
Children's Hospital of San Francisco
Thanks you for attending
Mardi Gras 1984

Carnival !

Saturday, March 10, 1984

Little Jim Club. March 10, 1984

Candidates
for
Queen of the Mardi Gras

Mrs. Judith Keer
Mrs. Alexandra McLagan — *alice*

Candidates
for
King of the Mardi Gras

Mr. Robert Cartwright, Jr.
Dr. William P. Enderlein

Music by Sal Carson's Orchestra
and The International Connection

Entertainment by "Batucaje" Brazilian Music and Dance
Directed by Jose Lorenzo

Benefactors

Mr. and Mrs. Vasant Advani
Anonymous Special Friend
Mr. Romeo Arguelles
 Philippine Consulate General
Campton Place Hotel
Chevron U.S.A., Inc.
Conacher Galleries
Mr. and Mrs. Christopher Covington
C.P.S., A Commercial Real Estate Co.
Mr. Peter H. Dailey
Mr. and Mrs. Ciro Duarte
Mr. Duncan Elkinson
Fireman's Fund Foundation
Mr. Craig Gordon
 San Francisco Comicle
McKesson Foundation
Mr. and Mrs. Robert W. Morey, Jr.
Robert Roth Furs
Sunworld International Airways

Insert for March 10, 1984

Mary Woods,
1984. Worked
with Sal on
many gigs.

Special Olympics party at McArthur Park Restaurant in San Francisco. 1984

Try Fisherman's Cafe for excellent seafood

The personal touch can make a big difference in any dining establishment and that's one of the reasons we return time and time again to *Fisherman's Cafe* at 7001 Geary Blvd. Owners *Tom* and *Shirley Panyacosit* treat customers like family and their friendliness is matched only by the food.

Our most recent visit was on a Tuesday night and our party of five included *Theresa* and *Phil Eubank,* she the proprietor of *Theresa's Beauty Salon* at 5847 Geary Blvd. After our meal, *Phil* said he no longer feels he has to drive his wife to Monterey for a great seafood dinner.

Dinner dancing

SAL CARSON and his band will provide music for dinner dancing the first Wednesday of every month at North Beach Restaurant, 1512 Stockton St. Music will start at 7 p.m. on the lower level of the popular establishment. The cover charge is $6.50 per person. For reservations, call 392-1700.

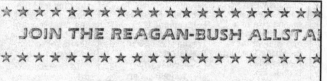

REAGAN-BUSH '84
The President's Authorized Campaign Committee

America needs Ronald Reagan again!
Spirit rides high — be a part of it!

Come hear:

★ **Rosey Grier** ★
L.A. Rams All Pro

★ **Don Newcombe** ★
LA Dodgers Pitcher, Cy Young Award Winner & MVP

★ **Tommy Mason** ★
LA Rams All Pro Halfback

★ **Jeff Kinney** ★
U. Nebraska All American Halfback

★ **Bob St. Clair** ★
49ers All Pro Offensive Tackle

★ **Don Defore** ★
Television Celebrity

★ **Charlie Hickox** ★
1968 Gold Medalist Olympic Swimmer

★ **AND OTHERS!** ★

Plus Sal Carson & his 49er Band
FOR MORE INFORMATION CALL: 986-1984

WHEN:
Thursday, October 18
Rally begins 11:30 a.m.

WHERE:
Justin Herman Plaza
5 Embarcadero Center

Reagan-Bush '84, October 18, 1984. One time Sal played at a political event and later in the day for the opposition party. A gig is a gig.

Bob Tuttle column in the San Francisco Progress. January 27, 1984

–245–

RONNIE SCHELL AND HIS FRIENDS

PHYLLIS DILLER	RONNIE SCHELL	KAY STARR	ROBERT RIDGELY	JACK RILEY	BILL MOEN
★ ★ ★ ★ ★	★ ★ ★ ★ ★	★ ★ ★ ★ ★	★ ★ ★ ★ ★	★ ★ ★ ★ ★	★ ★ ★ ★ ★

PHYLLIS DILLER

This irrepressible lady with her outrageous laugh returns for the second year in a row to Richmond on behalf of the Brookside Hospital Development Foundation.

Miss Diller is recognized as the leading female stand-up comic in the world today. Internationally famous, she has entertained presidents and royalty. She makes frequent appearances in England, Australia and Canada.

Miss Diller is an accomplished pianist and during the past 10 years has appeared as a soloist with more than 100 symphony orchestras across the country.

RONNIE SCHELL

No stranger at all to Bay Area fans, Ronnie returns to his hometown of Richmond for a second year to raise funds for Brookside's special Oncology Unit.

Tonight's stars are hand-picked by Ronnie who has worked with all of them during his more than 25 years in radio, television, movies and the stage.

Born in Richmond's old Cottage Hospital, Ronnie has adopted Brookside as his hometown hospital and sits as a member of the Development Foundation's Associate Board of Trustees.

KAY STARR

The "Wheel of Fortune" started spinning for Miss Starr in the 1950's and turning out hits became second nature for tonight's performer.

To the Oklahoman's credits are "Bonaparte's Retreat," "Side By Side," "The Lonesomest Gal in Town," and "Angry."

Acting is no stranger to Miss Starr's career. She was a regular guest for four years on the Danny Thomas Show.

Her list of accomplishments include awards, gold records, commendations and the sharing with Frank Sinatra "Hit Parade's No. 1 Male and Female Entertainer's" Award.

ROBERT RIDGELY

Bob, who modestly bills himself as "A Star For All Reasons," has more than 100 television drama, sitcoms, and specials to his credit, including appearances on the Bob Newhart and Steve Allen Shows.

A regular in Mel Brooks productions, Bob has exhibited his acting skills in "High Anxiety," and "Blazing Saddles."

Producers of commercials have long recognized his talents, he has been in more than 100. For Saturday morning cartoon buffs, Bob has been heard as the voice of Tarzan, Thundarr the Barbarian, Flash Gordon and scores of other heros, fiends and tiny animals.

JACK RILEY

A favorite of prime-time viewers, Jack has a string of successes, including the "Bob Newhart Show," "Barney Miller," "M.A.S.H.," "Mary Tyler Moore," "Hart to Hart," "Love Boat," "Different Strokes," and "One Day at a Time."

Jack has also done several movies which include "Catch-22," "McCabe and Mrs. Miller," "Frances," and "Butch and Sundance-The Early Years."

"The pinnacle of my film career," Jack says, "came when I was asked to play in a science fiction spoof, The Attack of the Killer Tomatoes. It made the list as one of the 25 worst films of all times."

BILL MOEN

Bay Area disc jockeys don't come any higher, figuratively-speaking, than KABL's morning personality, Bill Moen.

For the second year in a row, Bill has swept the Oakland Tribune contest to determine the area's "Top Jock." Bill has been with KABL 24 years and his talent for distilling the fun from the events of everyday life— even his wife, daughter and son are not spared—has consistently put him on the top of various listener polls.

Bill is designing a shrine for the plaque he won as "Top Jock." He describes it as "something with a waterfall and madonna, something simple and tasteful."

Insert, Ronnie Schell

Evening with Ronnie Schell. October 28, 1984. Benefit for Brookside's

Flyer for the benefit.

Program for Ronnie Schell benefit.

HORSE SENSE: Bandleader Sal Carson has a sideline, operating a horse ranch outside of Reno. Every morning he practiced on his trumpet which at first startled the 32 riding horses but since Sal gave them carrots and apples after each solo concert all went well the first week. Then, calamity. Horses that were rented out for trail rides, upon hearing the glissandos and tripple tongueing would, despite all the tugging of reins, turn and bolt for home and those Carson handouts. Sal is no longer the early morning bugler.

Sal's ranch article probably by Herb Caen.
Mid '80's

At the ranch,
1985.

SAL CARSON'S RENO PROPERTY
INTERSTATE 80
ON THE TRUCKEE RIVER

Four miles West of downtown RENO on the Mogul off-ramp (Exit 7 of Interstate 80) is the location of the Sal Carson Ranch.

Prime location for a Resort-HOTEL-Casino and/or Townhouse or Retirement Center. This beautiful 49 acre ranch along the Truckee River, runs along Interstate 80 with both On & Off Ramps leading directly to the property. Contiguous to the all new RIVER INN HOTEL CASINO and European Style Health Spa that is scheduled to open in May 1987.

PROPERTY INCLUDES:

1) Valuable WATER Rights (50 Miner's Inches) or 98 Acre Feet.

2) Joins to United States Government Land.

3) 2,000 ft. of TRUCKEE RIVER frontage on each side of the river.

4) South of the river is a fantastic possibility for a Ski Resort & Cross Country Skiing area.

5) Geo-Thermal possibilities and development of Hot Sprins. The Hot Springs of the River Inn are only 150' from the Carson Property.

6) Improvements include a six bedroom home, 12 stall stable, corrals and tack room.

LOCATION:

1) Along Interstate 80, West from downtown RENO, Next to the RIVER INN CASINO.

2) West of the property, The BELLI RANCH PROPERTY has completed construction Of 70 luxury home sites.

3) 1 ½ miles west of the property is the BOOMTOWN HOTEL/CASINO COMPLEX. The complex plans include an 18 Hole Golf Course, a 525 Room Hotel, A Shopping Area plus a 300 unit RV Park.

4) Across Interstate 80 (north of the Property) are several beautiful new sub-divisions which includes MOGUL HEIGHTS, MOGUL MEADOWS, and CENTEX HOMES. About 400 homes are completed and sold. There are 200 new sites now under development.

5) Between the Carson Property and downtown RENO, (on the north side of Interstate 80) is the NORTHGATE DEVELOPMENT. Which includes 1500 homes and a new Championship Golf Course.

6) On the property across the Truckee River (south-east from the Carson Ranch) is the INDIAN HILL DEVELOPMENT. A 300 Homes planned community.

Water and Sewer lines from Reno are at an expected hook-up date of Fall 1987. This cancels any need for septic tanks or water wells.

Sal's property on the Truckee River. Mid '80's.

"San Francisco Long Ago", 1985

SCOOP

published weekly by the
press club of san francisco
• established 1888 •
2,198 members
180 reciprocal clubs, world-wide

GEOFFREY FISHER, Editor

Volume 34, Number 18   Monday, April 29, 1985   (415) 775-7800

Terry Lowry to Get Plaque At Cinco de Mayo Festival

When Terry Lowry is honored as the special guest at the Press Club's celebration of Cinco de Mayo, Friday, May 3, Terry will be presented a special plaque for her contributions to the medium of television and for her service to the community.

Terry, the co-host of Channel 7's morning talk show "AM San Francisco," is one of the Bay Area's most popular television personalities.

Terry began co-anchoring the weekend news at KGO-TV in February 1981 after having started her broadcasting career at Channel 4 (KRON-TV) in December, 1970 when she translated the evening news into Spanish for simulcast on radio. She later did weather reporting, hosted and produced a bilingual public affairs program for the Hispanic community and hosted a variety of public affairs programs. In 1975 she became co-anchor of the noon news and eventually moved into the weekend news slot.

In September, 1982 she began co-hosting A.M. San Francisco with her husband, Fred LaCosse.

Terry Lowry has always given generously of her time to community organizations and has received numerous awards for her community work, including being named Woman of the Year by the League of United Latin American Citizens (LULAC) for 1982.

Another major feature of the Cinco de Mayo dinner will be the Sal Carson band that will provide the music for dancing. Carson, who has received rave notices from a broad spectrum of luminaries, including former First Lady Rosalynn Carter, Mayor Dianne Feinstein, former San Francisco Mayor Joe Alioto and former Governor of California Jerry Brown, tells SCOOP that he will play a wide range of "my favorite oldtime swing and bee-bop hits along with the newest from the Top 40 such as Michael Jackson, Neil Diamond and Lionel Ritchie."

With Sal Carson calling the shots there will probably be some favorites from Glenn Miller and Harry James.

As the former band leader for the San Francisco 49ers, Sal Carson composed and

Sal Carson And His Trumpet

recorded the 49ers song, "49ers So Proud and Bold." He has recorded the album "Vic Damone In San Francisco," an album that was recorded live in North Beach. The album is available in leading music stores.

San Francisco Progress columnist Jack Rosenbaum says that Carson "known as San Francisco's Music Man is an accomplished trumpeter, composer and vocalist. His band has a reputation for being able to please every type of audience."

Cinco de Mayo is a day for celebration for

See LOWRY Page 3

Transportation Seminar In Monterey, May 10 & 11

The San Francisco Transportation Council, an operating organization of the Press Club, will hold its annual Spring Transportation Seminar Friday and Saturday, May 10 and May 11 at Del Monte Hyatt in Monterey.

The theme of the Seminar will be "Transportation Bridges International Trade and Domestic Commerce."

Cinco de Mayo Festival. April 29, 1985. Scoop

Lindy Rockey, 1985. A vocalist who worked with Sal. "A gorgeous person and singer".

Letter from the Chief of Police. July 9, 1985

EXIT SMILING: "By golly, when I go I want a brass band playing 'When the Saints Go Marching In'," and by golly, that's what he got. Those words were uttered by atty. John Philip Coghlan Jr., a partner in Chickering & Gregory and a one-time mayor of Hillsborough, who died at 70. At the funeral services in Old St. Mary's last Thurs., attended by hundreds of his friends, Sal Carson's Dixieland band played tunes throughout what the priest called "a celebration," and most of the men honored Coghlan's request that they wear bow ties, his trademark. As the huge crowd filed out — the family hand-in-hand — Carson played "Saints," and the tears that everybody had tried to hold back came rolling down.

Herb Caen's column. San Francisco Chronicle. May 7, 1986.

The annual Festa Italiana, October 3-5, 1986

SCOOP

Volume 38, No. 3
Monday, January 26, 1987
415/775-7800

Established 1888

A Melody For The Consular Corps

Press Club President, Al Burgin and Tina Burgess Coan honor Columbia's Consul General with a commemorative plaque.

The Consular Corps celebrated a tea dance at the San Francisco Press Club, and it was a wonderful affair. The music of Sal Carson brought the old and the young to the dance floor.

Led by the Consul General of Spain, Don Domingo Sanchez, the Consular Corp paid tribute to one of its members, Dr. Joaquin Mejia Figueredo, Consul General from Columbia, and to his wife, Maria Teresa who will be departing for their homeland soon.

Assisting in the celebration was Ines Llano-Wells, the retired Consul of Col-

umbia and Rev. Dr. Jack Hencier, CMF, who recited the prayers of St. Francis. Vaya con Dios mi amor.

By Tina Burgess Coan

SCOOP DEADLINE

All written contributions to the weekly *Scoop* are due by 5 p.m. Friday. Photos should be in no later than noon on Tuesday.

—The Editor

Scoop January 26, 1987

3/27/87

Sal Carson Band at two benefits

Sal Carson and his 28-piece orchestra will team up with *Vic Damone* for a dinner dance tomorrow, March 28, at the *Fairmont's Grand Ballroom*.

It will be a benefit for the National Italian-American Foundation and the Casa Costanza Home for Aged Italians. We can't imagine a more enjoyable combination of show, dinner, and dancing. Here is a chance that may not come again. Call 467-3500 for reservations.

Sal can also be heard live with his six-piece Dixieland group on *KGO* and *ABC's* radio telethon tonight, Friday, March 27. Sal's band will kick off this worthy event at 7 p.m. and play till 8 p.m. The donations pledged will go to fight cancer and leukemia.

Casa Costanza Home benefit. Vic Damone joined Sal for the event. March 27, 1987 <u>San Francisco Progress</u>

Vic Damone
A publicity photo.

Tea Dancers. January 26, 1987

The news has just leaked that *Sal Carson* and his 27-piece orchestra will team up with *Vic Damone* for a dinner dance on Saturday, March 28, at the *Fairmont's Grand Ballroom*. It will be a benefit for the *Na-*

CARSON

tional Italian-American Foundation and the *Casa Costanza Home for Aged Italians.* Call 467-3500 for more information.

More Casa Costanza
coverage

The following prominent citizens have made important contributions to the Italian Amerian Community of Northern California and have been so recognized by the Foundation:

John Bracco
Irene Dallis
Romano Della Santina
Ralph D. Giovanniello
Senator Milton Marks
Marino Nibbi
Frank J. Petrini
Senator David A. Roberti
Joseph P. Russoniello
Hon. John A. Volpe

The National Italian Amerian Foundation is dedicated to promulgating the positive contributions and achievements of Italian Americans in our society. They seek to be advocates for Americans of Italian ancestry by recognizing outstanding accomplishments of individuals, by providing funds for scholarships and internships, and by promoting a greater understanding of those values that are uniquely derived from our Italian heritage.

Proceeds from this event will also benefit San Francisco's **Casa Costanzo,** the only low-cost housing project for aged Italian and Italian Americans in our community.

*The National
Italian American
Foundation*

*Seventh Annual
Awards Dinner
San Francisco, California*

Cover of program. March 28, 1987

Casa Costanza, inside the cover

GOLDEN GATE BRIDGE 50th ANNIVERSARY CELEBRATION
ENTERTAINMENT SCHEDULE OF EVENTS
★

SMALL MARINA GREEN

1:00	Dana Smith & His Performing Dog, Sunshine Backyard Circus
1:30	Brassworks of San Francisco
2:00	Dana Smith & His Performing Dog, Sunshine Backyard Circus
2:30	Brassworks of San Francisco
3:00	Bill Okal, The Congenial Conjurer Backyard Circus
3:30	Brassworks of San Francisco
4:00	Bill Okal, The Congenial Conjurer Backyard Circus
4:30	Brassworks of San Francisco
1:00 - 5:00	Clowns, Jugglers, Mimes, Stilt-Walker
	Corey Foreman
	James Hamilton
	Skip Hines
	Marti Kate
	Drew Letchworth
	Tracy Long
	Squeaky the Clown
	Mary Struthers
	Paul Willis
	Pat Wyatt
2:00 - 4:00	Japanese Wheat Gluten Blower

AQUATIC PARK

1:00 - 1:45	60th Military Airlift Wing Band
1:45 - 3:45	Navy Band
3:45 - 4:30	1st Marine Division Band

CRISSY FIELD PERFORMANCE AREA

2:00	U.S. Army Band
2:30	Peninsula Banjo Band
2:55	The Flips
3:05	Murphy's Irish Dancers
3:45	Taiko Do Jo
4:00	Coast Guard Search & Rescue
4:20	Samba de Alegria
4:50	Air Force Fly By
5:05	Dinosaurs
5:30	Precision Parachutists
5:40	Helicopter Demonstration
5:45	Zasu Pitts Memorial Orchestra
6:30	The Flips
6:45	Tony Marty, Official Song/Dick Crest
6:55	Event of the Year with Michael Pritchard
7:15	Maxine Andrews/Dick Crest
7:35	San Francisco Symphony set up
8:00	U.S. Army Band, Fifty State Flags, Color Guard
8:02	National Anthem
8:04	Mayor Dianne Feinstein
8:06	Carol Channing
8:15	San Francisco Symphony
8:55	Tony Bennett/San Francisco Symphony
9:10	Finale
9:15	Fireworks

Entertainment Schedule for the bridge anniversary. Page 1

FORT POINT

10:30 - 1:00	Sal Carson Trio - Original Songs and Poetry
10:30 - 10:45	Introduction and Kick-Off Dance Through Time Performers
10:45 - 11:00	3rd Place Original Poem and Song
11:00 - 11:15	Original Songs and Poems
11:15 - 11:30	2nd Place Original Poem and Song
11:30 - 11:45	Orignial Songs and Poems
11:45 - 12:00	Original Songs and Poems
12:00 - 12:15	1st Place Original Song and Poem
12:15 - 12:30	Sal Carson Trio
12:30 - 12:40	Presentation of Exerpts from "San Francisco USA"
1:00 - 1:20	The San Francisco Synthesizer Ensemble
1:30 - 5:00	Turk Murphy Tribute — Dixieland and Jazz Concert
1:30 - 2:15	Bert Carelli and the Royal Street Band
2:15 -3:00	The Golden State Jazz Band
3:00 - 4:00	Don Neely's Royal Society Jazz Orchestra *Sal, contractor*
4:00 - 5:00	Pat Yankee with Phil Howe and the Jazz Band

GREAT MEADOW
MC for the day — Jeremy S. Kramer

10:45 - 11:00	Filipiniana Dance Troupe
11:00 - 11:15	De Zevensprong Holland American Club of Seattle
11:15 - 11:30	Cornmashers/Appalachian Cloggers
11:35 -12:05	Los Danzantes Folklorico's with Mariachi Azteca
12:10 - 12:25	Chitresh Das Dance Company
12:30 - 1:00	ODC/San Francisco
1:20 - 1:50	Sal Carson Orchestra
2:05 - 2:45	Tropical Sounds with Dancers
3:00 - 3:10	Chinese Fold Dance Association/The Festival Dance
3:10 - 3:20	Lay Tap Floor
3:25 - 3:40	Rosie Radiator and her Super Tappers
3:55 - 4:30	Glide Ensemble
4:45 - 5:15	Swing Fever with Mary Stallings
5:30 - 6:00	Bandido

MARINA GREEN

1:00	Pottstown, Pennsylvania High School Marching Band Northern California Combat Model Airplane Demonstration Team
1:15	Mira Loma High School Marching Band
1:30	Capuchino High School Marching Band Dos Pueblos High School Jazz Band World Champion Frisbee Dogs
1:45	San Francisco City Freedom Day Marching Band and Twirling Corps San Francisco Flag Team Dos Pueblos Concert Band
2:00	San Francisco Hoover Middle School Jazz Band National Champion Acro Sport Team Riata Ranch Cowboy Girls Trick Ropers The Outdoor Recreation Bike and Skate Demonstration Team of San Francisco
2:15	Foothill High School Show and Marching Band
2:30	San Francisco Aptos Middle School Jazz Band Northern California Combat Model Airplane Demonstration Team All-Star Professional Street Demonstration Skateboarders
3:00	Fortuna and Arroyo High School Marching Bands San Francisco Mission High School Jazz Band Matt Plendle Hula Hoop Champion Cardio Kids Jump Rope Demonstration Team Quick Silver and Kitemakers of San Francisco Demonstration (until 5:00 PM)
3:15	National Champion Acro Sport Team with Dan Hoff Riata Ranch Cowboy Girls Trick Ropers
3:30	California High School Marching Band Richmond High School Jazz Band The Outdoor Recreation Bike and Skateboard Demonstration Team of San Francisco
3:45	San Ramon High School Marching Band Matt Plendle Hula Hoop Champion
4:00	Stanford University Marching Band Wu Shu Martial Arts Demonstration All-Star Professional Street Demonstration Skateboarders
4:30	Santa Barbara High School Marching Band World Champion Frisbee Dogs
ALL DAY	Antique Car Display with 150 Vehicles Dixieland Bands Golden Gate Bridge 1937 Cheerleaders

Entertainment Schedule for the bridge anniversary. Page 2

Turk Murphy was born December 16, 1914 in Palermo, CA and died May 30, 1987 in San Francisco. His band was at the bridge anniversary.

Golden Gate Bridge. 50th anniversary. May 24, 1987. Sal was the contractor for five bands including his band.

Pat Yankee was there with Phil Howe's
Jazz Band

USF Banquet

The *Sal Carson* band
will provide music for
the 100th annual ban-
quet of the USF Alum-
ni Association schedul-
ed April 16 at The
Galleria, 101 Henry
Adams St. Nine
members of The God-
fathers Club will be
r e c o g n i z e d f o r
celebrating their 50th
class reunion from
USF.

USF Banquet. Late 80's

Entertainment

Bandleader

Trumpeter's at home in Bay Area

By Deborah Carvalho
Staff writer

Many people recognize the
name Joe Carcione, TV's Green
Grocer. But how many know the
name Sal Carcione? How about Sal
Carson?

Carson is one of the Bay Area's
best-known bandleaders. When his
name began appearing on marquees he changed it from Carcione
to Carson. Oh, and yes, he is related to the Green Grocer — they are
first cousins.

Today, Carson, who has recorded with many artists including Vic
Damone, said he plays "everybody's favorite music" including
some pop songs.

A Moraga resident, Carson is
best known for his 16-piece big
band. However, he does have
smaller Dixieland groups, two of
which will be featured at the upcoming Golden Gate Bridge celebration on Sunday along with his
big band.

The 58-year-old bandleader was
born in San Francisco but moved
to Oakland when he was about 10.
Carson graduated from University
High School in Oakland in 1947.

Music has always been a big
part of Carson's life. His father,
Guiseppi Carcione, was an opera
singer with an San Francisco company. Carson recalled going to rehearsals and watching his father
perform. "It gave me respect for
good music."

However, instead of singing,
Carson took up the banjo when he

MORAGA RESIDENT Sal
Carson, above, leads his big
band, right, at San Francisco 49er games, where the
band held forth from 1974
to 1979.

The Sal Carson Band
16-piece big band at Great Meadows
above Fort Mason in San Francisco 2
p.m. Sunday. Two Dixieland bands at
the Marina Gardens in San Francisco
1:30 p.m. Sunday. Carson will be guest
disc jockey at Magic 61 (610 AM) noon
June 12.

was 11. He later switched to the
trumpet. "I remember going to the
Golden Gate Theatre in San Francisco and listening to to this guy
step up to the microphone and do a
trumpet solo. From that moment
on I knew the trumpet was the
right intrument for me," he said.

Ever since Carson has keyed in
on the trumpet and has opted to
sing only on a rare occasion.
"When I do sing it's usually stuff
like Frank Sinatra. Singing just
isn't my forte."

As a teen-ager Carson had his

Deborah Carvalho column, <u>Contra Costa Times</u>. May
21, 1987 (Continued on opposite page 257)

Carson has a comfortable niche

own eight-piece band that played at Oakland's Clarmont Junior High School. Later, he studied trumpet with Oakland's Leo DeMers.

It wasn't until Carson did a three-year stint in the Army during World War II that he honed his band directing skills. He was in charge of a band in Sioux City, Iowa and also traveled the USO circuit.

Carson said he was influenced by many of the big-band leaders in the '30s and '40s such as Benny Goodman, Harry James and Glenn Miller. "I remember listening to their records when I was growing up."

The musician recalled first no-

ticing the big bands back in 1937. "After hearing that music, I knew it was my future. That was my only ambition from then on. To be a bandleader and have my own band was like a dream come true."

Carson formed his first professional seven-piece band in 1946 to play at Hoberg's Resort in Lake County. His shows would draw 2,000 people.

The bandleader also admitted that he once had dreams of a national career, but felt he was at a disadvantage. "Bands like Dorsey and Miller were in a league by themselves. They established their careers with recordings during the war years and it was impossible for

anyone to break in after that."

Still, Carson believes he has built a good following in Northern California. He has several recordings to his credit including appearing on the "Vic Damone In San Francisco" album. Carson plans to release a cassette of his music on the Astro label this summer. "Everybody's Favorite Music" will feature his 16-piece band and include such standards as "Evergreen."

"We did research to find out what kind of music people wanted to hear. There is even the pop hit "MacArthur's Park" on the cassette. The back side includes an opera aida."

Aside from playing the Bay

Area venue, Carson has done the Lake Tahoe-Reno circuit and played with the San Francisco 49ers band from 1974-79.

Looking back on his career, Carson said the Damone album, which featured Carson's 33-piece band, ranks high on the list. He also enjoyed his six years with the 49ers and has fond memories of playing at Hoberg's. "That's where I really got my start. I played there for 20 summers from 1948 through '68."

Musically, Carson plans to continue playing his brand of big-band music. "That's what I enjoy the most."

Deborah Carvalho column, <u>Contra Costa Times</u>. May 21, 1987 (Continued from opposite page 256)

S.F. bandleader Sal Carson, sitting quietly in the audience at The Nugget in Sparks, suddenly found himself spotlighted. The star of the show, Barbara Eden, had seen him and launched into a recital how Carson "discovered me in San Francisco more years ago than I care to rememember." As Barbara Huffman, she was a secretary at S & C Motors by day and sang with the Carson band on weekends. She became Miss San Francisco in 1951, went to Hollywood — and, as Barbara Eden, found triple-threat fame, TV, movies and stage.

Article about Barbara Eden and Sal. ca 1989

Carson, Fennerman will help entertain

Sal Carson

by Mary Pusheck

He is called "San Francisco's music man" for a good reason. Few men have captured the mood and admiration of a city as Sal Carson has in San Francisco.

Carson and his orchestra will be brought to Rossmoor by Home Savings and Loan Association to entertain in the afternoon program at All States Day on Saturday, Aug. 15.

Carson and his orchestra were at the hub of the famous "Battle of the Bands" that was held at the St. Francis Hotel in the 50's. Since then, Carson has been a featured performer at many of San Francisco's top entertainment spots, including the Hyatt Regency, Sheraton Palace, Fairmont and Hilton hotels. Out-of-state engagements at Harvey's Hotel "Top of the Wheel" in Lake Tahoe and the Ponderosa Hotel and Holiday Lodge in Reno have offered his music mastery to vacationers, but Sal has always maintained his base of operation in San Francisco.

Groucho Marx as the straight man on radio and TV versions of "You Bet Your Life."

Groucho paid Fenneman the ultimate compliment saying he was the "perfect straight man." That really choked Fenneman up, who, as a high school student in San Francisco, worshipped the Marx brothers and particularly Groucho, who he thought was the funniest man in the world.

Fenneman was born in Peking, China. His father, in the import export business, returned to the United States with his wife when George was nine months old. He grew up in the West Portal section of San Francisco and attended S.F. State College, receiving his bachelor's degree in English and drama in 1942.

Hoping to make more money than his new school teacher wife, Peggy, George began auditioning for local radio shows. KSFO hired him at $35 a week. In six months time he was earning the comfortable salary of $55 a week at the ABC radio affiliate in town.

Among Fenneman's early radio credits are Dial for Dollars, Serutan News, "Dr. Kate," and the Abbott and Costello show.

A move to southern California in the mid-40's led to "You Bet Your Life." He is often asked if the people on the program were set up. "We had a staff who

George Fenneman

looked for regular American folk, although we did get some way out ones. They were thoroughly interviewed so we would know their life story and funny areas but Groucho never met them before they came on camera," he says. Each show had a $10,000 budget in the hopes that someone would win the big prize.

Today Fenneman keeps quite busy as a representative of Home Savings and Loan. He is also anchorman for the Southern California public service television program, "On Campus." Recently he was off-camera announcer for the Donny and Marie Osmond show. As host for NBC's "Talk About Pictures" he won an Emmy in 1974. That program, which deals with the work of famous photographers, is currently in syndication.

All of Rossmoor is invited to attend and enjoy this fine entertainment. A complete time schedule for the day will be printed next Wednesday.

Sal and George Fennerman. August 15, 1987

Sal Carson's dance bands have long been music to our ears

By Ed Levitt
The Tribune 10/4/87

The band leader known as "San Francisco's Music Man" spent his early life in Oakland and the last 21 years in Moraga.

But the cities all seem to blend together if you're Sal Carson.

"If it's out West," he says, "I've played them all."

The Sal Carson band appeared at the Holiday Lodge in Reno one night several years ago when in walked Harry James.

"I spent the next few hours entertaining my idol," Carson recalls.

Imagine — playing the trumpet and featuring all the James classics for Harry James himself, the top trumpet player of his time.

"Harry loved it. We ended the evening drinking 19 martinis."

Carson knows the number, he says, "only because the bartender told me the next day."

But nobody has to tell Carson about musical numbers. "In 40 years as a band leader," he says, "I've played thousands of songs — mostly for dancing."

Yet his most memorable engagement was not for dancers. From 1974 through 1979, the Sal Carson band played at all San Francisco 49ers home games.

"I remember playing the Star Spangled Banner for the first time at Candlestick Park and getting the jitters," he says.

Eastbay PEOPLE

"I walked alone to midfield. I began playing my trumpet solo. I felt nervous. My legs shook. My hands shivered. But I did it — I finished playing the National Anthem without missing a note."

On another afternoon, he recalls, "Drew Pearson of the Dallas Cowboys streaked downfield for a pass — and ran right into the bandstand, wiping out our trombone section."

A football fan, Carson enjoyed playing for 49er fans. He even composed the 49er team song.

"Then they brought in some rock and roll outfit," he says with a shrug.

But Carson is still busy. One recent weekend he led his band at the Sheraton in Concord, Sigmund Stern Grove in San Francisco and for a wedding in Napa.

He also has made a recording with singer Vic Damone, leading a 33-piece orchestra.

But Carson, whose real name is Carcione ("I'm Joe 'The Green Grocer' Carcione's first cousin"), performs mainly at parties.

He has played for former first lady Rosalynn Carter, Gov. Deukmejian, 49ers owner Edward DeBartolo Jr., San Francisco mayoral candidate John Molinari and film director Francis Coppola.

He also books bands — all carrying the Sal Carson name.

"More than half of our dates are scheduled out of San Francisco — mostly within 50 miles of my Moraga home," he says.

By Lonnie Wilson/The Tribune

Proud Sal Carson brandishes a trumpet and recently cut album in the yard of his Moraga home.

Carson assembles bands for virtually all musical tastes: jazz, Dixieland, ballroom, top 40 rock.

"Private parties," he says, "that's where the band money is today. The ballrooms, nightclubs, hotels are vanishing as sources for big band jobs."

Forced to change with the times, Carson now puts together trios and six-piece combos.

"This is the '80s. You must be versatile to survive. So I hook up electrical instruments. I play the hit tunes of today. I also incorporate songs from the '50s — all very popular now. And I play our favorites from the '40s.

"We bring our own electric Yamaha piano, our own public address system and our own speakers. You've got to use your own equipment to get the right sound — the sound of the '80s."

He may have been less particular when he started leading a band in 1947 at Hoberg's, then a resort in Lake County.

"I played at Hoberg's 20 straight summers. More than 2,000 people danced to my music every night. I met my wife on the dance floor."

Ed Levitt column in <u>The Oakland Tribune</u>. October 4, 1987

Astro Records. 1987

St. Francis Hotel, San Francico.   Menu cover, 1988

The Band at the St. Francis Hotel, late 80's. (l to r) Top: Tom Markem, Sal, Mary Woods, Jerry Stucker, Tony Ramos. In front: Gordy Fels

St. Francis Hotel postcard

THE BAND THAT COMES TO PLAY!

SAL CARSON BAND AND COMBO'S

MARY WOODS, vocalist

Swing, Jazz, Rock, Dixieland, Latin, Country, Ballads, Big Band, and Single Entertainer

Carson's outstanding success and expertise over the years will provide you music and entertainment for any occasion

Remember! Live music *makes* the party

SAL CARSON BAND AND COMBO'S
Tel/Fax 925.254.1881
127 Hardie Drive
Moraga, California 94556

Band mailer, late 80's

Mary Woods and Sal, late 80's

Mary Woods,
1989 at The
Fairmont
Hotel

Friends of the Alameda Parks Present

"*Follow Me*"

Friday Evening
February Nineteenth,
Nineteen hundred and eighty-eight

Dancing 8:30 till 11:30 P.M.
To the Big Band sound of
Sal Carson and his Orchestra

$15.00 per person
The Elks Rathskeller

2255 Santa Clara Avenue   Alameda, California 94501
TICKETS: 522-4100 Alameda Rec. Dept. OR 522-3467

*Proceeds to be used for the Alameda Parks

Alameda Parks dinner dance.
February 19, 1988

THE 5 CALIFORNIAS

California Office of Tourism • 1121 L Street, Suite 103 • Sacramento, California 95814 • (916) 322-1396 • Telex

March 21, 1988

Mr. Sal Carson
Sal Carson's Orchestra
127 Hardie Drive
Moraga, CA 94556

Dear Sal,

On behalf of Governor Deukmejian, the California Office
of Tourism, and myself, please accept our thanks for
your participation in the Fifth Annual Governor's
Conference on Tourism, March 2, 1988.

This year marks the fourth year your marvelous orchestra
has provided music for the Governor's reception and dinner
and each year it adds a "high note" to the festivities.

The Conference has become the premier event for the leadership of California's tourism industry, attracting repre-
sentatives from every area of the state. It provides a
forum for learning about tourism trends and offers an
opportunity to exchange ideas with the people who help
shape the state's $35 billion industry.

As you know, much of the business of tourism consists of
providing ways for people to have a good time. Thanks again
for doing your part to bring good music to the Conference.

Most cordially,

Diane

Diane Donian
Deputy Director
California Office of Tourism

California Office of Tourism letter. March 21, 1988

SAN FRANCISCANS FOR THE
HOMEPORTING OF THE U.S.S. MISSOURI
CORDIALLY INVITES YOU
TO A BENEFIT DINNER
AT THE

FAIRMONT HOTEL
ATOP NOB HILL
IN THE GRAND BALLROOM
WEDNESDAY, JUNE 15, 1988

Master of Ceremonies: The Honorable Joseph Alioto

Guest Speakers: United States Senator, The Honorable Pete Wilson
Speaker of the Assembly, The Honorable Willie Brown
California State Senator, The Honorable Quentin Kopp
The Honorable Dianne Feinstein
Captain Theodore Krumm, U.S.N.
Joseph P. Mazzola

Honored Guests: Congresswoman Nancy Pelosi, California State Senator Milton Marks,
Supervisor Wendy Nelder, Supervisor John Molinari, Supervisor Willie Kennedy, Supervisor Thomas Hsieh
Supervisor Jim Gonzalez, Supervisor Bill Maher

Music and Presentation of Colors, Provided by the U.S. Navy Band

No Host Cocktails 6:30   Dancing to the music of   Semi-Formal
Dinner   7:30   Sal Carson Orchestra   R.S.V.P. Card Enclosed

Home porting
of the USS
Missouri.
June 15,
1988

Cinco de Mayo   Dinner-Dance

Friday May 5, 1989
555 Post
San Francisco

Cinco de Mayo dinner dance. May
5, 1989

6:00pm Mariachi Music 2nd Floorloung

7:30pm Dinner Tapestry Room

Brazilian Samba Floor Show

Presentation of Awards

Dancing until Midnight to the

music of Sal Carson

Rsvp: Please make payable
and mail by April 20 to:

Senora TINA BURGESS COAN
59 Chabot Terrace, S.F. 94118
(415) 668-8686

Cost $30 (No Host Cocktails)

Cinco de Mayo program

Goodby Kezar, 1989. "It was a big party the day before the demolition. Lots of football players were there".

The San Francisco Recreation and Park Department
and
Friends of Recreation and Parks

PRESENT

GOOD-BYE OLD KEZAR

Schedule of Events:
7:00 to 7:45	Sal Carson and his Orchestra
	Riordan High School Band
7:45 to 8:00	National Anthem with Scott Beach
	Mary Burns
	R. C. Owens
	49er Gold Rush
8:00 to 8:45	Sal Carson and his Orchestra
8:45 to 9:15	USF Cheerleaders
	R. C. Owens introduces Alumni Players
	Auction of Signed Footballs--Scott Beach
	49er Gold Rush
9:15 to 10:00	Sal Carson and his Orchestra
10:00 to 10:15	USF Cheerleaders
	Polytechnic Cheer
	All Schools Pep Rally
	Auction of Signed Footballs--Scott Beach
10:15 to 11:00	Sal Carson and his Orchestra

Kezar program.

Forty-Four Years of Service
BOYS' TOWNS OF ITALY
BALL OF THE YEAR

SATURDAY, MAY 13, 1989
FAIRMONT HOTEL
SAN FRANCISCO

"Ball of the Year"

PROGRAM

Welcome .... Larry Nibbi

Entertainment .... Sergio Franchi

Greetings from the Children .... Rt. Rev. Monsignor
John Patrick Carroll-Abbing
Founder and President

Presentation of Awards:
"Man of the Year" .... John Bracco

"Michelangelo D'Oro Children of the World Award" .... Larry Nibbi

Music .... Sal Carson
and his Orchestra

Closing Remarks .... Larry Nibbi

"Ball of the Year". May 13, 1989

"Ball of the Year" program

Sergio Franchi was born April 6, 1926 in Italy. He died May 1, 1990 in Stonington, CT. which was a very sad day for Sal.

Tea dancing flyer. Gig was once a week for five or six months.

DEPARTMENT OF THE NAVY

USS CARL VINSON (CVN-70)
FLEET POST OFFICE
SAN FRANCISCO. CA. 96629-2840

6 September 1989

Mr. Sal Carson
127 Hardie Drive
Moraga, CA 94556

Dear Mr. Carson,

On behalf of all the Battlestar crewmembers, I want to express our sincere gratitude for the entertainment of the "Big Band" sounds provided by your group on our recent Dependents' Day Cruise.

Even today, we continue to receive numerous letters from people who experienced "a day at sea" with "San Francisco's Own."

Enclosed you will find 22 "CARL VINSON" ballcaps and 22 rare 5X7 photographs of the ship returning to San Francisco with all the aircraft on board, as suggested by a close friend of the ship, Mr. Jack Block. What makes the photograph rare is the normal operating procedure is to launch all the aircraft back to their home air stations, along the West Coast, prior to entering the bay. They fly back and land on board when we leave.

Again, thank you for everything you did that made our cruise such a tremendous success.

Sincerely,

DOUG HOCKING
Lieutenant Commander, U.S. Navy

Letter from the Lieutenant Commander, U.S. Navy. September 6, 1989

HYATT RICKEYS

IN PALO ALTO

4219 EL CAMINO REAL
PALO ALTO, CALIFORNIA 94306

Hot Sounds
Poolside

Fridays 5 PM to 8 PM
Dancing•Listening•Entertainment

Featuring Sal Carson Big Band
August 4 - August 25

Magic 61
and the
Bob Dini Orchestra
September 1, 1989

Clip this coupon for Hot Sounds Poolside
$1.00 off per drink
Limit 1 coupon per person
Valid August 4 - September 1

Hyatt Rickeys. August 4-25, 1989

Sacramento Hilton Inn flyer for New Years Eve

Mr. Sal Carson
127 Hardie Drive
Moraga, CA   94556

Reference: April 25, 1990
              SUZANNE SOMERS SHOW
              OVERTIME

Dear Sal:

Enclosed is our check in the amount of $614.00,
which is the overtime you billed us for the
above date.

The tape of VIC DAMONE arrived, and it is very
good, and we really appreciate your sending it
to us.

You did a fine job on the show, and we look
forward to working with you the next time we
have a San Francisco date.

We leave on Thursday for Chicago, where we have
HARRY CONNICK, JR. on a date, and we return on
May 21st. Should you want to contact us for any
reason, you can always reach us through our office.

Again, our thanks, Sal.

              Cordially,

              Phillip J. Consolo

PJC:ec
enc. chk. $614.00

(sidebar, vertical text) UNITED ATTRACTIONS, INC. 213 WILD HORSE DRIVE PALM DESERT, CA 92260 619-340-0582

Suzanne Somers Show letter, April 25, 1990

Jerry Stucker,
Interstate – 80 Band
Sal's other band.

Chapter 10
The 90's

The 90's will be remembered for all the afternoon tea dances in the Greater Bay Area. Sal played quite a few tea dances and the Hyatt Regency in Palo Alto booked him for six months.

He continued to be involved with the Special Olympics which he supported enthusiastically for many years.

A very big event was Frank M. Jordan's Inaugural party that required being held at the Bill Graham Civic Auditorium because of the large number attending the event.

Sal's other band, Interstate-80 Band had a series of gigs.

The Marvin Hamlisch Show with Sal was well received. Turk Murphy once told me that Hamlisch's arrangements of Scott Joplin's music for "The Sting" was brilliant and others thought the same as he received an Oscar. Needless to say, Sal enjoyed the fact he was in the same show.

So, Sal was busy in the 1990's even with some health problems he ended the decade with a New Years' Eve dinner dance at the Fairmont Hotel

Tea dance at Hyatt Regency in Palo Alto. This was a six month gig. (l to r) Kevin Porter, Bob Belanski, Ray Lockley, Sal, Mr. Unknown, Mary Woods and Shota Osabe.

San Francisco Special Olympics
A California Non-Profit Corporation
Co-Sponsored by the San Francisco Recreation & Park Department
741 - 30th Avenue, San Francisco, California 94121
415 221-6575

Linda S. Lovelace
AREA DIRECTOR

Tom Mannion
LEGAL COUNSEL

Freda Motak
VOLUNTEER
COORDINATOR

May 1, 1991

Mr. Sal Carson
Sal Carson Productions
127 Hardie Drive
Moraga, CA 94556

Dear Sal,

First of all, I want to apologize for the tardiness in sending this letter to you.

On behalf of the San Francisco Special Olympics Advisory Board, I would like to thank you and your band's generous donation to the December 4, 1990 Special Olympics Christmas Party.

As you know, the party was a great success and largely due to the wonderful entertainment you and your band provided. Your donation made the event special and memorable one for all.

Again, that you for your kind contribution.

Sincerely,

Adeline Guerrero
Christmas Party Chair
S.F. Special Olympics Advisory Board

AG:MO/qa

SPECIAL OLYMPICS
Created by The Joseph P. Kennedy, Jr. Foundation.
Authorized and Accredited by Special Olympics, Inc. for the Benefit of Mentally Retarded Citizens

Special Olympics letter, May 1, 1991

Valentines dance party.
February 15, 1991

Loch Lomond Resort.
August 1991

USS Carl Vinson
aircraft carrier, 1991.
Tom Hart on sax

Frank M. Jordan
Inaugural Community Open House
Civic Auditorium
January 8, 1992

Acknowledgements
and Special Thanks

Adeline Bake Shop
The Balloon Lady
Bill Graham Presents
The Bobby Murray Band featuring Freddy Hughes
Dick Bright
Chevy's Mexican Restaurant
Val Diamond
Donatello Ristorante
El Grupo Folklorico Madruga
Embarko
Fairmont Hotel
Fillmore Grill
Golden Phoenix Restaurant
Grand Palace Restaurant
Harbor Village Restaurant
Harris' Restaurant
Hyatt Regency Embarcadero
Izzy's Steaks & Chops
Ray Jason
Jeff Pollack's Original Joe's Marina
Los Kimbos
Madeline Eastman Trio
Marina Safeway
Mary O'Shea & Associates
Max's Restaurants
Miriwa Restaurant of San Francisco
New Sun Hong Kong Restaurant
North Beach Restaurant/Basta Pasta
One World Taiko
The PBN Company
Perry's Restaurant
Robot Redford (courtesy of Star Robots USA)
The Sal Carson Band
Salud Restaurant
Sandy's Restaurant
San Francisco Hilton Hotel
Sam Jordan's of California Catering
Sheraton Palace
Slim's
Stars
Ray Taliaferro
Tommy Toy's Haute Cuisine Chinoise
Toulouse Foods
Vocal Minority (courtesy of Jon Sims Center for the Performing Arts)
Washington Square Bar & Grill
The Westin St. Francis
Yau Kung Moon Kung Fu Sports Association

Sal on the USS Carl Vinson. 1991

Mayor Frank Jordan. January 8, 1992

Frank M. Jordan, Mayor of San Francisco,
Inaugural party. January 8, 1992. Bill Graham
Civic Auditorium

The band on stage, USS Carl Vinson, 1991. Mary Woods was the vocalist.

Band members: Mayor Frank Jordan party. January 8, 1992, at the Bill Graham Civic Auditorium. (l to r) Front row: Sal, Mary Woods, not known, Rudy Paladini, Dick Mathus, H. Streil. Back row: Walt Battagello, Jim Schlicht

Another shot of the band at Jordan's party.

An intimate
party for
Mayor
Jordan

Mary Woods and Sal. Sir Francis Drake Hotel.
ca 1992

RHEEM
PERFORMING ARTS
THEATRE
350 RHEEM BLVD., MORAGA
510-376-1490

SAL ★
CARSON

and his

★

16 PIECE BAND

FRIDAY NIGHT DANCE

APRIL 10,   8:30

Flyer for Sal's Band. April 10, 1992

–272–

Rheem Theater, Moraga.
April 10, 1992.

Office of the Mayor
SAN FRANCISCO

FRANK M. JORDAN

March 17, 1992

Sal Carson
127 Hardie Drive
Moraga, CA 94556

Dear Sal:

One of the most exciting "aspects" of being a brand new Mayor in San Francisco is the opportunity to head up the 5th annual Celebrity Waiter Luncheon scheduled for Wednesday, April 29 at Pier 35 - and to co-chair, along with Superintendent of Schools, Ramon Cortines, this truly "only in San Francisco Event" with the legendary Bill Walsh!

Thanks to _you_ -- and so many other sports, entertainment and media celebrities who volunteer each year to be a "Celebrity Waiter or Waitress", local athletic directors have been able to keep a large number of sports programs running which, in turn, keep our kids off the streets and on the playing fields.

INDEED, IN FOUR YEAR'S TIME WE HAVE RAISED OVER $400,000 FOR OUR LOCAL MIDDLE AND HIGH SCHOOL SPORTS PROGRAMS.

The money raised by this year's Event will again go directly to the San Francisco School Department to purchase uniforms and equipment, repair athletic facilities, and maintain intramural and competitive sports programs.

Your presence and participation adds significantly to the credibility and prestige of this Event -- helping to bring in not only "Celebrity Watching" guests, but over $100,000 each year.

I want to _personally_ - as well as _officially_ - invite you, once again, to be on hand to both serve our guests and "serve our schools!"

I very much hope that you will be able to participate to be a Celebrity Waiter or Waitress, and to that end, have enclosed a response card for your convenience. I will look forward to hearing from you in the next few days.

Sincerely,

Frank M. Jordan

200 CITY HALL, SAN FRANCISCO, CALIFORNIA 94102
(415) 554-6141

Letter from Mayor Jordan for Celebrity Luncheon

Sal at the Celebrity Luncheon. April 29, 1992

Herb Caen column.
September 23 1992

Just Kiddin' Around

SPINOFF: Did you notice that classified ad offering a restored 1909 cable car — one of the cute-as-hell O'Farrell Jones & Hyde dinkies — for $80,000? It's being offered by Paul Brown of San Marino, whose grandpop, Howard, bought it here in 1951 for $10,000 and used it on his ranch. It's not motorized, thankgawd. God never intended cables to run on rubber tires ... What is definitely annoying: Caesar salad with the romaine lettuce leaves untorn or uncut. That's not a Caesar, by Jove ... It's Warren Maloney's great idea — the all-city high schools' reunion at the Hilton Sat. night, with music by Sal Carson's big band. More than 1,000 tickets have been sold to old-timers who graduated from our high schools in the 1940s. Warren's pop was the noted politico Pete Maloney, whose name is memorialized on the Fourth St. bridge ... A quizzical Norm Goldblatt after waving bye-bye to the honeymooning Frank'n'Wendy: "I wonder if mayoral sex is all it's cracked up to be."

★   ★   ★

Sal Carson and his Big Band play at 8 tonight at the Rheem Performing Arts Center.

Another performance at the Rheem Theater. June 12, 1992

San Francisco Special Olympics
A California Non-Profit Corporation
Co-Sponsored by the San Francisco Recreation & Park Department
741 - 30th Avenue, San Francisco, California 94121
415 221-6575

January 1, 1993

Mr. Sal Carson
Sal Carson Bands and Productions
127 Hardie Drive
Moraga CA 94556

Dear Sal:

On behalf of the athletes of San Francisco Special Olympics, our thanks go to you and your band for once again playing for our Christmas party. Your music was as terrific as always, and the athletes (and volunteers) had a blast ... what more is there to say?

Here's to a healthy and prosperous new year!! Thanks, Sal, for all you do for San Francisco Special Olympics.

Sincerely,

Ralph + Kris Johnson

Ralph and Kris Johnson
Christmas Party Committee

Special Olympics letter. January 1, 1993

Yes, I will attend the "All City Forties Reunion" on Saturday, September 26, 1992 at the San Francisco Hilton Hotel — Grand Ballroom. Cocktails at 6 PM, dinner at 7 PM. Dining and Dance to the Big Band sounds of Sal Carson until Midnight. Tickets are moving fast so get your check in as soon as possible. You won't want to miss this "Once in a lifetime" Event!

NAMES _____

_____

_____

ADDRESS _____

TELEPHONE NO. _____ SCHOOL & YEAR GRADUATED _____
* *

FOR COMMITTEE USE ONLY _____ PAYMENT RECEIVED _____

TABLE ASSIGNMENT _____ SPORTS OR ACADEMIC HONORS _____

_____

ALL CITY FORTIES REUNION, 1055 LAUREL ST., SAN CARLOS, CA 94070 • (415) 281-8466

**All City Forties Reunion.
September 26, 1992**

DEPARTMENT OF THE NAVY
USS CARL VINSON (CVN-70)
FLEET POST OFFICE AP
96629-2840

Mr. Sal Carson
127 Hardie Drive
Moraga, CA 94556

Dear Mr. Carson,

I would like to invite you and your two bands to join CARL VINSON in our upcoming Family Day Cruise on Monday, August 9, 1993. This would be a unique opportunity to entertain as well as meet the crew and families on "San Francisco's Own."

The cruise is scheduled to last from 7:30 a.m. to 6 p.m. and will originate and end at NAS Alameda.

Many activities are scheduled for the cruise, including an air power demonstration with aircraft from our air wing. Static displays, tours and a variety of entertainment will also be a part of the day's fare. Breakfast and lunch will be provided.

My MWR Director, Mr. Toby Reed, will be in contact with you to coordinate any details for this event. He may also be reached at (510) 263-2153.

I hope you are able to join us for this event. It promises to be an enjoyable day aboard the "Gold Eagle."

Sincerely,

J.S. PAYNE
Captain, U.S. Navy
Commanding Officer

Thanks for helping us out + entertaining our many families and guests.

**Carl Vinson Family
Day Cruise.
August 9, 1993**

–275–

```
          USS Carl Vinson CVN-70
           Dependents Day Cruise
              August 9, 1993


            Entertainment Schedule
               - Out Bound -
            ─────────────────

    6:30 a.m. to 7:30 a.m. - Navy Band - San Francisco -
                    on Stage.


    7:30 a.m. to 8:00 a.m. - Michael Pritchard, M.C. Comedian
             Star T.V. Comedy, on stage.


    8:00 a.m. to 8:30 a.m. - 12 Piece Bag Pipe Band - Parade Hanger
                   Bay Deck.


 8:30 a.m. to 9:30 a.m. - Sal Carson's 20 Piece Big Band - on stage
              Featuring - Vocalist Mary Woods.


 9:30 a.m. to 10:00 a.m. - "Sons of the Sea" Ray Truman on stage
              16 Man Chorus Group


   10:00 a.m. to 10:45 a.m. - Rock Band - 6 Piece "Interstate 80", on
                    stage.


 10:45 a.m. to 11:00 a.m. - Marine Detachment Drill, Hanger Bay Deck
              USS Carl Vinson CVN-70 Detail


   11:00 a.m. to 11:30 a.m. - Dave Marty - Banjo Star - on stage
              "The Singing Banjo"

     11:30 a.m. to 1:30 p.m. - Carl Vinson DJ on Stage -
```

Carl Vinson entertain-
ment schedule.

Sal on board.
August 9, 1993

Mary Woods and Sal in front. August 9, 1993. Between Mary Woods and Sal is Tom Hart.

Another band shot. August 9, 1993. Carl Vinson ship.

Mary and Sal.

VAN KASPER & COMPANY

Private Brokerage 50 California Street, Suite 2400 San Francisco, California 94111
Telephone: (415) 391-5600

August 17, 1993

Mr. Sal Carson
127 Hardie Drive
Moraga, CA 94556

Dear Sal:

Thank you and your wonderful musicians and technicians for a
marvelous performance on board the USS Carl Vinson CVN-70 for the
Dependence Day Cruise. The Big Band, singer Mary Wood, the
Interstate 80 group, and the great sound staff. It was something
the crew will never forget. They said the show was the best one
ever. The hats are ordered and are coming. I am grateful and
indebted to you. You are the greatest.

Thank you.

Sincerely,

L. Jack Block
Mayor's Committee Chairman
USS Carl Vinson CVN-70

Thank you letter. August 17, 1993

Maria Kozak
and Sal on a
liberty ship at
Christmas.
1994 or 1995.
Maria was
very helpful to
me when I
wrote the Earl
Watkins book.

UNITED BROTHERHOOD OF
CARPENTERS AND JOINERS
OF AMERICA

LOCAL UNION NO. 22, A.F of L.

TELEPHONE: 468-8610
FAX: 468-8698

2660 NEWHALL STREET, ROOM 200
SAN FRANCISCO, CA 94124-2527

Jim McPartlan
nancial Secretary

73

November 10, 1993

Sal Carson
127 Hardie Drive
Moraga, Ca. 94556

Dear Sal:

I wanted to take this opportunity to thank you for the wonderful job you did at our dinner on Friday, October 29th at the S.F. Hilton. *and Oct. 11, 1996*

Your band was delightful, as usual, and the rock band was also enjoyed by all. It was a great combination for the variety of ages that were in attendance, what a wonderful suggestion on your part! I couldn't help but notice how full the dance floor was throughout the evening, not to mention the numerous compliments I received as well. Also, thank you for your recommendation and advice on the PA system, your expertise was very helpful in making the evening such a success.

Once again, thank you for a wonderful evening you can be sure we will book you for future events and recommend your band to others as well.

Sincerely,

Jim McPartlan
Financial Secretary

JMP/js
opeiu-3-afl-cio (38)

Letter from Carpenters and Joiners Union. November 10, 1993

Fairmont Hotel

Mary Woods and Sal. Fairmont Hotel. 1994

SAL
CARSON

San Francisco Olympic Club. 1994. (l to r) "Chip" Trombley, Sal and Dave Broni

!!!!! DANCE !!!!!

to

SAL CARSON'S

INTERSTATE 80
BAND

WITH VOCALIST MARY WOODS

Great music of the 50's though the 90's!
Great Place to Meet People!

Friday, September 16
5:30 to 8:30pm

Holiday Inn Union Square
Ballroom
480 Sutter St. at Powell

$10 admission — No host bar
Profits to be donated to San Francisco Special Olympics

Event Committee
Ralph Johnson, Chairperson
Pamela Weston, Co-Chairperson

$10 Pre-Paid Admission
for One Person

PLEASE PRESENT THIS TICKET AT THE DOOR

Interstate 80 Band. September 16, 1994

Proudly Presents

An Evening With

Marvin Hamlisch

with

Opening Act

Sal Carson Big Band

This evening with
Marvin Hamlisch
has been made possible, in part,
by a generous grant from
The Hofmann Foundation.

1994

Marvin Hamlisch Show. 1994

George Habit
10-19-94

Page 7B

☆☆☆

We were dining over at WOODLAKE JOE'S on Peninsula Ave. the other night, when we ran into Big Band Leader Sal Carson. Sal told us he loves Woodlake Joe's since the introduction of their all new upgraded menu with lower prices. We were glad to hear it because this place is great. They have live entertainment in the lounge, and a large and comfy dining room overlooking the CharBroiler in their Exhibition Kitchen. So come sit back, relax, and enjoy the best in Old Fashioned S.F. Style Italian Cuisine...

Sal Carson

☆☆☆

George Habit column. October 19, 1994

Columbus Day at St. Peter and Paul Church in San Francisco. (l to r) Front row: John Fiore, Sam Stern, Silvia Gaylord, Sal. Back row: Not known.

MARVIN HAMLISCH

A blockbuster evening of laughs and top-notch music.
The Post-Standard, Syracuse, New York

Marvin Hamlisch was admitted to the Juillard School of Music at age seven, and graduated cum laude from Queens College in 1967, with a B.A. in Musical Composition.

In the 1960s, it was Sunshine, Lollipops and Rainbows, the hit song recorded by Lesley Gore, and other pop singles, as well as the beginning of a career scoring motion pictures, with The Swimmer that brought him to our attention.

He is the composer of over forty motion picture scores, including his Oscar award winning score and song for The Way We Were, and his adaptation of Scott Joplin's music for The Sting, for which he received his third Oscar.

Other film scores include Sophie's Choice, Ordinary People, Ice Castles and Three Men and a Baby.

For the theatre, he has written the music for A Chorus Line and They're Playing Our Song.

"Music can make a difference," Hamlisch says. "There is a global nature to music which has the potential to bring all people together. Music is an international language, and I hope to contribute by widening communication as much as I can."

Hamlisch has written One Song, a "global anthem", with lyrics by Alan and Marilyn Bergman, which he performs at symphony concerts. His Anatomy of Peace, a 25 minute symphonic piece commissioned by the Dallas Symphony Orchestra, premiered in November, 1991.

Marvin Frederick Hamlisch was born on June 2, 1944, in New York City. He and his sister, Terry, were raised in a musical household by their father, Max, an accordionist and conductor, and their mother, Lilly.

Mr. Hamlisch will participate in the second Acorn Educational Series event, when he hosts students from the upcoming Junior Bach Festival "Encore Concert" during his afternoon rehearsal.

Marvin and his wife Terre reside in New York City.

SAL CARSON

Known as "San Francisco Music Man", Sal Carson is an accomplished trumpeter, composer and vocalist.

For six years, Carson led the 49ers Band, composing the official team song, 49ers So Proud and Bold.

A first cousin of Joe Carcione, local radio and television's Green Grocer, he has backed such outstanding performers as Bob Hope, Barbara Eden, Phyllis Diller, & Kay Starr, and has several recordings to his credit, including appearing on the album, "Vic Damone In San Francisco".

The Sal Carson Big Band provided backup for Diahann Carroll and Vic Damone on the Opening Night at the Regional Center, and most recently for Shirley Jones.

Mr. Carson spent his early life in Oakland, and has lived in Moraga for the past 25 years.

Marvin Hamlisch and Sal Carson notes for the Hamlisch Show. 1994

USS CARL VINSON CVN -70
MAY 12, 1995

**ENTERTAINMENT
THE BIG SHOW**

1) NAVY BAND SAN FRANCISCO
    TREASURE ISLAND, S.F. CA 94130   14 - SHOW BAND
    415-395-5085

2) SAL CARSON SHOW BAND
    127 HARDIE DR., MORAGA CA 94556   22 - BIG BAND SOUNDS
    510-254-1881

3) THE TONY HALL BAND
    127 ROCKAWAY AVE, S.F. CA 94127   6 - SWING
    415-753-3511

4) SCOTT ANTHONY BAND
    889 DEHARRO ST., S.F. CA 94107   8 - BANJOS
    510-826-6193

5) NATURAL GAS JAZZ BAND
    DR. PHIL CRUMLEY
    26 MARTLING AVE, SAN ANSELMO CA   8 - JAZZ
    415-453-9043

6) BEN WIATRAK MYLC BAND
    25 VIA CAPISTRANO AVE, TIBURON CA 94920   8 - ROCK
    415-435-9043

7) INTERSTATE - 80
    c/o SAL CARSON
    127 HARDIE DR, MORAGA CA 94556   5 - ROCK
    510-254-1881

8) JANICE RICHEY PIPE MAJOR
    MACINTOSH PIPE BAND
    654 CHERRY ST, NOVATO VA 94945   22 - SCOTCH PIPE & DRUM
    415-892-5565

9) THE GOLDEN CHORISTERS
    WALTER TINGLEY
    1090 - 26th ST, S.F. CA 94107   20 - BARBER SHOP SINGERS
    415-648-5419

Carl Vinson. May 12, 1995

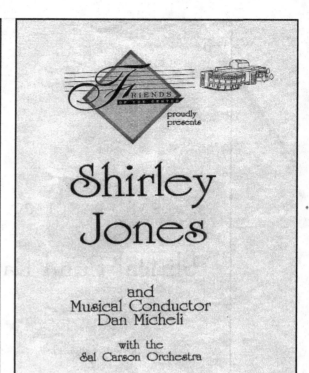

FRIENDS OF THE CENTER

proudly presents

Shirley Jones

and
Musical Conductor
Dan Micheli

with the
Sal Carson Orchestra

Shirley Jones Show. Mid 1990's

(Below) Art Rosenbaum column.
November 14, 1995

ROSENBAUM: A hint to Muni

continued from page 11

Francisco's serial killer of the 1970s, is growing in fame, thanks to author Robert Graysmith. His book, "Zodiac," first published 10 years ago, is now in its 19th printing in paperback. It remains an unsolved mystery, and retired police inspector Dave Toschi is still receiving tips on the killer who boasted of 37 murders, though officially charged with six.

Overheard: A uniformed security guard from a nearby building was arrested for stealing a pair of shoes from the Ross store at Fourth and Market. Guess the shoplifter took the store's slogan, "Dress for Less," literally.

A lengthy Chronicle sports feature on Joe DiMaggio implied that — unlike Mickey Mantle, Stan Musial, and other baseball greats who capitalized on their fame by opening restaurants — Joltin' Joe wouldn't stoop to such commercialism. No? How about longtime DiMaggio's at Fisherman's Wharf, where Joe often acted as greeter?

Sal Carson, the San Francisco bandleader, has a new appreciation for police. He was driving at midnight from Sparks to Reno when suddenly came the ominous sound of a police siren. A woman officer stepped out of her squad car and asked the quaking Carson, "Did you stop for gas back there?" Carson wildly imagined being hauled off for robbery. "Yes," he stammered. The officer said, "You left your gas cap on the trunk." Then she added, "Don't bother getting out of your car, sir, I'll put the cap back on." Reno never looked brighter to Carson.

Oddity: In the changing of holidays, Thanksgiving wasn't switched to a Monday. But hear this: The first Thanksgiving was celebrated November 13, 1631, a Monday.

Infamous last words (thanks to Max Millard): "I'm not exaggerating..."

–283–

SAN FRANCISCO
LABOR COUNCIL

Political Fund Raiser

Wednesday
November 8, 1995

Sheraton Palace Hotel
San Francisco

Political Fund Raiser. November 8, 1995

MENU

Mixed Greens
With Eggplant, Tomato, Cucumber,
Olives, & Feta Cheese
Lemon Basil Vinaigrette

Grilled Filet Mignon
Chipotle and Red Chili Butter
Scalloped Potato Tart
Fresh Seasonal Vegetables
Dinner Rolls

Chocolate Truffle Tort
Dusted with Cocoa Powder
and Served with Sour Cherry Sauce

Coffee, Tea, Decaffeinated Coffee

MUSIC BY

Sal Carson Band
Mary Woods, Vocalist

Graphics by Zetta Design
Printing by Black Sheep Press

Fund Raiser program

Rita Rubinatti vocalist. Did
some work with Sal. Could
speak five languages. Film
and stage experience. ca 1996

October 19, 1996. Photo of Valeria Bulgo, Sal and Silvia
Norton. Courtesy of Elk's Lodge #3, San Francisco.

On the Jeremiah O'Brien troop ship, San Francisco, 1996. (l to r) Earl Watkins, Sal, Darrel "Hutch" Hutchison and Joe Terzian.

"Hutch" Hutchison at a gig. The pretty lady was a waitress. ca 1990's

Earl Watkins, 1996 on the troop ship. We miss Earl. What a wonderful man!

A hotel gig in 1996. That's Art Dougherty on the far right.

Regional Center, Walnut Creek. Flyer. 1997

New Year's Eve, 1996. Sacramento Hilton Hotel. The vocalist is Mary Woods. The two men are Dick Matias and Rudy Paladini.

Tribute to Walter Shorenstein. June 17, 1997.

A Tribute to Shorenstein

by Organized Labor and the Building Trades

Tuesday, June 17, 1997

**Fairmont Hotel
Grand Ballroom**

~ Program ~

Bruce Lee
Chairman of the Board
UAW - LETC

The Honorable Willie L. Brown, Jr.
Mayor, City and County of San Francisco

Stanley M. Smith
Secretary - Treasurer, San Francisco Building Trades Council

Multi-Image Presentation ~ *"A Tribute to Shorenstein"*

Presentation of Awards to Walter and Douglas Shorenstein

Remarks by Walter Shorenstein

Dessert and Dancing

Music by the Sal Carson Orchestra

Carson tunes up big band for 'big

By TONY HICKS
Staff writer

Sal's been there.

Casinos? Lounges? Sal's played 'em — in Vegas, Tahoe, Reno. Dance halls, vacation resorts, convention centers, private parties, football stadiums. He's walked out of gigs next to glowing marquees lighting the name of Elvis, and given a young San Francisco secretary a boost up a showbiz ladder. (She later climbed to camp-television immortality as Larry Hagman's magical servant.)

Sal Carson's been there and is still doing that.

The longtime Bay Area band leader and Moraga resident brings a lifetime of music and musical history, as well as his 18-piece big band, to Walnut Creek's Dean Lesher Regional Center for the Arts on New Year's Eve.

With a little luck, Carson may put his trumpet down or stop singing between crazy swing sessions and talk a bit about himself. The stories are almost as good as the swing.

The San Francisco native grew up in the 1930s and '40s longing to be on the bandstand next to idols Harry James, Jimmy Dorsey and Count Basie. He finally got there in the early 1950s — only to watch rock 'n' roll steal his audience.

"I'm one of the very few that stayed with it," he said. "When I started about 80 percent of it was over. Had I gone 10 years earlier I could have been the big time — a Dorsey or one of those."

The son of an immigrant Sicilian father who sang in the San Francisco Opera for many years, Carson settled for playing his music in smaller venues. Every summer for 17 years in the 1950s and '60s, he'd tote his trumpet and the orchestra up to Hoberg's resort in Lake County, spending nights with a ballroom full of people re-en-

SAL CARSON, second from left, helped Barbara Eden get her start in show business — as a singer.

acting what used to be.

Other than some of the albums he's made with singers such as Vic Damone, the closest Carson ever got to the big time was the trips to Nevada, either wailing with the big orchestra or downshifting into a lounge act with a smaller six-piece unit.

Carson spent the 1970s leading the official San Francisco 49ers band at home games. He can reel off stories about Dallas Cowboy Drew Pearson taking out his trombone section on a deep route or his knees knocking the first time he soloed "The Star-Spangled Banner" at midfield. He also can tell stories about being Creedence Clearwater Revival's booking manager in the Bay Area from 1967-'69

before they made it big.

But what he really likes to talk about are his brushes with greatness — the people he considered great.

One Reno gig that began just like any other brought Carson face-to-face with a honeymooning legend he'd dreamed of being as a youngster.

"I get up on the stage and low and behold there's Harry James out there with his new wife," he said, voice rising and eyes widening at the memory. "Later, somebody said to me, 'Do you want to meet Harry?' and I only said, 'Oh, wow.'

"There I am — entertaining Harry James. He stayed all night and danced," he said, shaking his head.

In the late 1950s Carson granted

the wish of a talent agency secretary who'd been pestering him for a chance to sing in his band. She went on to become the most famous pre-Robin Williams genie in Hollywood.

"Barbara Eden started with my band," he said, through a toothy smile. "She was a good singer and she was absolutely gorgeous. I took her on a job and she sang a couple of songs — but she didn't even have to sing."

Eden sang in Carson's band for about a year before going off to Hollywood. After she became famous, Carson appeared on an episode of "This Is Your Life" highlighting Eden's career. She also introduced him at some shows she did in Las Vegas.

Tony Hick's column. Late 90's (Continued on next page)

Jeremiah O'Brien troop ship, 1997. (l to r) Earl Watkins, Bill (?) Sal and Jim Schlicht

night'

PREVIEW

What: Sal Carson and his big band

Where: Dean Lesher Regional Center for the Arts, Civic Drive at Locust Street, Walnut Creek

When: 9 p.m. Tuesday

How much: $50 (including champagne and hors d'oeuvres

Call: 943-SHOW

"She said she wanted to introduce the man she owed it all to. It made me feel wonderful."

He said he can still picture the signs next door and across the street during a string of Vegas gigs in the early '70s. The names read Elvis Presley and Perry Como respectively.

If Carson has bitterness over missing the big years of big band, it's buried somewhere under the excitement of watching swing music have a rebirth of sorts.

"All of a sudden the last couple of years, people have been calling for it," he said. "Today they're asking for the swing and the jazz. People are appreciating the big-band era. If we started playing rap, they'd walk out."

Carson said he loves, and has played, just about every type of music and still does, depending on who the audience is. He plans to pepper the New Year's swing with a little Top 40.

"That's all I do," he said, shrugging. "That's all I ever do. I blow my horn all day, I practice my singing. I rehearse the band. We've done about the best we can do in this era."

And now he gears up for New Year's Eve — "the big night," he calls it.

"Playing New Year's Eve is wonderful," he said. "Scott Denison (the Regional Center's general manager) and I saw eye-to-eye on this one. I loved the idea, I live in Moraga — I said, 'Let's do it.' "

Tony Hick's column. Late 90's (Continued from page 288)

Rheem Theater, Moraga. 1998

Labor/Neighbor Cope. 1998 (Program on next page)

–289–

Program for Cope. 1998.
(Cover on previous page)

(Upper right)'
Columbus Day Parade. Late 1990's

Ramada Plaza Hotel.
October 17, 1998

Linda Bulgo, Sal's niece.

Linda Bulgo publicity photo

Linda Bulgo

Born and raised in San Francisco, Linda attended San Francisco City College and received a degree in music. She has also attended the American Conservatory Theater, and is continuing her musical education at San Francisco State University. Linda has been singing professionally since she was seventeen years old.

Brief bio of Linda

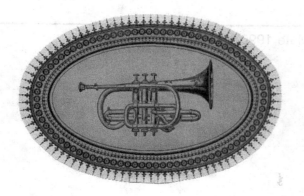

Sal Carson's Big Band plays the best Dixieland around!

ALSO AVAILABLE:
Solo musicians (piano, violin, trumpet, guitar) for all occasions, including soloists for the National Anthem.

Sal Carson's Interstate 80 Band can easily expand from a 3-piece jazz combo to a 17-piece Big Band, depending upon your entertainment needs.

**SAL CARSON IN THE
PRO FOOTBALL HALL OF FAME!**
Click here to read a letter of appreciation to Sal Carson for his musical contributions to the San Francisco '49ers.

LINDA BULGO
**formerly of *"Beach Blanket Babylon"*
Click here for information.**

Sal flyer, late 1990's

San Francisco's 12th Annual
Celebrity Waiter Luncheon

Friday, April 23, 1999
at the Fairmont Hotel
Hosted by the Committee to Save SF School Sports

May 6, 1999

Sal Carson
127 Hardie Dr.
Moraga, CA 94556

Dear Sal:

Certainly — this photo is worth a "thousand words." Better yet, it's actually worth thousands of dollars which is what this year's Celebrity Waiter Luncheon netted for San Francisco's school sports thanks to you and all who made this Event a rousing success.

Kind personal regards,

Art Blum
President
Committee to Save SF School Sports

Celebrity Waiter Luncheon. May 6, 1999

A TRIBUTE TO WALTER JOHNSON
Secretary Treasurer of the San Francisco Labor Council, AFL-CIO

1999 Labor /Neighbor C.O.P.E. Dinner
San Francisco Labor Council

OCTOBER 26, 1999 • ARGENT HOTEL • 50 THIRD STREET
SAN FRANCISCO • CALIFORNIA

6:30 PM Cocktails
7:30 PM Dinner

PROGRAM

Invocation: Pastor Merton Johnson

Introductions

Tributes and Presentations

Guest of Honor: Walter L. Johnson

Entertainment: Sal Carson & His Band

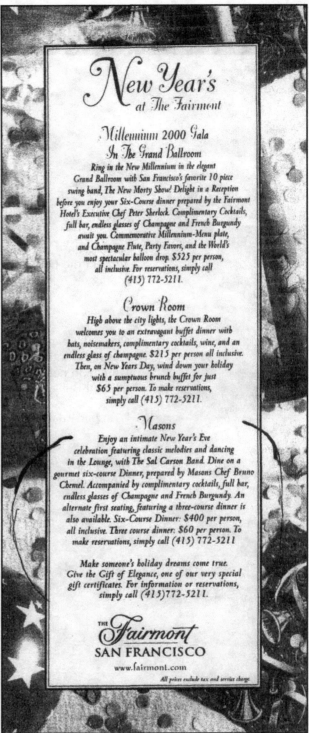

New Year's
at The Fairmont

Millennium 2000 Gala
In The Grand Ballroom
Ring in the New Millennium in the elegant
Grand Ballroom with San Francisco's favorite 10 piece
swing band, The New Morty Show! Delight in a Reception
before you enjoy your Six-Course dinner prepared by the Fairmont
Hotel's Executive Chef Peter Sherlock. Complimentary Cocktails,
full bar, endless glasses of Champagne and French Burgundy
await you. Commemorative Millennium-Menu plate,
and Champagne Flute, Party Favors, and the World's
most spectacular balloon drop. $525 per person,
all inclusive. For reservations, simply call
(415) 772-5211.

Crown Room
High above the city lights, the Crown Room
welcomes you to an extravagant buffet dinner with
hats, noisemakers, complimentary cocktails, wine, and an
endless glass of champagne. $215 per person all inclusive.
Then, on New Years Day, wind down your holiday
with a sumptuous brunch buffet for just
$65 per person. To make reservations,
simply call (415) 772-5211.

Masons
Enjoy an intimate New Year's Eve
celebration featuring classic melodies and dancing
in the Lounge, with The Sal Carson Band. Dine on a
gourmet six-course Dinner, prepared by Masons Chef Bruno
Chemel. Accompanied by complimentary cocktails, full bar,
endless glasses of Champagne and French Burgundy. An
alternate first seating, featuring a three-course dinner is
also available. Six-Course Dinner: $400 per person,
all inclusive. Three course dinner: $60 per person. To
make reservations, simply call (415) 772-5211

Make someone's holiday dreams come true.
Give the Gift of Elegance, one of our very special
gift certificates. For information or reservations,
simply call (415)772-5211.

THE *Fairmont*
SAN FRANCISCO
www.fairmont.com
All prices exclude tax and service charge.

New Years at the Fairmont. Ad in the San
Francisco Sunday Examiner & Chronicle.
December 12, 1999

(Upper left) Tribute to Walter Johnson.
October 26, 1999

(Lower left) New Years Eve at Regional
Center for Arts in Walnut Creek. 1997

–294–

Chapter 11
2000 – 2007

The years of the 2000's found Sal's musical activity decreased because of health problems resulting in operations that kept him on the bench for some time.

Some of the high and lows were:

2000:
Gig at the Crown Plaza Hotel with vocalist Mary Wood

Marine Fireman Union gig.

2001:
A very sad moment was the death of his favorite bass player, Vernon Alley

Letter from the Pro Football Hall of Fame informing Sal that his composition for the 49 'er Football Team was made a part of the Hall of Fame archives.

2002
He enjoyed the "Bye-Bye, Beatle" performance on March 1, 2002

Labor/Neighbor COPE dinner. October 24, 2002

2003
Holiday recording

Another COPE dinner

2004
A gig Sal always enjoyed was on the Jeremiah O'Brien

March 1, 2004, their daughter, Kathy, died. A very sad time for Sal and Kathleen.

2005

Joyce Whitelaw performed with the band for various gigs.

Performed at the "Musical Celebration of Oakland".

2006

Another sad moment was the death of Lou Rawls, January 6, 2006

July 28 Sal was in the hospital for an operation

A very happy moment was Sal being invited to attend the Celebrity Football Players Shootout at Lake County. August 26, 2006

Sal spent much time in 2006 and 2007 in the hospital or in the office of physicians; however, his enthusiasm for finalizing his life story was still there although some time he had to limit the time devoted for interviewing. We continued to talk on the telephone and he told me he had some more material that he wanted to include in his book. His phone calls were always welcomed by me. Life does not always work out the way one would like, certainly Sal's death on October 19, 2007 was a very sad moment for me because I truly loved that man.

2007

Kathleen received numerous letters expressing condolences and telling of some special memory they had about Sal. How friendly he was, of dancing to his superb orchestra, his helping a young musician trying to be a professional are examples of the letters.

The closing paragraph of one letter seemed to me said just what Sal was:

"I will never forget Sal's kindness to a retarded girl in my daughter's middle school dance party in Piedmont. No one would ask her to dance so Sal got off the bandstand and danced with her...Love that guy!"

How many big band leaders do you know that would have done that? Yes, Sal Carson was truly a special person. Those of us who knew him, loved him.

Linda D'Arezzo displaying a Sal poster. Photo by Jim Goggin. 2005

The Crown Plaza Hotel in San Francisco, 2000. Mary Woods wondering if playing trumpet is easy

An outside gig. October 2000. (l to r) In back: Ed Turdici, Bill Catalano, Jr., Bob Balanski and in front: John Fiori, Sylvia Gaylord and Sal.

Marines Fireman Union, 2000. (l to r) Jerry Stucker, "Chip" Trombley, Mary Woods Sal, Darrel Hutchison

SATURDAY, NOVEMBER 3, 2001

S.F. Chronicle

A worthy tribute to bassist Vernon Alley

Anyone who skipped the "Legacy of Vernon Alley" concert at the Palace of Fine Arts on Wednesday missed one of the San Francisco Jazz Festival's finest and most memorable presentations in its 19-year history.

Nine hundred mainstream jazz fans came early and stayed late.

PHILIP ELWOOD
Jazz

They dug master of ceremonies Noah Griffin's elegant introductory remarks and his singing (Alley on bass), and enthusiastically greeted the 15 musician friends of Alley whose lengthy ensemble "C-Jam Blues" rendition ended the 3½-hour concert.

Although ad hoc tributes, benefits and memorials in the jazz community are often haphazardly produced and short on quality, this one moved with swinging precision, mainly because one of Alley's oldest friends, the superb trumpeter Allen Smith, chose all the musicians, approved the selections and organized the sequence

Trumpeter Allen Smith's performance was one of the standouts at the San Francisco Jazz Festival's tribute to bassist Vernon Alley.

JOHN O'HARA / The Chronicle 1995

of performances.

Smith's was one of the many outstanding individual performances of the evening, which also included magnificent pieces by pianist Richard Wyands, guitarists Eddie Duran and Bruce Forman, and saxophonists Chuck Travis, Noel Jewkes and Jules Broussard. Trombonist Danny Armstrong and drummers Vince Lateano, Harold Jones and Benny Barth were also aboard.

The warmth and spirit for which Alley is famous seemed to be a part of every performance, beginning with his own. He was onstage more than half the time, at one point singing "Big Fat Butterfly," a song written and recorded by Saunders King, in whose Jack's Tavern band Alley played more than 60 years ago.

Wyands, a Berkeleyan who has lived in New York for decades,

was in the same San Francisco State music classes (late-1940s G Bill) as Cal Tjader, Paul Desmond, John Coppola and Alley. He flew in from New York, he said, "just to play with Vernon a some of my old friends again."

Alley was presented the 2001 SFJAZZ Beacon Award, and Oct 30 was proclaimed "Vernon Alle Day" by Mayor Willie Brown. C sy Swig bestowed the honors du ing the show.

■ ■ ■

What happened to the Fillmore jazz district project that seemed so near a few years ago? The plans, and dreams, of the Fi more Jazz Preservation District seemed dashed when development difficulties and political shuffling brought it to a standsti Perhaps hope can be revived by the next Fillmore Jazz Preservation District concert and get-together, Feb. 17, in the West Bay Conference Center.

E-mail Philip Elwood at pelwo @sfchronicle.com.

Tribute to Vernon Alley by Philip Elwood, San Francisco Chronicle, November 3, 2001. Alley was Sal Carson's favorite bass player. What a pleasure it was to know Vernon Alley. The musicians were chosen by Allen Smith who also worked with Sal in the 49'er band and a top notch trumpet player.

Pro Football Hall of Fame
2121 George Halas Drive, N.W.
Canton, Ohio 44708

TEL: 330.456.8207
FAX: 330.456.8175
LIBRARY FAX: 330.456.9080
MUSEUM STORE FAX: 330.456.5084
www.profootballhof.com

November 26, 2001

Sal Carson
127 Hardie Dr.
Moraga, CA 94556

Dear Mr. Carson:

The Pro Football Hall of Fame wishes to express its appreciation for your recent donation of the cassette of your band that performed at San Francisco 49er games. Your gift is a valued addition to our extensive historical collection and will be used in furtherance of our educational purposes. Your donation will be carefully preserved with all other treasured momentoes and sound recordings that have been collected through the years.

Since the Pro Football Hall of Fame is a tax-exempt charitable organization, you may deduct the fair market value of your gift for federal tax purposes. Attached is an IRS receipt that describes the property donated and is for your records.

Also enclosed is a gift agreement that you should read and sign in order to complete the donation. Again, please accept our sincere appreciation for your generosity.

Very truly yours,

Jason Aikens
Collections Coordinator

Letter from the Pro Football Hall of Fame. November 26, 2001

"Bye-Bye Beatle". March 1, 2002

–299–

THE SAN FRANCISCO LABOR COUNCIL, AFL-CIO

2002 LABOR/NEIGHBOR C.O.P.E. DINNER

HONORING

LARRY MAZZOLA
NANCY WOHLFORTH
HOWARD WALLACE
BILL LLOYD

AND SPECIAL RECOGNITION TO
HERE LOCAL 2
FOR YOUR OUTSTANDING ORGANIZING VICTORY

THURSDAY, OCTOBER 24, 2002

WESTIN ST. FRANCIS HOTEL
6:30 P.M. RECEPTION • ITALIAN ROOM
7:30 P.M. DINNER • GRAND BALLROOM

PROGRAM
INVOCATION
INTRODUCTIONS
KEYNOTE SPEAKER   ART PULASKI
CALIFORNIA LABOR FEDERATION
TRIBUTES & PRESENTATIONS

ENTERTAINMENT
SAL CARSON ORCHESTRA

(Upper left) Labor/Neighbor COPE dinner.
October 24, 2002

(Upper right)
Happy Holidays. 2003

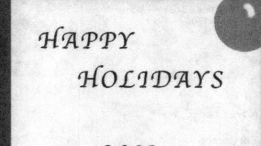

HAPPY
HOLIDAYS

2003

The
SAL CARSON ORCHESTRA

MARCH 23, 2004

Sal Carson Orchestra

Have you heard?

It was a banner day last Saturday at **Joe's of Westlake** Restaurant in Daly City. Well known orchestra leader Sal Carson (former San Francisco Forty-Niners Band Leader and a resident of Moraga) announced that his new CD "Swinging in San Francisco," featuring the song "San Francisco Forty-Niners so Proud and Bold," composed by Sal and Mabel Dafer is now in the Pro Football Hall of Fame in Canton, Ohio, and will soon be in the S.F. 49er Hall of Fame in Redwood City.

Have you heard?   March 23, 2004

Labor/Neighbor COPE
dinner. 2003

San Francisco Labor Council, AFL-CIO
2003 C.O.P.E. Dinner

• Welcoming Remarks •

• Invocation •
Pastor Richard Rubio, SEIU Local 250
Interfaith Committee for Worker Justice

United States Senator Barbara Boxer

• Dinner •
Music by the Sal Carson Band

• Recognition of Awardees •
Tho Thi Do
Secretary-Treasurer,
H.E.R.E. Local 2

Stan Warren
Secretary-Treasurer,
San Francisco Building & Construction Trades Council

Kristina Zinnen
Office Manager Emeritus,
San Francisco Labor Council

Art Pulaski
Secretary-Treasurer,
California Labor Federation

• Tribute to Bob McDonnell •
Song by John Fromer

opeiu3afl-cio(ii)

On the Jeremiah O'Brien in 2004. (l to r) Ken Fishler, Sal and Joe Terzian

Bassist **Vernon Alley**'s not going away so fast. **Sal Carson** says Alley played with his 49er band for six years. "Whenever we played a **Count Basie** arrangement," said Carson, "I'd turn around during the game, and he'd have a cute little grin on his face. And then he just swung the band."

Asked whether there was any music Alley hated, piano man **Mike Lipskin** (just married to singer **Dinah Lee**) said that like most pro musicians, Alley "would tend to compliment rather than denigrate." But if they were both playing at Moose's, or the Washington Square Bar & Grill, "he would occasionally yell, in his low rasp of a voice, 'That's not the right chord.'"

Carson mentions his new CD, "Sal Carson Orchestra, Swinging in San Francisco." And Lipskin is playing at a Davies Symphony Hall Salute to **Fats Waller** on Nov. 7. Alley would have understood the tribute/plug combo; the point is, the man was a pro.

Article about Vernon Alley. San Francisco Chronicle, October 20, 2004

Musical Celebration of Oakland. May 14, 2005

IN 2005, THE CHAMBER OF COMMERCE IS CELEBRATING 100 YEARS OF SUCCESSFULLY SERVING THE NEEDS OF BUSINESS & COMMERCE.

A MUSICAL CELEBRATION OF OAKLAND

OAKLAND METROPOLITAN CHAMBER OF COMMERCE

100TH ANNIVERSARY GALA

SATURDAY, MAY 14, 2005 ▪ OAKLAND MARRIOTT CITY CENTER
JEWETT BALLROOM ▪ RECEPTION AT 6 P.M.
DINNER, MUSICAL REVUE & DANCE BEGIN AT 7 P.M.

Joyce Whitelaw publicity photo.
May 2005. She did a number of
gigs with Sal's band.

Letter about the Oakland Musical Celebration

May 26, 2005

Sal Carson
San Francisco Music Man
127 Hardie Drive
Moraga, CA 94556

Dear Sal,

On behalf of the Oakland Metropolitan Chamber of Commerce Board of Directors, please accept this memento of our 100th Anniversary Gala.

The comments received from our guests exceeded our expectations. We knew we had planned a good party but it took our 650 guests to bring the glitter and laughter necessary to make a party successful.

Herewith this letter is your gift box included a CD of the 10 original songs performed at the Gala and the book '*IMAGINE*' published especially to celebrate the 100th Anniversary. We hope you will enjoy this gift.

Our vision for the next 100 years is to accelerate our economic development programs to expand jobs, housing and the quality of life in Oakland. You have played a significant role in our past and we hope you will be part of our success in the coming years.

Sincerely,

Joseph J. Haraburda
President & CEO

Celebrity Football Players Shootout. At Lake County Buckingham Golf Club. August 26, 2006. Roger Craig and Sal.

Five gals, Sal and Dwight Clark. August 26, 2006. (l to r) First four were former employees of the 49'ers as was Judy Greeran. That's our guy on the far right

Lou Rawls had a silky voice in jazz, pop and fundraisers

By Jeff Wilson
ASSOCIATED PRESS

LOS ANGELES – Lou Rawls, who earned fame with his glorious voice and respect through his prodigious fundraising for the United Negro College Fund, died Friday of cancer.

Mr. Rawls began as a gospel singer and spent nearly five decades working his velvet-voiced magic on classic tunes including "You'll Never Find Another Love Like Mine" and "Lady Love."

"His voice was so unique," said legendary producer Kenny Gamble, who with Leon Huff wrote "You'll Never Find." "The other thing was that he had a sense of community. Thousands and thousands of young kids benefited from his celebrity."

With his wife, Nina, at his bedside, Mr. Rawls died at Cedars-Sinai Medical Center, where he was hospitalized last month for treatment of lung and brain cancer, said his publicist, Paul Shefrin. Mr. Rawls' family and Shefrin said the singer was 72, although other records indicate he was 70.

A longtime community activist, Mr. Rawls played a major role in United Negro College Fund telethons that raised more than $200 million. He often visited and performed at black colleges.

"He's just someone who recognized, like many African Americans of a certain generation, that education was something that our kids didn't get access to and that it was critically important for their future, and for our communities' future and for the nation," said Dr. Michael Lomax, president and CEO of the UNCF.

In September, Mr. Rawls performed in the organization's "An Evening of Stars," which was to be televised nationwide through the weekend.

"He appeared frail, but he was in good voice, and he was in great spirit," Lomax said.

Associated Press file, undated
Singer Lou Rawls

Frank Sinatra once called Mr. Rawls' smooth, four-octave voice the "silkiest chops in the singing game."

Starting in a church choir, Mr. Rawls ultimately applied those silky tones to a variety of musical genres and more, including movies, TV shows and commercials. As a pitchman for Anheuser-Busch breweries, he spoke the familiar slogan, "When you've said Budweiser, you've said it all."

Mr. Rawls was raised on the South Side of Chicago by his grandmother, who shared her love of gospel with him. He also was influenced by doo-wop and harmonized with his high school classmate Sam Cooke.

When he moved to Los Angeles in the 1950s, Mr. Rawls was recruited for the Chosen Gospel Singers, then moved on to The Pilgrim Travelers. He enlisted in 1955 as an Army paratrooper. Sgt. Rawls rejoined The Pilgrim Travelers three years later.

While touring with the group, Mr. Rawls and Cooke were in a car crash that nearly ended Mr. Rawls' life. Cooke was slightly hurt, but another passenger was killed and Mr. Rawls was declared dead on the way to the hospital, according to Shefrin.

Mr. Rawls was in a coma for 5½ days and suffered memory loss but was completely recovered a year later.

He was singing for $10 a night plus pizza at Pandora's Box in Los Angeles in 1959 when he was spotted by Capitol Records producer Nick Venet, who invited him to audition. He was signed by the label soon after.

The album "Stormy Monday," recorded in 1962 with the Les McCann Trio, was the first of Mr. Rawls' 52 albums. That same year, he collaborated on Cooke's hit "Bring It On Home to Me."

In 1966, Mr. Rawls' "Love Is a Hurtin' Thing" topped the charts and earned his first two Grammy nominations. He also opened for the Beatles in Cincinnati.

During that period, Mr. Rawls began delivering monologues about life and love on the songs "World of Trouble" and "Tobacco Road," each more than seven minutes long.

His "Dead End Street" in 1967 won him his first Grammy for best R&B vocal performance. The singer won three Grammys in a career that also included the hits "Your Good Thing (Is About to End)" and "Natural Man." He released his most recent album, "Seasons 4 U," in 1998 on his own label, Rawls & Brokaw Records.

Mr. Rawls' main musical legacy is "You'll Never Find," released in 1976 after he signed with Gamble and Huff, architects of the classic "Philadelphia Sound."

"That was the first record we put out on him," Gamble said. "It captured the best of his voice. It had all the dimensions, it had the low and it had the excitement."

Mr. Rawls also appeared in 18 movies, including "Leaving Las Vegas" and "Blues Brothers 2000," and 16 television series, including "Fantasy Island" and "The Fall Guy." He voiced Garfield the cat in the animated project "Here Comes Garfield."

Lou Rawls obituary, The Sacramento Bee. January 7, 2006. He was born December 1, 1932 in Chicago, IL. Died January 6, 2006. Los Angeles, CA

Joe Montana autographing Judy Grerran's shirt. Notice that Dwight Clark got there first. Judy was Sal's secretary when he had an office in San Francisco. Joe seems to have a steady hand.

Death Notices and Guest Books for "Carson"   Modify your Search

Search Results   Page 1 of 1 (2 total results)
    Show 25   complete notices   per page

Carson, Sal (Carcione)   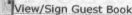 View/Sign Guest Book

Sal Carson (Carcione) Passed away peacefully on October 19, 2007 at the age of 86, surrounded by family, after a dignified and courageous battle with congestive heart failure. Sal was born in San Francisco and raised in Oakland where he graduated from University High School. He started his band at the age of 15 and became a very successful band leader. People remember his band at Hoberg's Resort, where he played for 25 plus years and his big band at the Forty Niners football games, where on many occasions he played, solo trumpet, the "Star Spangled Banner" on the 50 yard line. Sal devoted much of his time to the Special Olympics and the Godfather Club for the Saint Vincent School for Boys. Sal is survived by his wife of 65 years, Kathleen; his two daughters JoAnne Grasso, Karen Loing and was predeceased by his daughter Kathy Carcione. Father-in-law to John Grasso; grandfather to Kerry, Kathy, Krissy, Tom, Laura and Forrester plus 10 great grandchildren. Brother to Sylvia, Valeria and Gloria; uncle to Donna, Linda, Dianna and other nieces and nephews. Also Matthew Baumann, Linda's husband, who was a good and kind friend to Sal. Funeral Services and a celebration of his life will be held at a later date on Cobb Mountain in Lake County. In lieu of flowers a donation can be made to the Special Olympics, St. Vincent's School for Boys in San Rafael or a charity of your choice.
Published in the San Francisco Chronicle on 10/26/2007.
Notice • Guest Book • Flowers • Gift Shop

Sal's obituary

The City and County of San Francisco

Certificate of Honor

Presented To

Sal Carson

November 1, 2007

Whereas, on behalf of the City and County of San Francisco, I am pleased to recognize and honor Sal Carson for his lifetime career in music. He led a full and productive life and continued to enjoy the companionship of his family and many friends before his passing last week. On behalf of the City and County of San Francisco, please accept my condolences on his death and know that our thoughts and prayers are with you during this difficult time.

THEREFORE, I have hereunto set my hand and caused the Seal of the City and County of San Francisco to be affixed.

Gavin Newsom
Mayor

Certificate of Honor

Chapter 12
Maurice Anger

There were so many people who had a strong influence on Sal Carson. Big Band leaders, various musicians, owners of resorts and night clubs, plus friends who helped him get gigs. Most of those were referred to in this book. I decided to select one for additional comment. That one is Maurice Anger.

This gifted pianist, band leader and arranger was born October 25, 1918 in Berkeley, CA where he died October 9, 2005, just short of his 88th birthday. When he was only fifteen years old he became a professional pianist, started his own band and for seven decades he brought joy to those listening and dancing to a good orchestra.

"When I was about seventeen years old and living in Oakland, I would go the mile and a half to the Anger's beautiful Berkeley home. Mr. Anger was a big shot in the Wells Fargo Bank. Maurice would invite me to rehearsals held at his home on Monday night. I was impressed with his tight seven piece band, his piano skill and arrangements. He had a lot of style.

"Maurice graduated from the University of California and had a band during that time playing many Cal gigs. "We became very good friends and I joined in with some jam sessions at his home on Sundays. He also helped me out with arrangements when I elected to increase the number of pieces in my band. When I went into the service and was lucky enough to head a band Maurice sent me arrangements".

There was stiff competition among the various bands in the Greater Bay Area, but Maurice and Sal worked together because of their friendship. When one could not take a job because of another commitment they would recommend the other. There were times when Anger's trumpet player (he only carried one) could not make the gig so Sal was asked to fill in much to his delight.

Sal referred to Maurice Anger as a wonderful friend who helped him so much and one he never forgot.

Photo of Maurice Anger by Romaine.

Maurice with
Jack Benny

Coda

Each year San Francisco celebrates Columbus Day with a parade. In the vicinity of St. Peter and Paul Church there always musicians playing up a storm of happy music on that day

For a number of years the trumpet player was Salvatore Carcione whose professional name was Sal Carson, the well-known band leader. He was there again in 2007 with his trumpet. Too weak to play, but he had to be there.

On October 20, I called my dear friend to give him a progress report about his book, to ask a few questions and to let him know we were almost finished. Working with him on his life story was a wonderful project. Sal was so enthusiastic and loved coming up with "Did I ever tell you about." I wanted to set a date to fill in some of the missing names, spelling of names and I know he wanted to talk about his sincere love of family which was foremost in his life. His wife Kathleen answered the phone and told me that Sal had died the night before. That's not right. I felt so sad that he did not live to see his life story in print.

For the Goggin family and countless others, Sal Carson made life better for all of us by just knowing him.

Acknowledgements

A book of this type requires the input and encouragement of many people who should be recognized for the contributions which they all made with enthusiasm.

Thanks and love to my wife, Maria, who not only did all the typing, but made constructive comments about my penmanship. Plus Katheen Carcione who was always there to help.

Without the guidance and sincere interest of good friend Wayne Pope, the owner of Pope Graphic Art Center, this book would never have passed the rough draft stage.

Here are others who also deserve my thanks.

Bill Bardin
John and Julie Barneson
Carol Clute
David and Joan D'Arezzo
Richard Feinberg
Greg and Susan Goggin
Jeff and Roxanne Goggin
John Grasso
Charles N. and Donna Ewald Huggins
Jack's Record Cellar, Wade and Roy
Donald and Donna Johnson
KQED, Hanna Lin
Kinko's in Folsom, Art and Danny
Ed and Dottie Lawless
Richard May
Bob Mielke
San Francisco Musicians Union, Local 6, John Hunt and Maria Kozak
San Francisco Public Library, History Center, Susan Goldstein, Archivist.
San Francisco Traditional Jazz Foundation, Bill Carter
Earl Watkins

Here's hoping no one was missed. If so, it was not intentional.

Jim Goggin

Bibliography

Chilton, John, *Who's Who of Jazz,* New York, Time-Life Records, 1978

Claghorn, Charles E., *Biographical Dictionary of Jazz,* New Jersey, Prentice-Hall, Inc, 1982

Clarke, Donald, *Popular Music,* Penquin Books, London, 1998

Clute, Peter; Goggin, Jim, *Meet Me at McGoon's,* Victoria, B.C. Trafford, 2004

Clute, Peter; Goggin, J*im, Some Jazz Friends,* Victoria, B.C. Trafford, 2005

Cogswell, Michael, *Louis Armstrong, The Offstage Story of Satchmo,* Portland, OR, Collectors Press, Inc., 2003. any Armstrong fan should have this book

Eckland, K.O., *Jazz West 2,* Donna Ewald Publisher, San Rafael, 1995

Erlewine, Michael; Bogdanov, Vladimir; Woodstra, Chris; Yanow, Scott, *All Music Guide to Jazz,* San Francisco, Miller Freeman Books, 1998

Feather, Leonard, *The Encyclopedia of Jazz,* New York, Horizon Press, 1955

Goggin, Jim, *Turk Murphy – Just For The Record,* San Leandro, San Francisco Traditional Jazz Foundation, 1982

Goggin, Jim, *Some Jazz Friends, Vol 2*, A Victoria, B.C., Trafford, 2006

Goggin, Jim; Clute, Peter, *The Great Jazz Revival*, San Rafael, Donna Ewald, Publisher, 1994

Goggin, Jim, *Earl Watkins – The Life of a Jazz Drummer,* Victoria, B.C. Trafford, 2005

Kinkle, Roger D., *The Complete Encyclopedia of Popular Music and Jazz* 1950, New York, Arlington House Publishers, 1974

Larkin, Colin, *The Encyclopedia of Popular Music,* London, Muze Books, 1997

Oxtot, Richard and Goggin, Jim, *Jazz Scrapbook,* Berkeley, Creative Arts Book Co, 1999

Sadie, Stanley, *The New Grove Dictionary of Music & Musicians,* London, Macmillan Publishers, 1995

Walker, Leo, *The Big Band Almanac,* Hollywood, DaCapo Press, 1989

OTHER BOOKS BY JIM GOGGIN

With Pete Clute

"The Great Jazz Revival"

"Meet Me at McGoon's" ($30.00- includes S & H)

"Some Jazz Friends"

With Dick Oxtot

"Jazz Scrapbook: Dick Oxtot – me and other stuff"

Jim Goggin

"Turk Murphy – Just For The Record"

"Bob Scobey, a Bibliography and Discography"

"Jazz Nightclubs and Ballrooms, Hotels and other addresses, 1930 – 2002"
($30.00- includes S & H)

"The Dude Martin Band Story"

"Some Jazz Friends, Vol. 2"

"Earl Watkins, The Life of a Jazz Drummer"

"Bob Mielke: A Life of Jazz" ($30.00 – includes S & H)

All books - $23.00 (includes S & H) except where indicated otherwise

For availability write to:
Mother Lode Productions
Attn: CAROL CLUTE
P.O. Box 2048
Morgan Hill, CA 95038 – 2048

INDEX

A

"LIVE" from BIMBO'S
in San Francisco

VIC DAMONE

And

THE SAL CARSON ORCHESTRA

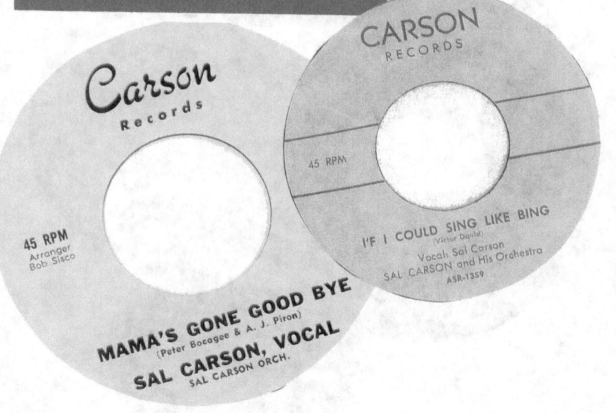

ASTRO
431 BRYANT STREET
SAN FRANCISCO, CA 94107

SIDE 2
1149 B
Produced by
Sal Carson

49ers PROUD and BOLD
(Sal Carson Mabelle E. De Fer)
Sal Carson Orchestra
Vocal - Sal Carson
Arranged by Rudy Paladini

ASTRO
49ers SO PROUD AND BOLD
(Sal Carson - Mabelle De Fer)

ASTRO
RECORDS
127 Hardie
Moraga, CA

STEREO
(4981)
CARSAL PUB.
BMI 1:28
R-6544

SAL CARSON
Big Band
Arranged by Rudy Paladini

CARSON
715 35th Avenue • San Francisco

SSR-45-1033

MOONLIGHT IN VERMONT
(Blackburn-Suessdorf)
SAL CARSON
and His Orchestra
featuring
LOU MADALONI
Vocal

ASTRO
431 BRYANT STREET
SAN FRANCISCO, CA 94107

Brown-
Henderson
ASCAP
2:30

SO BEATS MY HEART FOR YOU
(Ballard-Henderson-Waring)
Sal Carson, His Trumpet & Orchestra

VIC DAMONE
LIVE
"CHRISTMAS IN SAN FRANCISCO"

with
The SAL CARSON ORCHESTRA
1. Christmas In San Francisco
2. 49ers, So Proud And Bold
(Sal Carson, vocal)

T p
T p

DATE Nov. 10, 1945
TITLE The Ladie IS A
Tramp —
Sal Carson

THROUGH ALL
THE YEARS
(Robert G. Brown)

ASTRO
RECORDS

Carleen Pub. Co.
BMI
(1373)
TIME: 2:21

SAL CARSON
With The
SAL CARSON ORCHESTRA

ASTRO
HELLO DOLLY
(Herman)

STEREO
(4982)
Edwin H. Morris
Co.
1:36
R-6945

ASTRO
RECORDS
127 Hardie
Moraga, CA

SAL CARSON
Big Band

CARSON
Records
230 Jones Street • San Francisco

SSR-1030

Vocal with
Orchestra

I LOVE YOU DEAR
(CARSON - CALHOUN)

SAL CARSON
and His Orchestra
GLORIA CRAIG
Vocal

FAR ACROSS
THE DEEP OCEAN
(Robert G. Brown)

ASTRO
RECORDS

Carleen Pub. C
BMI
(1372)
TIME: 2:35

SAL CARSON
With
THE GLENNS
And The
SAL CARSON ORCHESTRA
Arranged By
BOB SISCO

SIDE 1
ASTRO
Century
RECORDS

127 Hardie Dr., Moraga, Ca. 94556

Produced By
SAL CARSON
CARSAL MUSIC
BMI

A-1007-A
STEREO
TIME:
3:08

"HOW MUCH HURTIN"
(Mabelle E. De Fer)
THE WHITTINGTON SISTERS
Music By The Marlins

45

HELLO DOLLY
(Herman)

STEREO
(4982)
Edwin H. Morris
Co.
1:35
R-6545

ASTRO
RECORDS
127 Hardie
Moraga, CA

SAL CARSON
Big Band

CARSON
Records
230 Jones Street · San Francisco

BRR-1029

INTERMEZZO
From "Cavalleria Rusticana"
(Mascagni)

SAL CARSON
and His Orchestra

HAPPY

HOLIDAYS

2003

The
SAL CARSON ORCHESTRA

THE BEST OF VIC DAMONE
LIVE

PROGRAM 1: (TT: 9:00)
IN THE STILL OF THE NIGHT
EVERGREEN
EASY TO LOVE

PROGRAM 3: (TT: 8:42)
ON THE STREET WHERE
YOU LIVE
COME IN FROM THE RAIN
AN AFFAIR TO REMEMBER

PROGRAM 2: (TT: 8:42)
I CAN'T SMILE WITHOUT YOU
FALLING IN LOVE WITH LOVE
YOU NEEDED ME

PROGRAM 4: (TT: 8:32)
YOU STEPPED OUT OF A DREAM
MAC ARTHUR PARK

R8T-8204
COPYRIGHT 1979 REBECCA

Ranwood Records, Inc., a wholly ow
of Teleklew Productions, Inc. ℗ Teleklew
Printed in U.S.A.

WARNING: It is expressly forbidden to c
this recording in any manner

CARSON
Records
230 Jones Street · San Francisco

Vocal with
Orchestra

SSR-1030

I LOVE YOU DEAR
(CARSON - CALHOUN)

SAL CARSON
and His Orchestra

GLORIA CRAIG
Vocal

RANWOOD
STEREO 8

THE BEST OF
VIC DAMONE
LIVE

RANWOOD

CARSON
Records
230 Jones Street · San Francisco

Vocal with
Orchestra

SSR-1031

BORREGO
(CARSON)

SAL CARSON
and His Orchestra

SAL CARSON
Vocal

CONTRA COSTA SHRINE CLUB

**POTENTATE
WALLY YORK**

**PRESIDENT
BILL HAYNES**

**CHAIRMAN
CHARLIE MEYERS**

"RETURN TO HOBERG'S"

Annual
FALL DINNER DANCE
1975

SAL CARSON
AND HIS BIG BAND